Officer of the West Yorks.

Officer of the West Yorks.

The Napoleonic Wars With
H.M. 51st regiment
Corsica, 1794 to Waterloo, 1815

A. F. Mockler–Ferryman
and

Samuel Rice

LEONAUR

Officer of the West Yorks.
The Napoleonic Wars With H.M. 51st regiment
Corsica, 1794 to Waterloo, 1815
by A. F. Mockler-Ferryman
and
Samuel Rice

First published under the title
The Life of a Regimental Officer During the Great War, 1793-1815

Leonaur is an imprint
of Oakpast Ltd

ISBN: 978-0-85706-260-4(hardcover)
ISBN: 978-0-85706-259-8 (softcover)

http://www.leonaur.com

Publisher's Notes

In the interests of authenticity, the spellings, grammar and place names used have been retained from the original editions.

The opinions of the authors represent a view of events in which he was a participant related from his own perspective, as such the text is relevant as an historical document.

The views expressed in this book are not necessarily those of the publisher.

Contents

Preface

The period of English history covered by the contents of this book is one of very considerable interest, for within that period Great Britain rose to be a mighty power, saving Europe from destruction, and gathering to herself the commerce of the world. One has only to glance at a chronological table of events to satisfy oneself that, from 1793 to 1815, the British Navy and British Army fought continuously and desperately in the making of the Empire, winning many great and glorious victories by sea and by land, and handing down to posterity the names of British sailors and soldiers to be sworn by as long as the British Empire shall exist. It was an age of heroic deeds by heroic men.

Let us call to mind how the Navy fought at Cape St Vincent, Camperdown, the Nile, Copenhagen, and Trafalgar; and how the Army fought in the Peninsula and at Waterloo. Let us think of the countless minor expeditions in all parts of the world in which army and navy together added to their laurels; of such sailors as Nelson, Cochrane, Collingwood, Duncan, Hood, Hawke, Howe, Hotham, Jervis, and others, and of such soldiers as Wellington, Moore, and all the former famous generals; and let us remember that it was by such victories, won by such men, that England gained her place in the world.

The stories of the lives of the great soldiers have been written over and over again; we know all about their strategy and their tactics, and how they guided the machines confided to their care; but of the lesser men, who, as it were, helped to turn the wheels of, or to apply oil to, the machinery, we know very little. Without their aid the machine must have come to a stop; and how they kept it going deserves to be remembered.

Samuel Rice, extracts from many of whose letters will be found in the following pages, was one of a host of Englishmen who played a part—even though it may have been an insignificant one—in the making of the Empire. He was, in every sense of the word, a Regimental Officer—one who never sought and never accepted employment outside the Regiment. Joining the 51st in 1793 as Ensign, he served with it, in good times and in bad, until 1831, the last fourteen years in command. He represents a type not uncommon at the commencement of the last century; and, at that period, probably most regiments of the British army contained men of the same stamp, who cared nothing for personal honour or glory, who cared little for the good or bad opinion of their superior officers, but who lived for the Regiment, finding their reward in a conscientious performance of regimental duty, and content to let their own actions go unnoticed so long as they helped to uphold the reputation of their beloved Regiment.

Nowadays, such men, from force of circumstances, are rare. The British officer can no longer afford to remain with his regiment; for, even if he is fortunate enough to possess sufficient private means to do so, he can stay in the regiment for only a limited number of years, and is forced to make way for others when still in the prime of life. And there are wider reasons for the disappearance of the regimental officer of the old school. Modern methods of warfare, resulting from the improvement in weapons and the invention of new means of locomotion and communication, require deeper thought and deeper study than was accorded to military matters by our ancestors. It is not enough that the officer of today should be acquainted only with such things as pertain to his own branch of the service; for he must be conversant with the tactics of all arms, and he must know a hundred and one other things which he cannot learn by remaining with his regiment.

Furthermore, the officer who nowadays has no ambition beyond regimental soldiering is liable to be regarded as lacking in zeal and efficiency; and if he allows himself to drift along into the regimental backwater, he is bound to find his progress barred before very long. But he has advantages such as his ancestors never had. By passing examinations he can qualify himself to hold appointments on the staff, and he can obtain other living-wage employment away from his regiment. A century ago there was nothing of this kind; examinations were little indulged in; and it is not too much to say that the majority of the staff officers came to the front and remained in the front by personal (and often political) interest—by a system of nepotism pure and simple. The officer, therefore, who knew that he had no friend at court to push him on made up his mind to remain with his regiment, and trust to good fortune to bring him rapid promotion. He affected to despise the staff officer as a butterfly and a place-seeker, and he threw all his heart into his regimental duties.

If proof of the value of these regimental officers is wanting, it will be found, writ large, in the account of every Peninsular fight, and by the aid of these men was Wellington's fame built up. "Their most marked characteristics," says Colonel Henderson, when discussing in his *Science of War* the officers of the Light Division regiments, "were that when they were left alone they almost invariably did the right thing; that they had no hesitation in assuming responsibility; that they could handle their regiments and companies, if necessary, as independent units; and that they consistently applied the great principle of mutual support." Such were the regimental officers who had received their initial training under the guidance of Sir John Moore, and such was Samuel Rice, of the 51st Regiment, himself one of the earliest disciples of that great master of the art of war.

By way of apology for bringing to notice a man unknown to fame, and who had no pretensions to be considered famous, I may, perhaps, be permitted to explain that, in putting this book together, my aim has been not so much to give a biographical sketch of one individual as to describe the lot of an ordinary regimental officer of the period; and it seems to me that there is no more satisfactory way of doing this than by following the career of one officer, chosen to represent the type. With such an object in view, I believe that it would be difficult to find a more suitable representative than Colonel Samuel Rice, who served with the same regiment for upwards of thirty-eight years—possibly in itself a record.

Moreover, he fought with his regiment in 1793, at the very commencement of England's great war in Europe, and he saw the final shots fired in 1815. From what is known of his character, it is probable that Samuel Rice would have been the last person to have desired notoriety; but his descendants have preserved, hitherto unpublished, letters written by him one hundred and twenty years ago, and I have thought that some of these, showing as they do the ways of the military world when England's reputation was being made, are of sufficient general interest to be worthy of publication.

My best thanks are due to Miss Lucy Augusta Rice for the loan of her great-uncle's papers, and to the past and present officers of the

King's Own Yorkshire Light Infantry—the old 51st—for information
concerning their gallant regiment.

A. F. Mockler-Ferryman.

St John's House,
Tavistock.

CHAPTER 1

Studying For The Army

Samuel Rice was born at Chislehurst on the 19th August 1775, and was the son of John Rice, one of an old Welsh family long established at Mydfai (Mythvey).[1] His mother was a daughter of Samuel Plumbe, who had married the sister of Henry Thrale, M.P., the then sole proprietor of what subsequently became Barclay & Perkins' Brewery, and the husband of the lady who has been named by posterity "Dr Johnson's Mrs Thrale."

Being one of a family of thirteen, young Rice was fortunate in having grandparents possessed of the wherewithal to give their grandchildren a start in life, and possessed, moreover, of sufficient intelligence to assure themselves that the money spent on education was well laid out. It is, perhaps, remarkable that, although very ordinary boys at school and not above getting into scrapes, all of John Rice's seven sons entered honourable professions and did well. The eldest took Holy Orders; two were in the Royal Navy; two in the Army; and two were lawyers, one of the latter becoming an Indian judge and receiving the honour of knighthood. John Rice himself, who was an only child, had been at Eton, but his sons were educated at Cheam (Mr Gilpin's), and Samuel, the second son, remained there until 1792, when, as was customary in those days, he was sent abroad to learn French before entering the army.

Those were stirring times. France was in a state of revolution, with her king and queen in prison; a republican Government on the point of being established, and Continental Europe up in arms, with the hope of being able to restore order in the country and prevent the

---

1. An account of the Rice family will be found in *Some Things we have Remembered*, by Percy Melville Thornton. London: Longman. 1912.

excesses which were likely to result from the indiscipline of a republican army in league with the mob. At first England maintained a strict neutrality, and held aloof from interference with the internal affairs of France; thus, when, in the spring of 1792, Sam Rice took up his residence at St Omer (some twenty miles from Calais), he found the French well-disposed towards his countrymen, though he, the true British boy of the period, was disinclined to regard his new hosts otherwise than as the natural enemies of his country.

In spite of the fact that he was kept hard at work, learning not only French, but also drawing, fencing, and dancing, he appears, from his letters home, to have found leisure for shooting, fishing, and riding, and he thoroughly enjoyed the change of scene as well as the novelty of being at a tutor s instead of at school. On this subject he wrote, soon after his arrival in France, to his elder brother, then at Cambridge—

"It gives me great pleasure to feel myself freed of my leading-strings, and to be my own master, doing what I will without being scolded and sworn at. I am like the Frenchmen; I like Liberty; but I think they have carried theirs too far, and will not do well without a little more steadiness. We find our own wine; I have bought for the present two dozen of claret and one of Burgundy. *You* cannot afford to drink such wine."

This matter of wine, which in those days was considered a necessity even for a young gentleman of barely seventeen, eventually led Sam Rice to complain to his father about the scanty allowance which he made him. Twenty guineas a-year for extras, including clothes, was, he said, a ridiculously small sum upon which to attempt to "live as other gentlemen do"; and he summed up his necessary annual expenses as follows: "Wine (weak stuff), half a bottle a-day, and occasionally giving to friends, eight guineas; washing, hairdressing, and hair powder, six guineas." His appeal, however, had little effect, and on his father's refusal to increase his allowance, the young student cut down his wine bill in order to have more money to spend on shooting.

That he benefited by his sojourn abroad is evident from the letters which he wrote in French to his father from time to time; and his knowledge of the language proved of the greatest value to him in after life. Living as he did at St Omer, in an atmosphere of military preparedness for war, he acquired at an early age habits of careful observation; he learned also to form his own opinions and to use his own judgment, and he became imbued with the true military spirit. His remarks on the situation as he found it at St Omer in 1792 are of interest—

"St Omer," he wrote, "is well fortified with ramparts and flanked with bastions; and there are several drawbridges before you get out of the town, which, of course, makes it very inaccessible, if well garrisoned. But the worst part is that they have got such a few meagre dogs that, I am sure, at the sight of an Austrian army they would be glad to accept of any terms of capitulation. To be sure there is one battalion of Swiss, who are undoubtedly good soldiers; but I believe that it is generally thought that they will not fight, because the Swiss remain neutral, and they cannot fight against the Germans, as they are allies. The people do not seem much afraid of the Austrians; [2] they stump and bully now, but when the enemy comes a little closer, I am very much mistaken if they will not draw in their horns."

Again, a little later, he wrote—

There is a great preparation for war here. I don't know how many hundred men are employed every day in repairing the batteries, in forming new ones, and in making new drawbridges, as well as in cutting rivers to surround the town. All this is done by order of General Lukener. Also vast quantities of stores and ammunition are daily brought into the town, and hay in abundance, for I never walk out of the town but I meet twenty or thirty waggon-loads of hay coming from the country to be laid up in the town in case of want. I heard yesterday that a party of hussars belonging to the French had killed no less than four hundred of the Austrian cavalry, but that General Gouire (or some such name), a French general, was killed. I cannot say that this is a fact; but, if it is, most likely you will have heard of it before this reaches you. Some gentlemen from here have been to see the camps at Valenciennes and Lille, and all along the side of French Flanders, which they say are so strongly entrenched that it will be impossible for the enemy to come into the country. They saw ten thousand hussars pass them all at once as they were in their carriage, and had to wait four hours to let the cannons pass. All the hussars had great moustaches, which gave them a savage appearance.

The wearing of moustaches by the French cavalry was a new idea, and the infantry soon adopted the same method of producing a "sav-

2. France declared war against Austria 20th April 1792.

age appearance." The British soldier of the period, on the other hand, prided himself on his clean-shaved face, with, at the most, a suspicion of side whisker, cut square with the line of the mouth. "Shaved clean, and with the hair neatly tied and powdered," was the regulation. Moustaches were not worn in the British army until many years after Waterloo, and the order to wear them was received with suspicion and dislike, being regarded as an attempt to Frenchify the British army.

It is recorded of one famous cavalry regiment that the officers paid no attention to the order until the inspecting general made strong comments on their shaved upper lips, and ordered the colonel to enforce the moustache regulation. Within a few days each officer appeared on parade fully equipped with a false moustache, and this appendage was removed when parade was over. How long this continued is not stated, but for a long time the officers of this particular regiment were observed to be clean shaved when in plain clothes and heavily moustached when in uniform. The British infantry shaved the upper lip almost up to Crimean times.

But the Frenchmen's moustaches did not impress young Rice in 1792, for he regarded the Republican soldiers as effete and useless, and likely to become an easy prey to the invading Austrians and Prussians. His dislike for the French as a nation was intense, and he prayed for their downfall.

"I think the French," he wrote, "a parcel of d—d rascals, and I heartily hope the Austrians will give them a good thrashing. We are to have a garrison of six thousand men here, for they expect this town to be attacked by the Austrians, who propose to burn the place by firing red-hot bullets, and so pass over its ashes to Brussels."

As events turned out, St Omer was not attacked, but it was hardly the place for quiet study, and it is wonderful that, under such circumstances, the boy learned anything.

As an experience, his seven months' residence in France must have been full of interest and excitement. He lived, as it were, on the outskirts of the fight—at times with the enemy's guns within earshot, and he constantly saw troops marching to the front to the tune of "Ça ira." He lived also in the midst of the Revolution, for although St Omer itself was comparatively quiet, the accounts which came from Paris sickened him and filled him with righteous indignation. In one of his letters he mentions that he has just heard of the massacre of some thousands of Aristocrats in Paris, and he gives vent to his feelings in no measured terms—

The cruelties and barbarities which have been committed will ever be a stain upon the national character. This French nation, which was once the most gentle, has now by its cruelties rendered itself the most savage and barbarous. I am now a strong Aristocrat, and I should imagine that people in England who favoured the Revolution must have changed their opinions since the recent horrible massacre in Paris.

It was, however, one thing to declare himself an Aristocrat in a letter home, but quite another thing to let it be known in St Omer, and he admits sailing under false colours, in that he wore "the cockaded tricolour, decreed by the National Assembly." He excuses himself thus:—

If you were to appear without one, you would be mobbed and called 'Aristocrat' by every saucy boy in the street. So much so that one of the actors last night at the Playhouse, during the time he was performing, was shouted to for his cockade, and they would not let him perform without it. One of the others brought him one, which he put to his breast, but that did not satisfy the audience, for they shouted again *à chapeau*, and he was obliged to put it in his hat, to save himself from a broken head.

Though Sam Rice held French revolutionary methods in general abhorrence, he appears to have approved of the treatment dealt out to the religious orders, for, in describing events at St Omer, he says:—

The nuns are all going to be turned out of their convents, and also the friars. Most of them have been sent away, and there only remains one church of them, from which they will be speedily dislodged. There were twelve capital houses with nice gardens which those rascals the monks inhabited—one for each, and they were allowed a considerable sum for their maintenance; but now the people have seen what rogues they were, and have turned them out neck and crop, and have sent them into the country to live upon twelve pounds a-year. Their library and church are turned into magazines for hay and different stores, and all the religious houses are to be converted into barracks for the soldiers.

It is perhaps worthy of remark that eighteen of these persecuted

Jesuit fathers of St Omer were granted, in 1794, an asylum in England, and, bringing with them several of their pupils, founded Stonyhurst College, for the education of Roman Catholics.

As time went on, the cloud over France grew blacker, and by the end of August the young English student was rejoicing in the thought that the defeat of the French army by the Allies was about to be realised, though he gave the French credit for offering a stubborn resistance.

"The French," he wrote on the 28th August (1792), "now that they have so long enjoyed their liberty, will never, I think, submit to a despotic government, and I believe that some would sooner blow themselves up in their towns than capitulate. They seem not to have the least idea that the enemy can enter into the kingdom, but I am very much of opinion that he will do so sooner than the French expect, and in that event the Prussians [3] will play the devil with them. The Duke of Brunswick in his manifesto was very severe. He said that all who did not submit to him, when his troops presented themselves before the towns, would be put, every one, to the sword, when taken; and he wrote especially to the Parisians, against whom he has vowed vengeance.

"Three parts of the officers of the army which was Lafayette's have deserted, and Lukener is suspended. It was reported that Lafayette had deserted, but it is said now that he has been stopped in endeavouring to escape with the *caisse militaire*. In my opinion, the situation is very bad. Longwy, a town on the frontier, is besieged by the Prussians. If they take it (and most probably they will), they may march straight for Paris, as there are no other fortified towns to obstruct their passage. Success attend them! I long to hear of their arrival at Paris. We are very quiet at St Omer, and most probably we shall continue so, as the Prussians do not seem to be inclined to make their attack on this side.

"*Wednesday evening.*—I have just read in the *Gazette* that Longwy is taken. The King of Prussia, at the head of his army, made the attack, and took the town in less than fifteen hours."

On the 7th September, just after the news of the September mas-

---

3. Prussia joined Austria on the 26th July, and the Duke of Brunsick held the post of commander-in-chief of the allied armies.

sacres had reached him, he discussed the situation again:—

The Allies have already taken two towns—Longwy and Verdun, and there are no fortified towns between them and Paris, but it seems to me that they cannot reach Paris without an immense army, otherwise they will be cut to pieces by the French armies. They say that on Sunday and Monday two thousand Aristocrats were massacred in Paris in the prisons.

His next letter was dated October 3, and in it he makes no mention of the brilliant victory of the French at Valmy, where, on the 20th September, Kellermann defeated the Prussians under the Duke of Brunswick, and thus gave heart to the Republican forces. He must have known of the victory, and he may have already referred to it in a letter which has not been preserved, for he seems to have begun to fear that all was not going well with the Allies.

"I make no doubt but what you have heard," he says, "that Lille is besieged. My father, I am afraid, will be anxious for my safety, but I assure you as yet there is nothing to cause anxiety; neither do I think that there will be. It is not possible that they can take Lille, as it is one of the strongest towns in France, and has a garrison which is determined to hold out to the last. They have kept up a brisk cannonading for these two or three days past, and even here I can hear the report of the cannons very distinctly. Most people think that it is only a false attack to draw off the French armies from Verdun, where the Prussians are being kept blocked up. I think this most probable, as they would never attempt to attack such a place as Lille with only 20,000 men. Lille is very much damaged, as the enemy fire red-hot balls, which, of course, have set fire to a great many houses. Numbers of people are saving themselves from Lille and taking shelter in St Omer. They come, some in carriages, with their children; others in carts, with their household furniture; and a pitiful sight it is to see the poor women and children reduced to such extremities. I was up at half after five this morning to see a regiment depart for Lille, and I was very well amused for my pains. The soldiers seemed to wear a melancholy air, though they marched to the tune of ' Ça ira,' which generally gives them courage and consolation."

The postscript to this letter shows that even an English visitor had to fall in with republican views:—

You must direct to me, '*A Citoien Rice, chez Citoien Boudeille, Rue de l'Egalité, St Omer*,' for you know that the title *Monsieur* has been abolished.

With regard to Lille (Lisle) Citizen Rice's forecast was correct; for, on the 7th October, the Prussians raised the siege and departed, thus shattering Rice's hopes of a speedy occupation of Paris by the Allies. The Duke of Brunswick's manifesto, which he mentioned in a previous letter, did more harm than good, as the insolence of its tone irritated the French into deposing their king forthwith, massacring Aristocrats wholesale in Paris, and putting forth all their strength to defeat the Austrians and Prussians. In this they succeeded beyond all expectation, for the victory of Valmy was repeated at Jemappes (November 6); and, a week later, the French entered Brussels and occupied the Austrian Netherlands.

St Omer appears now to have settled down to comparative quiet, and the young Englishman to his studies and amusements; but, before the end of the year, his father began to be anxious about the state of affairs in France, and wrote, "the complexion of the times is such as, in my opinion, renders it no longer proper for a young man designed for the British army to remain in France." The people of England realised that the climax was approaching. A revulsion of feeling against the French had set in with the suspension of King Louis in August; the September massacres had increased it; and the arraignment of the unfortunate king on December 11 raised it to boiling-point. Neither was this all, for England saw in the high-handed acts of the victorious Revolutionary leaders a menace to the "rights and liberties of Europe."

Sam Rice, therefore, quitted France early in December, only a month before his return would have been made compulsory by the French Government, when, upon the execution of Louis XVI. (January 21, 1793), an open rupture occurred between England and France. His education was now considered to be complete, and his father set to work to obtain for him a commission in the army.

Chapter 2

Ensign of the 51st

On the 12th February 1793 (a few days after the declaration of war by France against England and Holland), Samuel Rice was appointed to an Ensigncy, by purchase, in the 51st Regiment (2nd West York).

At that time, under ordinary circumstances, young gentlemen obtained commissions in the army in one of two ways. Free commissions were granted to a limited number of the sons of officers who had performed good service for their country, and all other commissions were purchased, upon the recommendation of two or more officers of high rank. There were no examinations or other means of ascertaining the standard of education of the would-be officer, and it may be taken that Sam Rice was better educated than most young officers who then joined the army.

The greater number of commissions were obtained by purchase, but in times of war, when the supply of officers was short, colonels of regiments were allowed to employ the services of young gentlemen (usually ensigns of militia), who were termed "volunteers," and who hoped, by distinguishing themselves on active service, to be granted free commissions. During the many years of war which terminated with Waterloo, a vast number of officers entered the army in this way, and being, for the most part, men whose very livelihood depended upon their zeal, proved themselves valuable officers.

The so-called purchase system, in one form or another, was almost as old as the British standing army itself, and dated back to the time when the colonel of a regiment was entirely responsible for his corps, which was known by his name. For many years there was no fixed scale of charges for commissions, the colonels charging more or less what they liked, and employing agents to sell the commissions, so that both the colonels and the agents feathered their nests very satisfactorily. In this manner many useless officers found their way into the army, and it was not until 1765 that the authorities took the matter up and issued strict regulations on the subject. Then the price to be paid to Government for a commission as Ensign, and for promotion to each subsequent rank, was clearly laid down, the colonels being forbidden to make any profit for themselves, though the matter of what was termed "over regulation" was not touched on, but left to the regimental officers themselves.

When Sam Rice entered the army he paid £450 for his first commission as ensign in an infantry regiment; and the regulation prices paid to Government at that time by officers of infantry on promotion were as follows: to lieutenant, £250; captain, £1100; major, £1400; lieut.-colonel, £1300. Consequently, by the time an officer had reached the rank of lieut.-colonel, he had paid to Government altogether £4500. But if he could not find the money to purchase any step, it was open to him to purchase promotion to the half-pay list, at a considerably reduced price, subsequently exchanging or purchasing back to full pay, if he desired to do so.

Eventually, on retirement, the officer received from Government a lump sum equivalent to the value of his commission, so that he got back the sums which he had expended. This was termed Retirement by the Sale of Commissions, but the regulations varied from time to time, and later on lieutenant-colonels were given the choice of taking the lump sum, or of retiring on full pay. The above is a brief outline of the purchase system, in so far as transactions between officers and the Government were concerned, but many and various complications arose from the over-regulation prices of commissions, with which the Government had nothing to do. These transactions were carried out among the officers of the regiment, with the assistance of the regimental agents, and the object of them was to maintain a healthy flow of promotion by buying out the senior officers.

Death was the only other way of displacing them, for there was no regulation by which an officer was forced to give up the command of a regiment after holding it for a certain length of time, and no age limit for any other officers. Every regiment appears to have had its own recognised tariff, depending principally on the purses of the officers; thus the over-regulation price of, say, a lieutenant-colonelcy of a cavalry regiment was considerably higher than that of an infantry regiment, and a lieutenant-colonel would not retire unless the officers junior to him subscribed the sum which he considered his rank and appointment were worth. In such a case the procedure would be something as follows: the lieutenant-colonel would name his price to the senior major, who would then see how the amount could be made up by voluntary subscriptions from such officers as would benefit by the retirement of the lieutenant-colonel. The senior major would, of course, pay the largest amount, and the senior captain and senior lieutenant would probably subscribe handsomely, if they intended to purchase their respective steps. It frequently happened, however, that officers could not afford to purchase their promotion, in which case a junior officer could purchase over the heads of his seniors, the latter deciding to wait for a death vacancy, for which no over-regulation money was required.

The injustice of a system which permitted men with money to buy their way to the front does not seem to have struck the officers— probably because they knew of no other system,—and its advocates maintained that it never interfered with the advancement of a good man, whom the authorities were able to reward with free promotion to half pay, or even to full pay. Still, there can be no two opinions about a system which induced officers of the army to give as a common toast, "A bloody war and a sickly season!"

The system lived long and died hard. Its abolition was debated for thirteen years, and even then a Bill relating to it which was introduced in the House of Commons was thrown out by the Lords, and purchase was only finally swept away by a Royal Warrant of 1871, at great expense to the Government, for compensation had to be paid to such officers as had subscribed over-regulation money for their different steps.

However, to return to young Rice. Getting the ensign properly outfitted caused a good deal of trouble, and eventually he was much upset at finding, when on the voyage to join, that his tailor had provided him with a "plain cap" instead of a "laced one." That was rather a dressy age, for ever since George the Second reorganised the uniform of the army on the Prussian model, tight-fitting clothes, lace, frills, and powder reigned supreme. Each year saw the introduction of some new ornamentation wherewith the soldier's dress was beautified; and much more attention was paid to the smart appearance of the men than to their professional training. The officers, therefore, had to be very particular about their uniform, as well as about their hair, and strict regulations were issued from time to time as to the mode of wearing the hair, changes taking place every few years.

In 1793, both officers and men wore their hair powdered and "clubbed"—*i.e.*, the long, flat, greased and powdered tail was rolled up, and bound round with a leather strap, upon which, by way of ornament, the officers had a rosette, and the men a small disc of polished leather. The head-dress of the period was a black three-cornered cocked hat, with a black silk cockade and silver lace and button; the full-dress coat, scarlet with grass-green facings, was cut away in front, with tails falling to the back of the knees; white breeches, and black cloth gaiters; the sword hanging on the left side from a white leather cross-belt, over the right shoulder and under the one epaulette; red silk sash wound round the waist, over the waistcoat, but under the coat, and having its tassels hanging towards the left side; a black leather stock filling the opening in the collar of the coat, a white starched frill beneath, and the silver gorget, with rosettes and ribbons, hanging at the neck. In this manner was Sam Rice dressed when he put on his "regimentals" for the edification of his sisters.

The 51st, under the command of Lieut.-Colonel John Moore, had left England for Gibraltar in March 1792, and young Rice, after fitting himself out, was ordered to embark in the *Neptune* transport at Portsmouth at the end of May 1793, and proceed to Gibraltar with a draft for the regiment. England was now at war with France, and the navies of the two countries were busy sweeping the seas. Transports were not permitted to put to sea without the escort of a fleet, and, as often as not, men-of-war were too much occupied to be available for convoy duty. Consequently the unfortunate men on the *Neptune* and other transports were kept on board in English ports for five weary months, every day hoping that the morrow would see the Blue Peter at the mast-head. Some of the letters written by Sam Rice under these trying circumstances are not without interest. Early in June he wrote to his father from Spithead, where the *Neptune* was lying at anchor—

I cannot say I much admire living at Spithead, and especially when in this state of uncertainty. It is not at all improbable but what we shall lay here some time longer, for I neither hear nor see anything that is like a preparation for a convoy. It is very unlucky for us that we lost the opportunity of going with Lord Hood. The *Venus*, which had an engagement with a French frigate, came in here yesterday. I fancy, if the truth were known, she got the worst of it, for she had two-and-twenty men and one lieutenant killed, as report says. By that I should think that the action must have been very smart. I was invited to dine on board the *Circe* [1] today, but could not go, as I am the only officer in the ship. She has taken a great many vessels, but chiefly priva-teers. Three were brought in this morning, with the British flag flying triumphant o'er the national one of France.

The soldiers confined on the transports appear to have given a good deal of trouble, and strong measures had to be resorted to in order to maintain discipline.

"In my last letter," wrote Ensign Rice, "I told you that I was to sit on a Court Martial, to be held on the *Granby* transport. The crimes alleged against the prisoner were: impudence to one of the officers, disobedience of orders, and defrauding one of his messmates. I being the youngest officer had to give first my opinion, so sentenced him to receive 150 lashes; the next, which was Williams, said 200, as did all the rest. I was present at the punishment. Two drummers were sent for from Portsmouth, to perform. But the commanding officer. Captain Wood, consid-ering he was but a raw recruit, or, I suppose, nothing but a wild Irishman, forgave him a little less than half the number, hoping that that would be sufficient for the present, and serve as an ex-ample to the rest. Our men, upon the whole, behave themselves tolerably well. We are obliged now and then to tie them up, for fighting or quarrelling, or suchlike things, but it is the nature of an Irishman to be quarrelsome. We cannot but expect it, and more especially when there are so many together."

Writing a week later, he again referred to the conduct of the troops on the *Granby*:—

The soldiers on board the *Granby* transport were yesterday very rebellious, but unluckily we could not pick out any to make an example of. These fellows will never be orderly till they have had, each of them, a good flogging, which, I think, they stand a fair chance of having before they have been many days at Gi-braltar. I am very confident that if we were not surrounded by men-of-war, and were to go to Gibraltar without a convoy, we should all be murdered.

The references to flogging in the two last letters must not be taken to imply that young Rice was shaping for a martinet in this early stage of his military career. In those days sentence of flogging was passed on a soldier for offences which nowadays would carry no higher pun-

1. His younger brother Charles Rice was at the time a midshipman on the *Circe*.

23

ishment than a few days' detention; and, in reading descriptions of military and naval punishments of a century ago, one marvels at their positive brutality. It may be that we have finer feelings than our ancestors had, or our natures may have become softer, but whatever has brought about the change, the fact remains that accounts of what took place on an ordinary flogging parade in time of peace make one wonder how a civilised country like England could have permitted such barbarities. Men were sentenced to receive so many hundred lashes—even up to two thousand, on the bare back, with a cat-o'-nine-tails—and the mode of carrying the punishment into execution was as follows:

The regiment having been drawn up in square facing inwards, and the "triangle," of solid spars,[2] having been erected in the centre of the square, the prisoner was marched in and ordered to strip to the waist. He was then secured by the wrists to the top of the triangle, and by the thighs and ankles to the side spars. At a given signal the drum-major and his drummers advanced, and were ordered by the commanding officer to "do their duty." The first drummer took off his coat, and delivered twenty-five lashes, when he was relieved by a second drummer, who delivered the same number, the drum-major standing by with a cane ready to strike the drummer if the lashes were not administered with sufficient strength. And these drummers were all trained to the work, by flogging the fleece off a sheep's skin, both with the right hand and with the left, so that alternate drummers should inflict the punishment from opposite sides of the triangle.

Near at hand stood the adjutant and the surgeon, the former to register the number of lashes, and the latter to observe the victim and order him to be taken down if he thought that further punishment at the time would endanger his life. But there was no question of respite, for the number of lashes awarded had to be given, if not at one time, then at several times. Immediately the man was taken down, he was marched to hospital, and carefully attended to until his back had healed; then, if he still had more lashes to come, he was taken out again, and his back cut open afresh; and we have it on the authority of Sir Charles Napier, the Conqueror of Sind, that a man was often brought to the triangle a third and a fourth time to receive the remainder of his punishment.

We spare the reader further details of this barbarous work, and we

---

2. Originally, on active service at any rate, the triangle was formed of halberds, lashed together. Hence the term "brought to the halberds."

have only said so much because it was necessary in order to show the spirit of the times, and in order to draw attention to some of the unpleasant duties of regimental officers.[3] It may be thought that corporal punishment was rarely inflicted, but official returns prove otherwise, and it is no exaggeration to say that, towards the end of the eighteenth century, a regiment on home service would parade round the triangle at least two or three times in a month.

> "In 1793," says Lord William Bentinck, "infliction by the cat-o'-nine-tails was the ordinary and general punishment for every offence, great and small, only varied as to the amount according to the different degrees of culpability, but always the lash; except in regard to the most trivial offences, corporal punishment was the echo in each and every one of the Articles of War."

It is not difficult to understand that, under such circumstances, recruits for the army were slow in coming forward. Moreover, the Government of the day neglected the soldier s comfort and welfare in every possible way, underfeeding him, underpaying him, and accommodating him in vile quarters. The majority of the recruits brought up for enlistment were produced by the "crimps," who resorted to every mean device in their prosperous business of catching men and selling them to Government, and one can scarcely wonder that such unwilling soldiers should have resented the harsh discipline to which they were immediately subjected. These were the men with whom young Rice first came into contact at Portsmouth—men, cooped up on board ship, without recreation of any kind, for weeks on end, and unable even to make a bid for freedom by desertion.

That there should have been a spirit of unrest on board the transports was not very strange, but the possibility of the disaffected troops murdering their officers was, of course, only wild talk on the part of a youthful subaltern. This, however, was not a very pleasant commencement to a young officer's service, but things seem to have settled down as time went on, and as more military officers joined the transports for duty. The only excitement was that provided by the arrival of a man-of-war, after a successful engagement.

> "I saw the *Nymph*," wrote Sam Rice on the 1st July, "as well as *La Cléopatre*, coming into the harbour. The latter had her

---

3. Flogging in the navy was carried out with even greater severity than in the army, the most brutal form of the punishment being that known as "flogging round the fleet."

mizzen-mast shot away, and was everywhere, I fancy, considerably damaged. I have not been on board either of them; in fact, the truth is, I have not been ashore since they came in. The brave sons of the Republic, I understand, fought with great courage, as did, as usual, the sons of Old England. The French captain was killed, or else, you may depend upon it, the engagement would have lasted till one of them had gone to the bottom. The *Phaeton* has taken a very fine French ship, named *La Prompte*. She only rates as a sloop in France, but is as big as any of our twenty-eights.'

In the middle of July the officers on the transports saw a chance of sailing with the fleet under Lord Howe, but he had other business on hand, and went without them. Sam expressed his disgust at his lordship's conduct:

We thought that we were to sail under the protection of Lord Howe's fleet, but in that we were disappointed, for he sailed last Sunday evening without having the politeness to take us with him. When we shall now sail I know not; but the report is that it will be very soon and suddenly. It needs be so, for they have given us a fair spell of Portsmouth. I now know enough of a transport, which means that I will never go in one again, if I can get my passage in any other vessel. I almost agree with Dr Johnson that it is as well to enter a jail as a cabin.[4] We have had a bad fever on board our ship for some time. Two have died of it, and many more are ill at the hospital. I should not be surprised if we were all to take the fever, after being so long confined in these old rusty colliers, now in His Majesty's service for the purpose of transporting us to Gibraltar.

We are to be joined by seven more transports, and Colonel Lindsay is to take the command of us all. He has sent us two thousand cartridges on board, and orders how we are to act in case of attack by the enemy. If one of us should be separated from our convoy, and see a Frenchman, we are to run immediately, and our men to be ordered to go betwixt decks. But, if the Frenchman sails better than us, and comes alongside, we are, with all our padding, to board, and play hell and the devil among them—that is to say, if possible. There has been a great

4. "Why, sir, no man will be a sailor who has contrivance enough to get himself into a jail."—Dr Johnson.

change among the officers from ship to ship.

I am the only one left upon this ship, and consequently am officer commandant, till a Captain Alcock, who is appointed here, comes on board. He has got a wife, whom he intends to take to Gibraltar with him. I'd just as soon have the devil on board as a woman; not that I have any natural antipathy to women, but I assure you they are a great nuisance, especially in such a confined place as a cabin. You might perhaps think a lady a wonderful acquisition to a sea party, but I am very certain, if you had ever been a voyage with a woman you would never desire it again.

Within the month he changed his mind about the lady, and on August 13 he imagined that he was within measurable distance of the end of all his troubles.

"I have just time to tell you," he scribbled in haste, "that we have received our orders for sailing. Our convoy fired a gun and hoisted a signal to get under weigh immediately. I do not suppose we shall go farther than St Helens today. I came ashore this morning at six o'clock to take leave of Old England, and to bring on board Captain and Mrs Alcock. We have the *Diadem*, sixty-four, and the *Active*, frigate, for our convoy."

Five days later he wrote again from St Helens, Isle of Wight, still jubilant at the thought that at last he had made a start for Gibraltar, though disappointed in being kept back by adverse winds. His letter shows how the vagaries of the wind upset all calculations in the days of sailing vessels, and he wrote as follows:—

I think I never beheld a finer sight in my life than the sailing of our fleet from Spithead. It consisted of about seventy-five sail. The *Diadem* led the way; and the *Active* brought up the rear. We had made about four leagues, when, to our great sorrow, our Commodore fired a gun as a signal to put back to St Helens, not thinking it prudent to put to sea, the wind not being very favourable. The 14th, we lay at anchor. The 15th, our Commodore early in the morning fired a gun for to get under weigh, which we immediately did. But we were again obliged to put back to St Helens, not being able to weather the land. The 16th, at anchor as before. The 17th, it blew a heavy gale, drove us from our anchorage, and carried us down almost as far as Spithead.

The same day we were nigh being run foul of by an Ostend vessel, which had also broken from her anchor. I never experienced such a gale before, and, indeed, it rather astonished the old seamen, especially at this time of year. The wind is still contrary. I hope we shall soon leave this disagreeable place, which is worse than Spithead. Captain Alcock, who, I told you, has the military command of the *Neptune*, is really a worthy man, and has behaved to me, since he has been on board, with the greatest friendship and civility. He is more like a father to me than a commanding officer.

He knows all the officers in our regiment, and has promised to introduce me, but more particularly to those whom he thinks it proper for a young man to associate with. Captain Alcock's younger brother is in my regiment, and is the oldest captain in it; he says that his brother will always stand my friend. I think I cannot be better off than I am at present. I am very well and happy in having met with such a worthy fellow as Captain Alcock. He has not been married above two months. His wife is a charming and agreeable woman, and we are all very comfortable together."

The fleet got away from St Helens on the 22nd August, but was overtaken by another gale, and had to run for Portland Bay, where the ships were forced to shelter until the 8th September. By that time the bay had become filled with ships bound for various parts of the world, the West India fleet of transports amongst them, and at length the wind showed signs of being favourable for departure. Yet, as Sam Rice's next letter shows, luck was all against them, and a few days later the ships turned about and anchored in Torbay.

Writing from Torbay on the 17th September he describes what had happened—

We left Weymouth on the 8th, the wind being in our favour. I believe never so large a fleet sailed from that place before, or ever will again. We were no less than two hundred sail in number. Many were the people who assembled to see us depart, and I do not in the least doubt but what the sight was highly worth seeing. We passed by this port, where we saw the Grand Fleet lying at anchor, and we little thought then that we should be obliged to go in. In a very short time we cleared the Land's End and steered on our course for Gibraltar. We had nearly reached the Bay of Biscay, when, to our great surprise, a frigate came up and spoke our Commodore, upon which a signal was made for us all to bear homewards as fast as possible. You may be sure we were all thunderstruck at this uncommon proceeding, and were not a little vexed at the thought of returning after having made so much way.

The next morning we passed by the Scilly Islands, and from thence bore away as fast as possible for this place, where we are safely riding with the Grand Fleet. The frigate above mentioned had been sent by Lord Howe, who, having had intelligence that the French fleet was not far off, and consisted of thirty-two sail of the line and nine frigates, very prudently, and fortunately for us, dispatched a frigate immediately with orders for us to return with all possible expedition. I was at first very much vexed at returning, but am now rejoiced to think that we have been fortunately saved from the rapacious claws of the French "*Sans culottes*."[5]

I hear we have taken Toulon, with a great deal of shipping, but that we have had bad success before Dunkirk.[6] Three regiments are gone from the garrison of Gibraltar to Toulon; so, if any regiments go to the West Indies, ours most probably will be one. Our men are now in a sad condition; we have now three hospital ships, and all full of men with fevers. Several have died, and, no doubt, more will, if they continue much longer on board a ship. It is thought that we shall sail with Lord Howe's fleet, but that is at present quite uncertain."

Eventually, after having put back no less than nine times altogether, the transports succeeded in getting away, and reached Gibraltar in November, when Ensign Rice and his two hundred recruits joined the 51st. He found war the one topic of conversation, and the prospects of the regiment proceeding on active service being freely discussed. He learned now the true story of Toulon, which, although actually in the occupation of a British and allied force, had not been "taken with a great deal of shipping," but had been peacefully garrisoned at the request of the Royalist (or Girondist) inhabitants.

---

5. The Royalists applied this term to the Republican leaders, who affected a carelessness in dress; and subsequently all Republicans were called "*Sans culottes*," i.e., ragamuffins. Nowadays the French use the term, in a more literal sense, as slang for our Highlanders.

6. The Duke of York defeated by Hoche, 7th September 1793.

Admiral Hood, who had brought his fleet to the Mediterranean, was cruising up the coast from Gibraltar, when he received a message from the Royalist Admiral at Toulon, asking him to co-operate in the defence of that place against the Republicans (or Jacobins), and to hold it until the monarchy should be restored. Hood agreed, and on the 27th August, troops having been sent from Gibraltar, and a Spanish squadron having joined the British fleet, the Admiral took possession of the forts and the many men-of-war in the harbour—amounting to not less than one-third of the navy of France. He at once dismantled the ships, and removed such of the sailors as were known to favour the Republican cause, and he then sought assistance from the Spanish, Neapolitan, and neighbouring Allies who, in the course of time, sent him some 12,000 men. This mixed force, with 2000 British troops under General O'Hara, essayed to protect Toulon from the ravages of the Republicans, who soon arrived—to the number of 25,000—to besiege the place, and by November became so active that General O'Hara sent to Gibraltar for reinforcements.

The 50th and the 51st, which, for some weeks, had been standing ready to go to the relief of the garrison of Toulon, at once embarked (December 5), and young Rice considered himself in luck's way in being called upon to take the field so soon after joining. Ill-fortune, however, still dogged his footsteps, for the captains of the transports delayed for three days in putting to sea, thus losing a fair wind, so that it was not until the 29th that the regiment arrived off Toulon, when it learned that the place had been evacuated in haste ten days before, the garrison having made an unsuccessful sally, in which General O'Hara was severely wounded and captured. Finding that the garrison was now too weak to hold the town against the vastly superior numbers of the Republican forces. Lord Hood set fire to as many as possible of the French ships in the harbour, blew up powder and stores, successfully embarked the British garrison, as well as nearly 15,000 Royalists, who feared for their safety when the Republicans should enter the town, and sailed for Hyères Bay[7] (a little to the east of Toulon), where, on the

7. It is perhaps worthy of note that there were present at Toulon on the eventful 19th December 1793, two men who afterwards became world-renowned. Napoleon Buonaparte, aged twenty-three, commanded the Republican artillery which was instrumental in hastening the withdrawal of the British from Toulon. Horatio Nelson, aged thirty-five, commanded the *Agamemnon*, forming part of Lord Hood's fleet. Napoleon was then on the winning side, but twelve years later Nelson wiped out his fleet at Trafalgar, and died on board the *Victory*, which had been Lord Hood's flagship at Toulon.

31st December, the transports conveying the 50th and 51st joined the fleet—to be received very coldly by the Admiral.

But Lord Hood's disappointment at the lateness of their arrival was no greater than that of the officers of the reinforcing regiments. That Toulon should have been abandoned, and that their prospects of honour and glory should have been torn from them by no fault of their own was bad enough, but, to make matters worse, the 51st lost all their regimental baggage and stores, including everything belonging to the officers, which had been placed on a separate vessel for conveyance to Toulon. Sam Rice, a philosopher even in those days, refers to this minor trouble very briefly. "The officers' and the regimental baggage," he wrote, "went into Toulon in the *Moselle* frigate,[8] which separated from the transports during the night and did not know that the town was evacuated, because the English flag was kept flying. You see we military gentlemen are subject to losses as well as the rest of the world." And the loss both to officers and the men was severe, for their colonel had been at great pains to stock the ship with everything that the regiment could want.

---

8. *La Moselle,* previously a French sloop.

CHAPTER 3

The Attack on Corsica

When Sam Rice joined the 51st, Lieut.-Colonel (afterwards Sir John) Moore had held the command for three years, but was even then only in his thirty-second year; for his promotion had been rapid, and he had reached the rank of lieutenant-colonel in the thirteenth year of his service. That Moore was a strong man goes without saying, and that he was a man of very exceptional talents the world discovered subsequently. A perfect gentleman, of unblemished character, a reliable and zealous soldier, he was able to bring a great influence to bear on those whom he commanded, and he had a special gift for training young officers. It was in this respect that Sam Rice benefited by being appointed to a regiment with such a commanding officer, and he learned under Moore things which he never forgot. At that time the condition of a regiment depended entirely upon the commanding officer, for in the last decade of the eighteenth century the British army was not in a very satisfactory state. Sir Henry Bunbury,[1] who made a study of such matters, wrote sixty years afterwards:

Men of the present generation can hardly form an idea of what the military forces of England really were when the great war broke out in 1793. Our army was lax in its discipline, entirely without system, and very weak in numbers. Each colonel of a regiment managed it according to his own notions, or neglected it altogether. There was no uniformity of drill or movement, professional pride was rare, professional knowledge still more so. The regimental officers in those days were, as well as their men, hard drinkers; and the latter, under a loose discipline, were

---

1. *Narrative of Some Passages in the Great War with France, 1799-1810.* By Lieut.-General Sir Henry Bunbury. Bentley, 1854.

much addicted to marauding and acts of licentious violence, which made them detested by the people of the country.

It is perhaps unjust to describe the officers as hard drinkers, if by that is meant that they were all drunkards, or that they drank harder than did their civilian friends and relatives. The morals of the army were possibly no worse than the morals of general society at that period, for it was an age of heavy drinking, when respectable and respected old gentlemen drank themselves under the table every evening, and boasted of the number of bottles of port which they could consume at a sitting. Yet, if the opinions of Bunbury and other writers holding somewhat similar views of the British army in pre-Peninsular times are to be accepted, it cannot be maintained that the tone among the officers of ordinary regiments of the line was of a high order. Some certainly drank a great deal more than was good for them; otherwise it would hardly have been necessary to put in print in the standing orders of a certain regiment the caution that "the Surgeon and his Mate must always be strictly sober."

Gambling was indulged in to an inordinate extent; and duelling was not unknown. The fact is that the army was suffering from long years of inaction, and from the pernicious effects of service in America, India, and the West Indies, where regiments went to pieces and took years to recover themselves. To this must be added the further fact that the regimental officer was promoted not by merit, but by purchase; so that it was only necessary for a man to bide his time, and to have sufficient money at his back to buy his steps when they came, and in due course he commanded his regiment, and continued to command it until he could be bought out.

But, it may be asked, if such was indeed the state of affairs, how came it that the British army rapidly emerged from this condition of darkness to save Europe? How came it that the hard-drinking British officer was able to pull himself together, and become transformed into an upright and zealous soldier, capable of enduring endless hardships and displaying great gallantry? The answer is that all regiments were not bad; that most regiments—even the bad ones—possessed some officers of high moral character and endowed with exceptional talents, and when war came in 1793 these officers, on the principle of the "*survival of the fittest*," came to the front, and gradually established a tone on active service which had been impossible to uphold in times of peace.

Some regiments possessed more of such officers than others, and some regiments, again, chanced to have a colonel with sufficient strength of will to give a short shrift to any of his subordinates who were not likely to be of value to him. As the war progressed many of the junior, and not a few of the senior, officers willingly or unwillingly fell out, to make room for better men; many were found wanting and were removed; and many had undermined their constitutions to such an extent that in their first campaign they were carried off by what was commonly described as "the fever," or the "distemper." While the weeding-out process was at work during the last few years of the eighteenth century, and during the opening years of the nineteenth, the annual wastage of officers was immense; after that, matters righted themselves.

Still, it is an error to suppose that the whole army was in so bad a state in 1793 as Bunbury would have us believe, for there are still in existence the printed standing orders of a few regiments of the line of about this date, and from these there is proof enough that very great attention was paid to the wellbeing of corps. The discipline was strict, though of the severe and mechanical order, and it was maintained solely by the lash; duties in quarters were performed with the utmost regularity; and if the standing orders were carried out, the regiments should have been in excellent order. It may, of course, be possible that such regiments as had standing orders were, from this very fact, good regiments, and that the strictures of Bunbury and others applied to the bad regiments, which were, perhaps, more numerous than the good ones.

It is, however, quite certain that when the 51st regiment went on service in 1793, its general condition left nothing to be desired, since Moore had paid attention to such weeding-out of officers as was nec-essary when he first took up the command in 1790, and all young officers who joined afterwards were kept under his ever-watchful eye until he was sure of them. "He felt that a perfect knowledge and an exact performance of the humble, but important duties of a subaltern officer, are the best foundations for subsequent military fame"; [2] and he required from his officers a punctilious attention to duty and a thorough knowledge of their profession, so that they might be looked up to and respected by the soldiers whom they were called upon to command. And, a perfect gentleman himself, he had no place in the 51st for any officer who was not the same. He was not a martinet, and

---

2. Extract from the General Order, issued 1st February 1809, by H.R.H. the commander-in-chief, on the death of Sir John Moore.

he did not ride rough-shod over his officers and men, but he knew exactly when the occasion demanded a right enforcement of discipline, and when discipline could be relaxed without detriment to the "machine," which he proudly described, in September 1793, as being in as good order as he could get it.

So much has been said here of Colonel Moore's characteristics,[3] because he was Sam Rice's first commanding officer, and because his teachings left their mark upon the man who served continuously with Moore's old regiment for thirty-eight years. To return to affairs in the Mediterranean: Colonel Moore, as senior officer with the reinforcements which joined Lord Hood's fleet in Hyères Bay, immediately went on board the *Victory*, and reported his arrival to the Admiral, who somewhat churlishly remarked that the reinforcements were meagre and had arrived too late to be of any use. He forgot that the delay was due to dilatoriness on the part of his own naval officers, and he forgot also that had the reinforcements arrived a fortnight earlier, they could not have prevented the evacuation of Toulon, since, on the 16th December, the enemy had captured the forts which dominated the anchorage of the British fleet.

The Admiral was now busily engaged in working out a plan for employing the troops on the transports in some enterprise which, while redounding to his own credit, would compensate in a measure for the abandonment of the great French arsenal; for he was aware that the evacuation of Toulon without destroying all the French ships, although the only step that, under the circumstances, was possible, might be regarded in England as a grave failure on his part. Something, he decided, must be done at once, and that something must take the form of providing for the British fleet in the Mediterranean a base deeper in than that afforded by Gibraltar, which was at that time the only British possession in the Mediterranean, and almost a thousand miles from Genoa, in the neighbourhood of which port the French and Austrian armies were operating. Lord Hood realised from the outset the broad principle that, as Captain Mahan [4] says, "the policy of Great Britain was to control the sea for the protection of commerce, and to sustain on shore the continental powers in the war against France—chiefly by money, but also by naval co-operation when feasible."

---

3. See also chapter 6, for Sir John Moore's remarkable success in training officers and men for war.
4. *The influence of Sea Power upon the French Revolution*, by Captain A. T. Mahan, U.S.N. 2nd edition. 1893.

Under these circumstances, the Admiral's thoughts naturally turned to Corsica, which, though still garrisoned by French troops, was known to be more or less in revolt against the Republican Government. The exact state of affairs in the island, however, and the strength of the French defences and garrisons, were things about which Lord Hood had little information; and though he regretted the necessity for delaying the capture of Corsica, he wisely accepted, on this occasion, the advice of the military commanders to send two military officers to reconnoitre and report on the practicability of making a descent on the island. Moore and a major of artillery named Koehler were selected for this duty, and on the 11th January (1794) left in the *Lowestoffe* frigate, in which also sailed Sir Gilbert Elliott, one of the King's Commissioners in the Mediterranean, who was to endeavour to persuade the Corsican inhabitants to assist the British force in ridding the island of the French interlopers.

It is unnecessary to dwell on Corsican history further than to say that from 1559 to 1768 the island was a dependency of Genoa, and that in the latter year, contrary to the wishes of the people, was basely sold to France. The Corsicans then made a bid for independence, but within a few months (1769) their army, under Pascal (or Pasquale) Paoli, was defeated and crushed by the Count de Vaux. It was with this Paoli, who, after a period of exile in England, had returned to Corsica, that Sir Gilbert Elliott opened up negotiations, and from him, without much difficulty, obtained the promise that the Corsicans would aid the British in every possible way. Moore and his companion made a careful reconnaissance of the various French posts and forts, and on the 25th January the former returned to the Admiral with his report. The fleet was then on its way from Hyères Bay to the island of Elba, and in a few days anchored off Porto Ferrajo, where it was proposed to disembark the Royalist refugees from Toulon and place them under the protection of Tuscany (to whom Elba belonged), while arrangements were being made for the leap on Corsica.

The story of the operations which followed, as told by the chroniclers, is somewhat marred in the telling by constant references to the bickerings and petty jealousies of the naval and military commanders, each of whom appears to have been afraid that the rival service would obtain all the *kudos*. Why, the reader may wonder, is it necessary to hark back to these regrettable incidents, which did not greatly affect the result of the operations? Only because at one time they threatened to destroy the reputation of John Moore, Colonel of the 51st, and did actually lead to his temporary downfall. Lord Hood, strongly backed up by Horatio Nelson, then captain of the *Agamemnon*, despised soldiers, and thought little of the opinions of military officers. The naval plan was to rush at everything, without weighing the consequences, and the suggestions of the General, David Dundas (who had succeeded O'Hara), and other military officers of experience, who counselled proceeding with caution, were blown away, as showing weakness and want of enterprise. Nelson himself said, "Armies go so slow, that seamen think they never mean to get forward; but I daresay they act on a surer principle, though we seldom fail."

Nelson was, of course, in a measure right, but he and other naval officers of the period failed to realise the great difference between the facilities afforded to the respective services—that whereas seamen always had at their back their ship, providing them with quarters, food, ammunition, and everything that they required; soldiers, when once put ashore on an expedition, had to take everything with them and look after themselves.

The three principal places in Corsica held by the French were St Fiorenzo (now St Florent) on the north, Bastia on the east, and Calvi on the west; and in that order Lord Hood decided to attack each place in succession. St Fiorenzo, the first to be dealt with, was situated at the head of a deep bay, studded on the western shore with detached forts, or towers, which, being constructed of solid masonry in a circular form, deflected the round-shots which struck them. The most formidable of these advanced works was the tower of Mortella,[5] and it was impossible to attack St Fiorenzo until these outworks had been carried. With the object, therefore, of reducing the Mortella Tower, Moore was ordered to land at a little distance away, and with the 51st (numbering 350) and a mixed force of soldiers and sailors (numbering another 350), and with two guns, to march inland and take the tower in rear, while the ships bombarded it from the sea.

Moore's force landed on the night of the 7th February, and after a long march among the mountains reached, on the following evening, a point from which the enemy's fortifications could be clearly exam-

---

5. General Sir J. F. Maurice, in his *Diary of Sir John Moore*, says that the tower was so named from its situation on the shore of Mortella Bay— *i.e.*, the Bay of Myrtles: that it was on the plan of this tower that the so-called "Martello Towers "on the English coast were afterwards built; and that the spelling "Martello" was an error in an early despatch. The derivation of the word as coming from an engineer of the name of Martel is said to be pure fiction.

ined. Moore, who had reconnoitred them on his previous visit, was surprised to find that the French had strengthened their position considerably, and he came to the conclusion that his handful of men was quite insufficient to assail all the fortifications in front of St Fiorenzo. He therefore sent a despatch to General Dundas, and reported that to attack with any prospect of success would require all the general's available troops.

That day was spent in getting the guns into position and in a further reconnaissance, while two ships bombarded the Mortella redoubt, though without breaching it. The ships, moreover, were set on fire by the enemy's hot shot, and were forced to sheer off, with a loss of some sixty men. On the next day more guns were mounted on land, but although they did little damage to the solid tower, their fire made it impossible for the enemy to show himself or reply, and the French officer in command, seeing that he could no nothing, surrendered. The next outwork to be disposed of was the Convention redoubt, and this gave a good deal of trouble. Moore, who was still conducting operations on land, inspected the ground with General Dundas and Major Koehler, and discovered an excellent artillery position, from which it would be possible to batter the Convention.

The difficulty was to get the guns up the steep, rocky hill, but, with the aid of a party of seamen with tackle, two 18-pounders and a howitzer were mounted within the next few days, and a mortar and some other guns were placed on a more accessible position, when the enemy's redoubt was subjected to a heavy cannonade for two days. Moore had now with him only the 51st, but on the 17th February the General gave him orders for the assault that night. The Royals were to join the 51st, and Moore was to assail the front of the redoubt, while the other British regiments and the Corsicans were to deliver simultaneous assaults on either flank.

Moore decided to attack in column of companies, the first company consisting of the grenadiers and light infantry [6] of the Royals, the second of the grenadiers of the 51st, the third of the light company of the 51st, then the battalion of the Royals (only sufficient to make five companies), then three companies of the 51st. The other five companies of the 51st followed in rear as a support; and in rear again came

---

6. At this period all regiments had ten companies, the flank companies being known as the grenadier company and the light, or light infantry, company. It was considered an honour to belong to these two companies, which consisted of picked men under picked officers.

130 sailors, under Captain Cooke, with entrenching tools.

At 8.30 p.m., by the light of a brilliant moon, Moore led the advance, which for a quarter of a mile could only be made in file. After a little he reached a spot open enough to form up the column; the enemy's piquets fired a few shots, as they realised what was taking place; and Moore immediately ordered his column to push on. When within fifty yards of the redoubt, they found themselves in a slight hollow, unexposed to the enemy's fire, and here Moore halted them for a few seconds preparatory to the final uphill rush. A moment later the Royals and the 51st leaped into the head of the work, and crossed bayonets with the Frenchmen, who stood their ground gallantly and fought with desperation. Eventually, however, the flank attacks pushed in and over-whelmed the defenders, though in the darkness it was difficult to distinguish friend from foe, and, to add to the confusion, the enemy holding the neighbouring redoubt of Fornali began to open with grape-shot upon the victorious British. But before midnight the latter had entrenched themselves, and within an hour it was learned that the French had abandoned Fornali.

Arrangements were now made for the attack on St Fiorenzo itself, but before they had been completed the enemy withdrew from the place and retired to the fortified town of Bastia, situated on the east coast of Corsica, and barely ten miles across the neck of the peninsula from St Fiorenzo. The coast near Bastia was quite open, and the town was not fortified on that side; elsewhere, however, it was defended by four detached redoubts and a citadel placed on heights at a little distance inland. On February 23, Moore and General Dundas went across the mountains to reconnoitre the enemy's position, and on the following day the 51st and 69th advanced to within a mile and a quarter of the French piquets, who were heard throughout the night digging entrenchments for their further security on the ground which it was necessary for the British to occupy in order to capture Bastia from the land side. Becoming aware of this. General Dundas, in the morning, ordered Moore to withdraw his force, and, to the surprise and disappointment of every one, the withdrawal took place.

Moore at first imagined that the general's idea was to perfect arrangements before delivering the assault, but after a while he discovered that, in spite of Lord Hood's constant request for co-operation from the land forces. General Dundas had refused to attempt the capture of the town with the small force under his command. This was a bitter discovery for Moore, who was longing to lead his regiment to the front, but he concealed his disappointment, as he considered that it would be "a species of mutiny for a subordinate officer to pass any opinion" on the action of his general.

Lord Hood, never on good terms with General Dundas, now brought matters to a head by sending a somewhat extraordinary letter, in which he said that upon the evacuation of Toulon the general's command had practically ended, and that he (Lord Hood) was in supreme command of both the fleet and the army. The general replied with calmness that, unless the admiral could produce his commission from the king, neither he nor his officers would acknowledge his pretensions to the command of the land forces. But Lord Hood's letter probably had the result which he desired, for on the following day General Dundas, on the grounds of ill health, gave up the command, and having appointed the next senior officer. Colonel D'Aubant, a brigadier-general, and given him the temporary command of the army, left for England on the 11th March. D'Aubant proved himself a useless commander, and being averse to an assault on Bastia, threw cold water on every plan laid before him.

In vain did Lord Hood urge the necessity for an attempt being made by the land forces; and, after holding several councils of war, he at length declared that he would take Bastia with the marines[7] and sailors. Already a month had been wasted in looking at the place—a month which gave the enemy leisure to perfect his fortifications and entrenchments. Almost another month passed before Bastia fell; and its fall was brought about not by assault or bombardment, but by starvation, resulting from Lord Hood's careful blockade from the sea and the Corsicans' watchfulness on land. There had been practically no fighting, and though Hood and Nelson dignified the operations with the name of siege, the army was never in position, and all that was undertaken by the ships was the maintenance of a strict blockade, and the landing of some guns and a fighting force under Nelson. The guns did little damage to the enemy or his works, thus wasting much valuable ammunition, and the force commanded by Nelson (consisting of 1183 soldiers acting as marines on board ship and 250 sailors) made no advance. On the 19th May Bastia was starved into surrender, and the 3500 men of the garrison gave up their arms to the British

---

7. Not the Royal Marines as we know them, but detachments of ordinary infantry regiments, detailed for duty as marines on board the ships, and under the command of the Admiral. The following regiments furnished marine detachments to Lord Hood's fleet at this time— the 11th, 25th, 30th, and 69th.

combined forces, which numbered no more than 3000 soldiers and sailors.

Attention was now directed to Calvi (on the west coast of Corsica), the only place of importance remaining in the possession of the French. It was known that they had been busy for some time victualling the place for a siege, and Lord Hood determined to operate before the garrison of Calvi could be further reinforced. Brigadier-General D'Aubant had gone home, on being relieved by General Charles Stuart, who had been sent out from England to succeed General Dundas, an appointment which met with the approval of every one and which gave confidence to the troops. The regiments in Corsica, though seven in number, were miserably weak, as they were required to furnish detachments for duty as marines on board the ships, and the climate had begun to tell on the health of the men. General Stuart's "army," available for operations against Calvi, consisted, therefore, of no more than 2300 men. These troops were conveyed in transports from Bastia to Mortella Bay, and, on the 19th June, after a further voyage, disembarked a few miles from Calvi, and marched inland to a camp on the high ground some three miles from the fortress.

Colonel Moore was given the command of a special "corps of reserve," consisting of the "flank companies of the Royal Irish, 50th, and 51st, and the remains of the 2nd Battalion of the Royals," so the command of the 51st devolved, for the time being, on Major Pringle. Two outworks of considerable strength lay in front, *i.e.*, on the land side, of Calvi—*viz.*, the fort of Mozzello and the fortified rock of Monteciesco. Batteries were immediately thrown up on commanding heights, about 500 yards from these outworks, and on the 7th July the enemy evacuated Monteciesco. The guns now turned on Mozzello, and for ten days endeavoured to make a practicable breach, the assailants suffering the whole time from the fire from Calvi itself and from some minor outworks, and Captain Nelson, who was present, unfortunately losing an eye, from splinters of stone being flung into his face by a round-shot striking the ground in front of him.

Before daylight on the morning of the 19th July, a breach having been effected in the walls of the Mozzello redoubt, the troops moved forward to the assault. Colonel Moore led the stormers, some of whom carried sandbags, and others ladders. Shot, hand-grenades, and live shells were hurtled down upon them by the defenders, but, nothing daunted, the grenadiers charged forward, and plying their bayonets with vigour, drove the Frenchmen out of the redoubt. In this desperate encounter Moore was wounded in the head by a splinter of a shell, but though knocked senseless for a moment, he continued to lead his men until he made certain that the place had been secured, and that entrenchments had been thrown up to cover the troops from the fire of the enemy's guns in Calvi.

With the capture of the Mozzello redoubt, however, the enemy's resistance virtually came to an end, and his guns ceased to fire. Yet the Frenchmen refused to capitulate, and the British prosecuted the siege with vigour, pushing forward new batteries and mounting upwards of thirty pieces of ordnance. Moore wrote at the time: "The men and officers fall ill daily; considerably more than a third of our force are in the sick report; perhaps there never was so much work done by so few men in the same space of time."[8] By the 30th July the enemy began to consider the matter of terms, as Calvi had been set on fire in two or three places, and the British guns were doing much damage. After this General Stuart stopped all firing, while he entered into negotiations with General Casabianca; and on the 10th August Calvi surrendered, the defenders laying down their arms and forthwith embarking on transports.

Young Rice, as a very junior subaltern in the 51st, of course had no opportunity of distinguishing himself in these operations, and he does not appear to have been much impressed by his first campaign. On the 2nd August 1794 he wrote to his father from "Camp before Calvi," as follows:—

A flag of truce having just gone in, or rather hoisted in the town by the enemy, and being not so much distracted by shot and shell, I embrace the opportunity (which I may say with truth is almost the only one I have had since the commencement of the siege) of writing these few lines. Do not expect now, when I begin, that I am going to give you minute details of all our operations here. In the first place, it would not be in my power, and, in the next, they would be very uninteresting. The papers will in all probability soon show the fate of Calvi and the operations before it. They are, in my opinion, better able to provide news of that nature than are private letters.

The most satisfactory news, I imagine, to you will be that of my health and safety. The flag of truce above mentioned will in all probability terminate in the capitulation of Calvi, which I am extremely glad to think likely, not on account of the danger

8. Maurice's *Diary of Sir John Moore.*

of shot and shell, but on account of the great sickness from which both officers and men are suffering. The disease, which is a fever, not only happens to the most delicate, but seizes in the most sudden manner on the most robust and healthy. We have now out of our army upwards of 2000 lying in fevers, and a great number of officers. It is not very dangerous, but two officers have died of it. In my opinion, the disease arises from our having to lie in the trenches exposed to the intense heat of the sun. I am quite tired of the siege.

We have taken all the enemy's outposts and silenced all his guns, and the town has been in flames for some days. If they continue stubborn, the General is determined to hearken to no more flags of truce, as he has so often been humbugged by them before; but to batter a breach and enter the town by storm, which will be easily effected, though perhaps not without a few broken heads. As yet only four officers have been killed, and six or seven wounded. Colonel Moore was slightly wounded on the head at the storming of the Mozzello redoubt, but is now, I am happy to say, quite recovered. An unfortunate shot killed an officer[9] of ours the day before yesterday in the trenches. He had only just joined, and was an excellent young fellow, and is much lamented.

I would thank you to tell Mr Greenwood [10] to write to Colonel Moore, as is customary, about my promotion; for until that time I do not take the rank of lieutenant in the regiment.

"I was at the taking of Bastia, though did not reap many laurels there. All I can say is that we were ready to do anything that there was to be done. My Lord Hood and his marines claimed the honour—if there was any—of taking that town. Bastia is a very good town, and will make very pleasant quarters. Calvi is to appearance no great things. Ajaccio is much the pleasantest place in the whole island.

August 4th.—My lieutenancy was this day noted to the regiment—the commission dated 1st April. We have not yet taken possession of the town, but are pretty certain the business is at an end. The General has not thought fit to divulge the great secret.

---

9. Ensign Thomas Boggis, killed 30th July 1794.—*Records of the 51st.*
10. The Regimental Agent, who would (presumably) have to write to the colonel to inform him that the purchase money had been lodged with him.

August 11th.—The enemy marched out of Calvi yesterday with the honours of war, and embarked on board transports for conveyance to Toulon. The town of Calvi is in a deplorable state.

Sir John Moore's *Diary* bears out this last statement.

"It is inconceivable," he wrote, "the destruction our fire has occasioned; there is literally not a house which has not been damaged by shot or shell. The whole is a heap of ruins."

Moore also often lamented the sickness from which the troops suffered, but an entry made in his *Diary* of the 16th August shows that Sam Rice's regiment was better off than most.

"The 51st," said Moore, "have fewer sick than any other regiment, owing undoubtedly to our surgeon, M'Cleish, who is a diligent and intelligent man; but also, in a great degree, to the good regulation of our regimental hospital for these three or four years past. This was one of the first things to which I attended on getting the command of the regiment. It has remained in good order ever since then. I am now rewarded by having three times the number of duty men of *any regiment here*."[11]

The cause of all this sickness among the troops was undoubtedly exposure, for there appears to have been no epidemic of any kind, and modern soldiers under similar circumstances would probably suffer equally. In the daytime the men lay out continuously beneath the fierce heat of a Mediterranean summer's sun, and their dress was that worn in England in the winter—*viz.*, tight-fitting cloth clothes, with their "clubbed" hair beneath a hat which, if anything, made their heads the hotter. At night they slept out, almost uncovered, among the mountains, at a temperature sometimes so low as almost to freeze the very marrow in their bones. That sunstroke and sun fever should have fallen upon them was little to be wondered at.

---

11. Maurice's *Diary of Sir John Moore.*

44

CHAPTER 4

Corsica Won and Lost

With the capture of Calvi French resistance in Corsica came to an end, and the island became a British possession, the Corsicans, some two months earlier, having declared their allegiance to the King of England. Sir Charles Stuart at once began the distribution of his troops in garrisons about the Island, and the 51st sailed from Calvi on the 19th August, going round to Bastia, of which place they were to form the garrison. Writing from Bastia on the 11th September, Sam Rice gives some account of events:—

I have the pleasure of telling you that we have quitted our canvas houses, and have taken up our quarters in this garrison, which is by no means an unpleasant one. How long we shall continue here Is very uncertain at present, as there are other places in the island which must be garrisoned. Our regiment will very probably go to Ajaccio, which is, by all accounts, one of the pleasantest and most healthy places In the whole Island. General Stuart, Colonel Moore, and some others of the great men set out, about a week ago, to take a tour of the island, for the purpose, I suppose, of finding out what places it will be necessary to garrison. The French, I hear, are making great preparations at Toulon, to endeavour to retake the island. I hope they will make the attempt, when we will give them a warm reception.

In the letter which I wrote to you after the surrender of Calvi, I think I mentioned the extreme sickness of our army. It was nothing then to what it is now. You will be astonished when I tell you that the 51st Regiment was almost 500 strong at the commencement of the siege of Calvi, but now, I am sorry to say, we have not a hundred fit for duty. The rest of the regiments are in the same way. The 12th Light Dragoons, who have had no fatigue, suffer alike from this shocking and unwholesome climate. The Corsicans say that, after this month is over, the climate will be very healthy until July. It is to be hoped so, else I am certain that in the course of three months we shall not have an English soldier in the island, if they continue to die as they have done for this sometime past. The officers have suffered just as much as the men. I am the only officer of the regiment who has not been sick, and how I have weathered it so long is to me astonishing. In the conquest of this island we have suffered little by the sword, but sickness has played the devil. This is a subject too shocking to dwell upon, though we are so habituated to hear of deaths, that the death of a man is scarcely more noticed than that of a fly.

I forgot to tell you that we left Calvi the 19th August—my birthday—and embarked on board transports for this place, which is not above a day's sail with a good wind, but we unfortunately were kept nearly a week at sea. I believe I never gave you an account of Bastia; indeed I don't know whether I can, further than that it is a large and populous place, and resembles very much the generality of French towns. We are very much crowded here with French refugees who came from Toulon, so much so that the officers cannot get lodgings, which I think a great hardship after having been so long in the field. I have been employed since I have been here in recruiting my kit, which was rather the worse for campaigning.

My bedding and cot I had the misfortune to lose the first week I was in Corsica, which was, I think, the greatest misfortune that could happen to a man, except the loss of his head. My softest bed for many months was the ground, with one blanket (which I purchased) to cover me. It was not really cold, so it did not much signify. You used to tell me what a lazy life a soldier's was. I don't know how it is, but I have not yet found it so, without you call lying in one's clothes for three or four months together, mounting out-pickets, and all such pleasant amusements being lazy. I assure you that the little service I have seen here has done me a great deal of good, and has shown me that there are more rough things than smooth in life.

We are going to be very gay here. An Italian Opera is shortly to open, which is to be patronised by the Governor, and is much approved of by the garrison. A coffee-house for English papers is also to be established, which I think a much better thing than the former. In fact, you do not know how grand we are going to be.

The *Moselle* frigate, which, as I told you, went into Toulon with all our baggage and was captured, fell into our possession again coming out of Calvi, but the '*Sans culottes*' took care that we should have none of our things with her. I shall come in for some prize-money for Calvi. Two fine frigates were taken with the town—*La Melpomonie* and *La Mignonne*, which, it is to be hoped, will fetch some cash.

This letter and the following one give some idea of the life of a subaltern in a marching regiment on foreign service in 1794, and for that reason are not without interest. They deal little with politics, because such matters did not concern a junior lieutenant in the army who had sufficient to occupy his time in looking after the welfare of his men, and in performing the ordinary routine duties of his regiment and of the garrison. And it may be taken as certain that a subaltern in Moore's regiment did not have much idle time.

Bastia, October 21, 1794.

Since my last, Sir Gilbert Elliott has been appointed Viceroy of the extensive kingdom of Corsica, on account of which the municipality gave a Ball to the officers of the garrison and inhabitants. It was 'perfect liberty and equality,' for I believe such a mixture of people never was seen at any assembly whatever. The supper induced a great many of the poor Toulon emigrants, of whom there are numbers here, to go. Without exaggerating, they eat more voraciously and in a more unchristianlike manner than any pack of hounds I ever saw. It was certainly the most beastly sight I ever beheld, though at the same time the most laughable. Some pulling fowls into pieces with their hands; others legs and shoulders of mutton, and many pocketing. In short, it was the most complete scramble that I ever saw, or, I believe, ever was seen. Colonel Hely, of the 11th, gave the garrison a Ball last week, which was done in a very genteel manner. General Stuart gives one tonight, which, I daresay, will excel them all in brilliancy. He is a very gentlemanlike, pleasant man.

Sir Gilbert Elliott went yesterday to Corte, where he is going to stay a few months, and then returns to Bastia. Corte is distant about five-and-forty miles from here, and is the place where the Corsican parliament is held. There is an excellent road all the way to it, which was made at considerable expense by the French. I cannot give you any account of the country, as I have seen so little of it. Those who have been round the island, and in the internal parts, do not speak very favourably of it. I am sorry I cannot tell you our troops get much better, though it is to be hoped that they soon will, as the weather begins to get cold and consequently more favourable to their complaints, which are chiefly the fever and ague. We continue daily to bury a great number of men, and I am afraid we shall for this some time to come. It is a shocking sight to go round the different hospitals, which are crowded with patients. It is a duty which we have frequently to do, and which, you may conceive, is not a very pleasant one, though at the same time very necessary.

Poor Tourle of our regiment has been extremely ill ever since we left Calvi, and has just gone, with another captain of ours, to the internal parts of the country for the recovery of their healths. Most of the officers who have had this complaint have gone over to Italy, which is no doubt the best place, the climate being so favour-able. We cannot muster above a hundred and fifty men fit for duty now, and I am afraid it will be some time before we can call ourselves a regiment again. The 12th Regiment of Light Dragoons embarked here for England the other day, and sailed with Lord Hood, who is also going home.

The French fleet still continues to be blocked up by us. What will be the event of the blockade is not in my power to tell. Some pretend to say that the French left Toulon through policy. It no doubt keeps that port open. I can scarcely imagine that that was their intention, but leave it to more able politicians than myself to judge. By the last accounts from the Continent, we heard that a general action was daily expected. What will be the result of it we are anxious to hear. Our loss in the West Indies, I see by the papers, has been very considerable both by the sword and by sickness. The French appear to still keep a very strong post in Guadaloupe, and before it is taken much blood will be shed, I imagine.

This letter contains two items of public interest—*viz*., that Sir Gilbert Elliott had been appointed Viceroy of Corsica, and that Admiral Lord Hood had sailed for England. To the subaltern Sir Gilbert's appointment and Lord Hood's departure meant little; to his colonel, who was behind the scenes, they meant a good deal; and to General Stuart they meant still more. It was the beginning of the end, and the end was the loss of Corsica to Great Britain. The veteran Admiral, who had already passed his seventieth year, resigned, ostensibly because England refused to send him the reinforcements for which he asked,[1] but in reality because he had had a "personal quarrel with Lord Spencer, then the head of the Admiralty."[2] Accustomed to carry all before him, and to win victory after victory, he became the idol of the people, and in the eyes of the navy he remained for many years the very essence of a fighting sailor who could do no wrong. His vanity was flattered, and, as he advanced in years, he began to consider himself infallible, refusing to listen to any advice which did not fall in with his own views.

We have seen how he treated General Dundas and his successor General Stuart, and, although it is evident that he was well acquainted with Moore's worth, his pride forbade him to acknowledge that any soldier could help him. With Sir Gilbert Elliott, as a pure civilian, his relations had always been different. Each knew that the other's good word would carry weight in England, and each showed an equal contempt for the opinions of soldiers. Sir Gilbert had lived on board the *Victory* with the Admiral for some months prior to his appointment as Viceroy, and had acquired the greatest admiration for the gallant sailor, who doubtless impressed upon the future Viceroy the importance of forming judgments for himself and not listening to the suggestions of the military commanders.

With the departure of Lord Hood, the navy ceased to be interested in Corsican affairs, so all cause for rivalry between the two services came to an end. A new rivalry, however, at once arose. Sir Gilbert, as Viceroy, became an autocrat, and although the exact terms of his commission had not yet been made known to him, he took a leaf out of Lord Hood's book, and informed General Stuart that he considered himself commander-in-chief. The General, however, was not the man to quietly accept a subordinate position in the force with which he had completed the conquest of Corsica, and he politely gave Sir Gilbert to understand that he intended to retain the command of the

1. Southey's *Life of Nelson*.
2. Maurice's *Diary of Sir John Moore*.

troops until the Viceroy should receive the King's commission authorising him to assume the functions of commander-in-chief, when he would be prepared to hand over the command.

Sir Gilbert was content to bide his time, but friction, of course, was inevitable, since, without a complete understanding between the heads of the civil and the military departments, it was impossible to establish any proper form of government in a newly acquired British possession. Moore's position is a little difficult to understand, as at that time he held no appointment other than that of lieut.-colonel commanding the 51st Regiment, although he had been recommended for the post of Adjutant-General, in place of Sir J. St Clair, who was going home. Yet all along Moore was General Stuart's right-hand man, and to all intents and purposes acted as his chief staff officer. Consequently, he upheld his General in everything that he did, and resolved to stand or fall with him. And the fall eventually came, though not for some months.

In the meantime the troops were moved about and garrisons established at various places, while three battalions of Corsicans were raised for home defence. The 51st continued to garrison Bastia until the end of the year, and from that place Sam Rice, on the 28th December (1794) wrote to his father as follows:—

I am sorry to tell you that, since my last, we have had the misfortune to lose poor Captain Tourle,[3] who died a martyr to the complaint of this climate. He was the handsomest and most healthy man I ever saw. No regiment, I believe, ever lost so worthy a fellow, both as an officer and man; nor was any one ever more regretted. He was buried with all military pomp, attended by the two generals and all the officers of the garrison. We have still two or three officers ill, but not dangerously so. The nature of the climate is such that, if once attacked, a person is subject to relapses. What is very singular is that the inhabitants throughout the country are subject to the same complaint, which carries off numbers of them.

There was a report the other day that the French fleet was off Ajaccio, but it was unfounded. Admiral Hotham's fleet is at Leghorn, and is daily expected at St Fiorenzo. We expect to

---

3. James Tourle entered the 51st as ensign, 1784; lieutenant, 1790; captain, 1791. He commanded the light infantry company, and died on the 6th November 1794. Colonel Moore mentions him as "a gentlemanly, spirited officer, as well as a worthy, cheerful companion."—Maurice's *Diary of Sir John Moore*, vol. 1.

march in a few days for Corte, to take up our quarters there. It is by all accounts a wretched place, but we are all happy at the thoughts of anything for a change. There are three Corsican battalions raised here. If they are to be drilled as our soldiers are, to stand the charge, which I suppose they are, I do not know how they will behave, as their manner of fighting is what we call bush-fighting—that is, to take a steady aim upon any one from behind a bush or tree,—in short, from any place from which the man can fire without being seen.[4] I see that there is a talk of peace. I am afraid that, if we make peace, we must resign the West India Islands and perhaps the famous island of Corsica, which will be a great loss to Government.

If I have made many blunders in this letter, I ascribe it all to a pretty Corse, who has been chatting to me all the time from the opposite window.

In the first week of January 1795, Sir Gilbert Elliott received despatches from home, giving him supreme command of the army in Corsica. There-upon General Stuart resigned, and at the same time General Trigge was appointed by the Viceroy to command the troops, and Colonel Moore was put in orders as adjutant-general, though, before taking up the appointment, he took the 51st to Corte and settled the regiment in its new quarters. Grave fears of a French descent on Corsica soon began to be entertained, and the defence of the island against a strong invading force gave the military authorities cause for apprehension. The British fleet in the neighbouring waters was still, however, of sufficient strength to give a measure of confidence to the sister service on shore, and if there were jealousies when the army and the navy were employed together, they were forgotten by the soldiers when they heard of the sailors' victories at sea. At any rate, so much may be gained from the following letter, written by Sam Rice from Corte on the 28th March 1795:—

What has been passing in this part of the world for this last month is certainly worth relating, but how to do it I am certainly much at a loss. I will begin with Admiral Hotham's engagement with the French fleet, but of course all I know of

---

4. The Corsicans were by nature true light infantrymen, and some years later Sir John Moore suggested the advisability of recruiting, for the British army, a light infantry corps in Corsica, whose inhabitants he considered to be the most suitable in Europe for the purpose.

the business is from hearsay. I can give you no days or dates, for when the French fleet came out and when ours attacked I know not, except that it all happened. A few days ago the French fleet appeared off Cape Corso, which did not a little alarm us, particularly as our fleet was not then in the Bay of St Fiorenzo. We concluded, of course, that a descent was intended, which was really the case. However, the Viceroy immediately sent an express in an open boat to Admiral Hotham, who was then with the fleet at Leghorn, and the next morning our fleet was in sight.

The French still kept in the same place, drawn up in *ligne de bataille*, and seemed resolved to meet us—like true Republicans, to conquer or perish in the attempt. Our fleet, coming up, soon made a change in the business, for the French set off as fast as possible, and we after them with a favourable wind. As the French ran, the fight could not be general, and, I believe, would not have taken place at all had not the *Inconstant* frigate—a remarkably fast sailer—borne down upon the French and en- gaged a 74, whereupon the French Admiral ordered two other 74's to her relief. By that time the *Illustrious* and *Courageux*— two of our 74's—came up and engaged the *Ça Ira* and *Censeur*, and I believe as desperate an action as ever was fought ensued. The French ships at last were obliged to strike, but not before having seven hundred men killed on board one of their ships alone. The *Courageux* lost all her masts, and the other was con- siderably damaged.

Those, I believe, were the only ships which came into action; the rest made the best of their way to Toulon, it is supposed, excepting the *Sans Culottes*, a first rate, who was obliged to put into Genoa, with the loss of her masts, carried away in a gale of wind which came on soon after the engagement. The intention of the French fleet in coming out of Toulon was to proceed immediately to Corsica, to enter the Bay of St Fiorenzo, to land ten thousand troops, cut out of the harbour four sail of the line (which they had been informed Admiral Hotham had left behind), and then set off with them. The scheme was excellent, but, fortunately for us, it did not succeed, for it would have given them a complete superiority by sea, and probably we all should have been made prisoners of war, as it would have been impossible, I should think, for us to have defended ourselves with so small a force of British as we have in the island. The French having troops on board accounts for the number of men who were killed on the *Ça Ira*.

Since I began my letter an express is arrived from Bastia with the news that, after the dispersion of the French fleet, five sail of the line fell into the hands of the Spanish fleet, which was coming from Carthagena to our assistance. This news is generally supposed to be authentic, which I hope may be the case. I forgot to mention to you before that the *Berwick*, a 74 of ours, who, I think I told you in my last, had rolled her masts overboard in a gale of wind, was going from St Fiorenzo to Leghorn to be repaired, when, unfortunately, she fell in with the French fleet off Cape Corso, and was taken. She, notwithstanding, made a very gallant action, in which her captain was killed. Our fleet is now in Porto Spezia, not far, I believe, from Genoa.

The details of the fight described above are substantially correct, though the engagement was carried on for two days, and the bulk of the fighting was done by the *Agamemnon* (Captain Nelson). Undoubtedly, by this action Admiral Hotham saved Corsica for the time being, but his victory was not as complete as it might have been, or would have been, if Nelson had been in command of the fleet. The latter recognised the necessity for staking everything on the destruction of the French fleet there and then, and endeavoured in vain to persuade the Admiral to pursue and prevent the enemy from reaching Toulon. Hotham's contentment at the result of the engagement bore fatal fruit, for the French ships which escaped to Toulon soon refitted, and having been joined on the 4th April by some ten others from Brest, formed a very powerful fleet, and became a serious menace to the small British garrison of Corsica, at the best of times not strong enough to resist invasion, and now much reduced by sickness. About this time the 51st lost another officer, and Rice inveighs against the climate again:—

"I am sorry to tell you," he writes, "that we have had the misfortune to lose Captain Alcock[5] of our regiment, who departed this life, like poor Tourle, a martyr to the complaint of this cursed climate. He had been but a short time ill at Bastia, from whence he went to Leghorn for the recovery of his health, but on his first landing was seized with a violent fever, which carried him off in the course of a few days, in spite of the faculty.

You may recollect my mentioning both him and his brother—the latter who was so civil to me on coming from England, and the former on my joining the regiment. Thus (in Alcock and Tourle) we have lost two of the worthiest, gentlemanlike, and handsomest men that ever any regiment possessed—the one captain of grenadiers, the other of light infantry. They were both great friends of Colonel Moore's, and, in short, of all the officers.

"We still continue to be very sickly in our regiment, having above one hundred privates sick in the hospital, and an equal proportion of officers, for of the latter we have here five sick in the hospital, one in Italy, two gone home for the recovery of their healths, two dead, and several others who have had a lucky escape from death. What great acquisition this island can be to the Crown of Great Britain I leave to abler politicians than myself to determine. It certainly has a tolerable bay for our shipping, and that is all. It has been a fine burying-ground for the British this last year, and if we continue during this next year to bury in the same proportion, I am afraid that the air will become more pestilential than it naturally is. In the time of the Romans this place was well known for its insalubrity, and the banishment of a criminal to Corsica was thought sufficient punishment. We expect Colonel Moore here daily, who is coming for change of air, he having been likewise ill."

Soon after this it appears to have gradually dawned on even the regimental officers that the defences of the island were not in too satisfactory a condition. Moore, who was indefatigable in touring the country, knew that the coast-line was open everywhere, and that the towns were defenceless. The Viceroy, generally optimistic, at times suffered from panic, and went so far as to consult the military authorities on the state of the defences and how they could be improved. He had his own views, however, on the subject, and as they differed entirely from those of the adjutant-general, little, if any, improvement took place. Moreover, intrigue was at work among the Corsicans, many of whom already doubted if British rule was any better than French. How much the "man in the street," otherwise the regimental subaltern, knew of what was going on is shown by the following letter from Sam Rice:—

---

5. Charles Alcock, ensign, 51st, 1781; lieutenant, 1786; captain, 1791.

I marched here about a fortnight ago with a detachment to assist in doing duty in this garrison. How long I shall stay here I cannot say. The number of French prisoners that we have in different parts of the island makes the duty hard, as they must, of course, be guarded. I went yesterday with a party to fetch above a hundred of them from near Fiorenzo, and brought them here the same day. They behave themselves very well at present, but should the French fleet appear off the coast I don't know what they may do.

A report prevails here that the French have received a reinforcement from Brest of six sail of the line. If such is the case I think we shall not long remain in the island. The French have a great party here, who would immediately join them in the event of a descent, and those who are now of our party would, I daresay, be better paid by the French, and so abandon us—such is the character of the Corsicans. If we may believe the French, they will not come here; they say that they are a nation too polished to ever think of so barbarous a country as Corsica. Barbarous as it is, I daresay they would be glad to chase us from it; not that it would be of any value to them, but, as long as we are here, they will be ever jealous, and indeed, in my opinion, very naturally so. We have orders to hold ourselves in readiness to take the field. Provisions and ammunition are constantly going to the interior of the country, in case of a retreat. Do not be surprised if my next is from some camp among the mountains. I send this by Captain St George, who takes home the Viceroy's despatches.

From this letter it would seem that the existence of two political parties among the Corsicans was a matter of common knowledge, and it would seem also to have been generally-known that one party favoured the French and the other the English. How the strings were pulled was probably only known to a very few Englishmen; possibly only to the Viceroy and Moore. Yet the puppets, placed upon the stage, played gaily to the audience for a while, then snapped their strings and played without them. From the beginning the Viceroy's methods had been distasteful to the people, and their beloved Paoli, the Corsican patriot, endeavoured to hint as much to Sir Gilbert, who, however, took the hint as unwarrantable interference.

From that time the Viceroy became distrustful of Paoli, and set up, in opposition to him, one Pozzo di Borgo, a man versed in intrigue, of few scruples, and hated by the Corsicans, who, though they continued to be loyal to the British Government, distrusted the influence which Pozzo had over the Viceroy. Had Sir Gilbert kept in with Paoli, and governed through him, all might have gone well. Instead, as Sir J. F. Maurice[6] puts it, he attempted to apply the British Constitution to a people to whom it was unsuited, and, in doing so, he used as his instrument a worthless man, who had not the confidence of the people.

Now, Moore was a personal friend of Paoli, and the Viceroy knew it, and he suspected Moore of intriguing against him, though, had he been a judge of character, he would have known that Moore was always too straightforward and outspoken to be capable of intrigue. Yet, believing that Moore was disloyal, he took the step which any man so placed would take. Not being an Oriental potentate, he did not have his enemy quietly poisoned off, but he wrote home and asked for his removal, and Moore was, in September 1795, ordered to quit the island within forty-eight hours.

On the 4th October Moore visited the 51st at Corte and shook the dust of Corsica from off his feet. After his departure the plot thickened, and in the early months of 1796 matters began to assume an uncomfortable attitude; disaffection among the people grew rife; and Paoli, in despair, went to England. From bad, things then went rapidly to worse, and the following letter from Sam Rice shows how, by the middle of the year, Corsican affairs were already approaching a crisis.

Bastia, June 27, 1796.

Our correspondence, I am afraid, will, every day now, become more uncertain and of course less frequent, owing to the French having overrun so great a part of Italy, and the rapid progress which they are still making. Our last news from Leghorn was that the Republicans were within a very few hours' march of that place; if so, the communication by that part of Italy will be entirely at an end. An officer from this garrison, who is going to England, and who will be the bearer of this, in order to be certain of avoiding the French, sets out this evening for Civita Vecchia, a seaport near Rome, and from thence will cross the Roman territories to some place on the Adriatic coast, whence

6. *Diary of Sir John Moore.*

he will take a vessel for Venice.[7]

I have the pleasure to tell you that the Regiment left Corte the beginning of this month. After what I have told you of that place in former letters, you may imagine that none of us regretted leaving it and its polite and agreeable people. Since my last, things in Corsica have been in a very disagreeable situation. The cause of the discontent of the Corsicans was first owing to the taxes, which they thought too oppressive. That discontent was not then by any means general, only some few villages refusing to pay by force of arms, but they were soon compelled by a party of our garrison from Corte. The last and most serious revolt happened about twenty miles from Corte, at a place called Bagnano. The Viceroy determined to put an end to such hostile acts, and came in person to Corte to give energy to the business. He was attended by a numerous suite of the most respectable people of the island, and also by a number of British and foreign troops.

The troops from Bastia were joined by our grenadier company and light infantry company, to which latter I have the honour of belonging. When everything was ready for the campaign we marched for the revolted country, our army consisting of near five thousand men—British, foreigners, and natives. The first impediment we met with was a fort, on a very commanding situation, built in the time of the French. The Corsicans, who were in possession of it, refusing to submit at discretion, the troops were immediately-ordered to surround it. Our two companies marched directly up to the fort and kept a very hot fire of musketry on it for some time, but, finding it impossible to scale the walls, we were obliged to retire, with the loss of our too brave captain of grenadiers, four privates killed and five wounded. It is since said that poor Shawe,[8] who was the person that fell, had no such orders as he was attempting to carry out. Whether he had or not it is now impossible to say. When anything fails the blame is generally cast on the sufferer.

No sooner had this unfortunate business happened than the news came from Corte that the town and foundry of that place were surrounded by natives, and that they were determined to

7. According to the postmark this letter was not delivered in London until the 19th August.
8. Robert Shawe, ensign, 51st, 1782; lieutenant, 1788; captain, 1793.

cut off" the Viceroy and the army, upon which we were immediately ordered to retreat on Corte. This rebel army was now so formidable near Corte, and so determined, that their chief sent word to the Viceroy that if he would not redress their grievances he should be under the necessity of doing it himself by force of arms, or something to that purpose. The Viceroy, wishing to spare blood, granted them nearly, I believe, what they wanted, which was the dismissal of his Corsican minister and some other men who had become odious to the people.

The short and long of the business is that the people, not approving of the Viceroy's choice of his ministers and people about him, took the opportunity I before mentioned of forcing him to act in a different manner. What was first thought to be the revolt of a few villages has ended in that of nearly the whole country. Things are at present pretty quiet, but there is still a very considerable republican party in the island, and it is said that the French have landed a great many arms here, and have sent over officers to incite the people against us.

I have the pleasure to tell you that I am now oldest lieutenant. If a vacancy should happen I would not wish to purchase, as it is very probable, if I have good luck, that I shall get on without, particularly as the war is not yet at an end.

Little did Rice think when he despatched this letter that within four months he and his regiment, together with the remainder of the British troops, the Viceroy and his staff of civilian officials, would be driven from Corsica. Yet during these four months events happened swiftly, and a combination of circumstances—many quite unforeseen—overwhelmed the Viceroy. He himself for a long while had been extremely unpopular with the people, who were for the most part in open rebellion. Napoleon Buonaparte was carrying all before him on the Continent, and the accounts of his many victories filled with admiration the minds not only of the French "emigrants," but also of the Corsicans themselves, who gloried in the knowledge that the conqueror was a Corsican. Then Spain, previously leagued with the other powers against the French Republic, basely deserted and went over to the enemy.

As soon as this was known in England, the British Government, fearing the worst, and aware that the British fleet in the Mediterranean was not equal to the combined Spanish and French fleets, decided forthwith to withdraw all the troops from the Mediterranean, and sent instructions to Sir Gilbert Elliott to evacuate Corsica.

But before this, the Viceroy, on hearing of the capture of Leghorn by Napoleon, had despatched Nelson to occupy the Isle of Elba, where he established a small force as a safeguard to Corsica, and he now proposed to withdraw altogether from the latter island, and assemble the troops at Porto Ferrajo, in Elba, preliminary to carrying out his orders to remove the troops from the Mediterranean. Nelson, on the 14th October, brought the British fleet to Bastia, for the purpose of conveying the troops to Elba, and he arrived only in the nick of time, for he found the garrison hard-pressed, the French "emigrants" and the Corsicans having surrounded the citadel, to which the garrison had withdrawn, and demanded its surrender. Bastia itself was also in the hands of rioters, who had seized British property and threatened to make a prisoner of the Viceroy.

Nelson at once rose to the occasion, and checked the riot by training his guns on the town, at the same time sending a message on shore to say that he was prepared to bombard the place and utterly destroy it. The embarkation of the troops then commenced, but took some time, and on the 18th, when the evacuation was nearing completion, news came that the French had landed near Cape Corso and were marching on Bastia. The guns were hastily spiked, but only just in time, for the last boat-load of soldiers had barely left the shore, on the 20th, before the French advanced guard marched into the citadel of Bastia. The dignified withdrawal suggested by the British Government resolved itself, therefore, into a somewhat undignified flight, and, but for the timely arrival of Nelson's fleet, worse things might have happened— possibly an ignominious surrender.

The embarkation of all the troops without the loss of a single man, albeit that a gale of wind was blowing at the time, was a very fine performance; and the excitement was increased by the knowledge that the Spanish fleet was bearing down upon Corsica, and could not be distant more than twelve leagues. Yet Nelson took the fleet safely to Elba, and there disembarked the troops.

Thus was Corsica lost to Great Britain.

"It was impolitic," says Southey,[9] "to annex this island to the British dominions, but, having done so, it was disgraceful thus to abandon it. The disgrace would have been spared, and every advantage which could have been derived from the possession

9. *Life of Nelson.*

of the island secured, if the people had at first been left to form a government for themselves, and protected by us in the enjoyment of their independence."

As things turned out, it is doubtful if any good resulted from the occupation of Corsica, beyond that, for a period, it may have been useful to the British fleet in the Mediterranean, although it provided no facilities for refitting or repairing damaged ships. Of the evils produced by the conquest and possession of the island, enough perhaps has been said. For a time, at any rate, the reputations of Hood, Dundas,[10] Stuart, and Moore were sullied; the Corsicans suffered oppression, hardships, and punishment for rebellion; Paoli, the Corsican patriot, retired to England, and died there in exile;[11] England's fair name was dragged in the dust, and many of England's soldiers found graves in the island. Only two men came off with flying colours: the ex-Viceroy, Sir Gilbert Elliott, was raised to the peerage, and Nelson added glory to his name.

---

10. Sir David Dundas, at the age of seventy-four, was (1809) appointed Commander-in-Chief of the Army, *vice* H.R.H. the Duke of York (who resigned on account of certain scandals), and held office for two years, after which the Duke of York again took up the appointment. Sir David was a fine old soldier of the pre-Peninsular type, but, as commander-in-chief, was not popular with the army. He published, in 1788, his famous book on drill, which became the first authorised Manual for the British army; and he lived to the age of eighty-five.

11. He was buried in the old St Pancras cemetery, London; but, in 1889, his remains were exhumed and conveyed to Corsica for reinterment.

CHAPTER 5

From the Mediterranean to Ceylon

The island of Elba, where the troops had taken refuge, belonged to Tuscany, which, with other Austrian and Italian states, was allied with Great Britain against the French Revolutionists. Tuscany, however, was too weak to withstand the French invasion, and had already lost Leghorn. For a time, therefore, it became doubtful whether the British force in Elba would be able to obtain sufficient provisions from the mainland close to the island, as there was always the danger of the French cutting off the supplies, and Elba itself had few resources. To make certain that the troops should not starve, it was decided to despatch a small expedition to the mainland, to dislodge the French from Piombino and the neighbourhood, and keep the communications open. This was satisfactorily carried out in November (1796) by Colonel Wemyss and a column consisting principally of the Royal Irish Regiment, and Piombino was held by the British for the next three months without being troubled by the French. Pure good fortune saved the troops, both on the mainland and in Elba, at this time, for before the end of the year the British fleet was withdrawn from the Mediterranean, and, had the French chosen, they could have captured the force left behind without much difficulty.

Sam Rice's letters during this eventful period were few, probably because there was no possibility of sending them home, but in the spring of 1797 he succeeded in getting a letter through. He wrote as follows:—

> Porto Ferrajo, Isle of Elba,
> March 22, 1797.

The *Fox* cutter, which arrived here the other day from Sir John Jervis, with the famous and glorious news of the Spanish fleet being defeated,[1] sails tomorrow for Gibraltar. There is no news whatever to tell you from this quarter. The French, so near neighbours, are very peaceably inclined towards us, for they have not even paid us a visit, which they might very easily have done, and to our great annoyance. The most unfriendly thing that they have done since we have been here was to stop about two hundred fat bullocks, which were coming for the use of the army. Our troops being withdrawn from the cantonment [2] was the cause of that. The French have resumed their old posts,[3] and if we stay here much longer, we must take them a second time.

We are all heartily tired of this place; there is not an amusement of any kind; it is badly supplied with provisions, and everything at an exorbitant price. We unfortunate subalterns can scarce live. Our pay barely finds a good breakfast. These are the pleasures incident to a military life. We are as much in the dark as ever about our destination. Various are the reports. Some are of opinion that we are to go back to Corsica; others that we shall go to Portugal. The latter, I hope.

It seemed as if the authorities had forgotten the existence of the small force at Elba.

But neither Jervis nor Nelson forgot that a detachment of the British army was marooned in a little island off the coast of Tuscany, in imminent danger of capture by the French, and soon after the great naval victory off Cape St Vincent, Nelson dashed back into the Mediterranean, ascertained that de Burgh and his troops were safe, and conveyed them safely to Gibraltar.[4]

So, within a few weeks of the date of Sam Rice's last letter from Elba, he and his regiment were on the way back to the Rock, and the evacuation of the Mediterranean was complete. That anyone should have thought that there was a possibility of the troops from Elba reoccupying Corsica at this juncture shows how little was known of the situation and of the intentions of the British Government. The idea of going to Portugal had more in it, and Sam Rice's hopes were shortly

---

1. Off Cape St Vincent (S.-W. Portugal), 14th February 1797, where the Mediterranean fleet (15 sail) defeated the Spanish fleet (27 ships), capturing four ships and sinking several others. For this victory Sir J. Jervis was created Lord St Vincent.
2. Piombino, on the Italian coast.
3. On the coast of the mainland opposite Elba.
4. Gretton's *History of the Royal Irish.*

to be realised.

What Captain Mahan calls the "Warfare against Commerce" had now set in with a vengeance. To put the matter briefly: Napoleon, already practically master of Continental Europe, aimed at being master of the world, but found himself held in check by Great Britain and her fleet. To destroy the power of Great Britain, therefore, became his immediate object, and he knew that the only means of bringing this about was by the destruction of her commerce with the world. From England, he swore, the commerce of the world should pass to France; but England was prepared not only to hold her own, but also to wrest from France her little all. The English nation was determined that even if the resources of the country were drained to the last dregs, the despot of Europe should be held in check, and as time went on many a financial crisis threatened, so that only by the most strenuous efforts was it found possible to provide the sinews of war. Fortunately, at this time the people of England were patriotic to the core, and they raised large sums of money as "Voluntary Contributions," which they presented to Government for the purpose of carrying on the war, only ceasing to subscribe voluntarily when, in 1798, the Government introduced the Income Tax, and declined free gifts of money.

Napoleon began by ordering the maritime powers of Europe to close their ports to British trading vessels; and England at once replied that she would cut off all trade between the Continent and the outside world; that only through England should there be any trade at all. Such was the condition of affairs when the troops from Elba arrived at Gibraltar in the spring of 1797. Spain had now become the mere catspaw of France, who dictated to her on all occasions, and the two powers set to work to coerce Portugal into joining them, threatening the occupation of Lisbon by a French force if Portugal should refuse to close her ports to English ships. Portugal, observing the heavy combination against her, and the removal of the buffer between herself and France, almost forgot her ancient alliance with England; but, remembering it before she had committed herself, she rejected the Franco-Spanish overtures, declared herself for England, and armed to resist invasion.

To support her in her brave resolve England sent Sir Charles Stuart and a body of troops to Lisbon, and, in June 1797, the 51st proceeded from Gibraltar to join that force. But although Napoleon, smarting under the insult offered to the Republic of France, desired above all things to bring Portugal to her knees, he was too deeply involved in other parts of Europe to be able to spare troops sufficient to carry out his threat of marching on Lisbon. The British force in occupation, therefore, was not called upon, during the next fifteen months, to do anything more than ordinary garrison duty, which, according to Sam Rice, was uninteresting to a degree, though the Portuguese did their best to show hospitality to their allies, and though Rice's younger brother, Henry, came into Lisbon in his ship on more than one occasion, and helped Sam to make merry.

In June 1798, Rice, with less than six years' service, was promoted captain in the 51st, and given the command of the light infantry company—a much coveted post. But, as he had been for some years a light infantry lieutenant, it was natural that he should have the command of the company, which happened to become vacant at the opportune moment. As we have already said, the grenadier and light companies of regiments were composed of picked officers and men, who wore uniforms different from the rest of the regiment. In the case of the light infantry company the hair was not "clubbed," and the head-dress consisted of a leather cap—almost a skull-cap, with a large round peak straight up in front. The red jacket worn was quite short, and the gaiters were much shorter than those of other companies.

The officers and sergeants were armed with fusils, and wore pouches; so light infantry officers had silver epaulettes on both shoulders, the sword-belt being held in place by the one and the pouch-belt by the other. And upon the epaulettes, as well as upon the cross-belt plate, was worn the light infantry badge—a silver bugle-horn. A distinctive uniform of any kind always carries great weight, and doubtless the light company officers held their heads high, though they had some reason for doing so, since they knew that on active service their place was with the vanguard—in the forefront of the fight. But their daily pay was no higher than that of their brother officers of the battalion companies—*viz.*, captain, 9s. 5d., and lieutenant, 5s. 8d. And they could not complain, for a lieutenant-colonel received no more than 15s. 11d., and a major 14s. 1d.—cheap enough food for powder!

While the 51st were eating out their hearts in inaction at Lisbon, the British Navy was doing splendid work, sweeping the seas in every direction, capturing French merchant vessels, and protecting British commerce. Then Napoleon, seeking new fields for conquest, suddenly bethought him of Egypt, and forthwith transported thirty thousand men across the Mediterranean for the enterprise; but Nelson, following him, utterly destroyed the French fleet in those seas at the battle of the Nile, on the 1st August 1798. After this serious defeat, there appeared to be little prospect of Napoleon being able to carry out his threat of marching on Lisbon, and the 51st began to speculate about their future movements, having little doubt that they would be sent either to the West Indies or to the East Indies.

In each quarter there was every prospect of fighting, for the West India Islands had been the scene of much conflict of recent years, their commercial value being considerable, and their possession being, consequently, of great importance. In the East Indies, also, much was doing; the East India Company was still struggling for supremacy over the native rulers; the great Mahratta war was being waged with vigour; and operations in the Carnatic were not yet at an end. To develop the trade of the East Indies was at this time of vital consequence to England, and since the insignificant French possessions in India (Chandernagore and Pondicherry) had already been captured, British trade had no competitors in that part of the world. It was necessary, however, to strengthen British rule in the country by reinforcing the land forces; and it was necessary also to keep open the long trade route between India and England by means of the Navy.

The convoy system was by this time in excellent working order, and all British merchant vessels sailed under escort of men-of-war. It will be remembered that as far back as 1793 Sam Rice described in some of his earlier letters how large numbers of merchant ships assembled at Portsmouth to be convoyed to their destinations, and how the ship in which he sailed to Gibraltar was one of a fleet of two hundred. But besides these convoys, the various trading routes were patrolled by frigates and sloops-of-war, ever on the lookout for the enemy's cruisers or merchantmen. So by the one means or the other British ships were given a possibility of security, though occasionally a venturesome merchant, to whom time meant money, refused to wait for a convoy, and sent his ship to sea without one, as often as not to be captured. In 1798 Government decided to put a stop to these risky proceedings, and passed an Act making a convoy compulsory for every British merchantman.

The East India Company at this time possessed a fleet of magnificent merchant vessels, and armed with guns; but they always sailed in a body with a convoy of men-of-war, and, considering the time taken in collecting a sufficient number of ships for a convoy, the service was fairly regular. As a rule, the convoy was relieved at St Helena, men-of-war from the Indian station being responsible for the eastern half of the voyage, and the meeting of the outward and homeward bound fleets at the little island was, from all accounts, a fine sight.

It was to the East Indies that the 51st eventually received orders to move, because news had reached England that some of the native rulers were leaguing themselves with the French to oust the British, and in October 1798 the regiment embarked at Lisbon, joined the fleet of East Indiamen, and sailed for St Helena. In January they put in at the Cape of Good Hope, and the following letter, written by Sam Rice, from that place, shows that the voyage had not been without incident:—

Cape Town, South Africa,
January 26, 1799.

Had not our water failed, I should not have had the pleasure of sending you these few lines, it being the positive order for the Commodore not to touch anywhere, except *en cas de besoin*. We arrived here three weeks ago after a passage of twelve weeks. Nothing material happened, only that one of the large Indiamen ran foul of us in the night and carried away part of our stern. I never was so frightened in my life. I thought that it was certainly all over with us. You can form no idea of the shock. Seamen think nothing of these things, but as for me, who am not a seaman and have no wish to be, I am in constant fear. Soon after our arrival we received orders to disembark, and to remain until such time as a reinforcement should arrive. I am happy to say that yesterday orders were issued for a re-embarkation. Our heavy baggage goes on board tomorrow; I imagine we shall do so the day after. The General, whose name is Dundas, reviewed us the other morning, and was highly pleased with our appearance, and not without reason. We no doubt are, for our numbers, *the prettiest and best-disciplined regiment in the Service*. You will excuse my mentioning it.

Here we see the true regimental officer's pride in his corps. The spirit which Moore had created in his officers still lived—to the 51st officer no regiment was equal to the 51st,—and without such a feeling, which was by no means universal in those days, a regiment was of little real value. That the 51st was in as good order as the officers thought is vouched for by General Dundas's Inspection Report, which is still in existence.

The presence of a British general and British troops at Capetown in 1799 is worthy of comment, because no part of South Africa belonged to Great Britain at that time, and Capetown was not actually captured by the British, to hold for their own, until 1806,[5] and not acknowledged as a British possession until 1814. The reason was this:

In 1794 the Cape had been for many years in the possession of the Dutch East India Company, whose rights no other Europeans disputed, and at the end of that year the French overran the Netherlands, the Hereditary *Stadtholder*, the Prince of Orange, taking refuge in England. Fearing that the French would proceed against the Dutch colonies, the Prince thought of his alliance with Great Britain and Prussia, and forthwith (February 1795) sent to the Dutch Governor of the Cape a despatch, ordering him to admit into the colony any British troops which might be sent, in order that they might protect the Dutch possession from a French invasion. This despatch was conveyed to the Cape by a British fleet, carrying British troops, but the Governor, knowing that the Netherlands had become a Republic and had joined France, refused to accept the orders of the exiled *Stadtholder*. The British General's position was a peculiar one; he had been ordered by his Government to occupy Capetown as a friendly measure, but this the Dutch Governor declined to allow him to do.

A month was spent in negotiations, and when these failed, General Craig took matters into his own hand, occupying Simonstown, and declaring his intention of carrying out his orders. The Dutch flew to arms, and expressed their determination to resist the unwarrantable intrusion, but in August were driven out of the position which they had taken up. In the following month a reinforcement of three thousand British soldiers joined General Craig, and against these heavy odds the Dutch could do little, so that the occupation of Capetown on the 16th September be-came an easy matter. From that time until 1803 the British held the Cape, nominally for the Dutch, but in reality for Great Britain; but by the Peace of Amiens, signed in March 1802, it was restored to the Dutch, with the proviso that the English East India Company could use it as a place of call.

In April 1799 the 51st disembarked at Madras, and took up quarters in Fort St George. Southern India (or the Carnatic, as it was then usually called), which, for some years past, had been in a state of unrest, owing to the tyranny of the notorious Tippoo of Mysore, was still the scene of military operations, but the 51st arrived just too late to take part in the great victory at Seringapatam, where, on the 4th May, the British force stormed and captured Tippoo's stronghold, annihilated

---

5. Sir David Baird, the hero of Seringapatam, commanded the troops, and Sir H. Popham the naval forces.

the Mysore army, and killed the infamous ruler himself. After that the country gradually settled down to comparative quiet, and the British troops, no longer required for keeping order, were free for employment elsewhere, the 51st receiving orders for Ceylon.

"The homeward-bound fleet leaves the Roads tomorrow," wrote Sam Rice, from Fort St George, Madras, on the 9th August 1799. "The mail is ordered to be made up this evening. Only one ship has left this coast for England since our arrival, which was with the news of the capture of Seringapatam. I was then with a detachment up the country, and did not know of her sailing, which accounts for my not having written before.

"I am sorry to say that we were not fortunate enough to share the honours with the conquerors of Mysore and divide with them the immense treasure of the tyrant in his capital. It is at least two thousand pounds out of my pocket, besides the chance of plunder—and being a flank company officer would have assisted me. It cannot be helped; better fortune another time. By the last news from Europe, this part of the world is likely to be the quietest for some time to come.

"The war seems only to be just begun; the fate of England and of Europe in general must soon be determined. We embarked for Colombo, in Ceylon, soon after our arrival here. After cruising in the Bay for three weeks, and beating against the monsoon in vain, we were at length compelled to put back, with half our men sick. Our loss has been very great, and the Regiment is still very sickly. It is yet thought that, when the monsoon shifts, we shall again attempt Colombo. I cannot give you a favourable account of India; the climate is so hot that, in my opinion, no real pleasure can be enjoyed; but this is always the cry of a newcomer; time and necessity may reconcile me to it."

Sam Rice's occasional references to prize-money and plunder sound nowadays very mercenary in a British officer, but a century ago such things added zest to the soldier's life, for, it must be remembered, rewards were for the few, and medals only for the most senior of the officers. Though plunder was not regarded as legitimate, prize-money was quite in order and regulated by Government. Everything taken from the enemy was sold by Government, and the amount realised was divided among the troops engaged, according to rank, so that, in the case of big captures, even a private soldier often received as much as £100; at Seringapatam, for instance, more than a million of money was divided amongst the troops, who, moreover, pillaged freely on their own account. Eventually, but not until after the middle of the nineteenth century, prize-money came to be considered degrading to the spirit of the British soldier, who, it was thought, should have higher motives for doing his duty. Moreover, the distribution of prize-money to a part of the army, because that part happened to make a fortunate capture, was certainly unjust to the remainder of the army who might have had an equally hard time, though with less luck.

Consequently, it was decided to substitute for prize-money a regulated rate of field-service allowance to all officers and men engaged in a campaign, and captures from the enemy became the property of Government. Private plunder, as a relic of barbarism, was generally denounced, and was often dealt with as a crime for which the punishment was death, yet, even in the Peninsular War, it went on to a great extent, and was at times openly winked at. And the Peninsular War cannot be said to have seen the last of open plunder, as witness the sacking of the Summer Palace in 1860, and somewhat similar, though perhaps less open, incidents up to forty years later.

Apart from the moral aspect of the question, plundering by an army is, of course, subversive of all discipline, as men once given over to plunder become irreclaimably out of hand. It has to be dealt with drastically—no other means can check it; for it is a curious psychological fact that, even in this present age of civilisation, men whose morals are above suspicion, and who under ordinary circumstances would not dream of misappropriating the smallest portion of another man's property, regard the property of the absent enemy as fair loot. The man's arguments are simple ones: if he did not take the thing, someone else would do so; when the enemy fled he abandoned all his possessions; and findings are keepings. All said and done, nations themselves have not always set the best example; and some of the art treasures of Europe have changed hands more than once as a result of conquest.

It was not until February 1800 that the 51st again embarked for the voyage to Ceylon, having in the meanwhile returned to garrison duty at St Thomas' Mount and at Fort St George, and on its departure the Governor-General of Madras, Lord Clive, issued a special valedictory order, in which he remarked on the splendid state of the regiment and its excellent discipline. Landing at Trincomalee three days after leaving Madras, the regiment encamped there for a week, and then went on again, by sea, to Colombo, at which place it eked out, for nearly two years, an extremely dull garrison existence, as may be gathered from the following extract from a letter written by Captain Rice at Colombo, on the 26th July 1800:—

> Our stay at Trincomalee was not long. This is by far the best place in the island, but, although it is surrounded by cinnamon gardens and many other fine things, I cannot say much in its favour. It is something cooler than the coast of India; existence may be endured; but there is no society whatever. It is most probable that our Regiment will remain some time on this island,—I am afraid longer than we wish. Everything here is very expensive, owing to the difficulty of getting supplies from the coast (India), which can only be done in the particular seasons. A secret expedition has lately been fitted out at Madras. Part has already sailed with H.M.'s 10th Regiment. We are always left out; better luck, I hope, for the future. Little is stirring in the country since the fall of the Mysorean tyrant, nor do I think there will be for some time to come. A Mahratta war was talked of, but I believe they are too wise.

Ceylon, when the 51st went there, had two principal British settlements on the coast—Trincomalee and Colombo, which had been captured from the Dutch as recently as 1796.[6] The British were also in possession of, or at any rate had control over, such a depth of coastline all round the island as could be dominated by ships' guns. The remainder of the island was ruled over by an independent chief, with whom the Dutch had attempted to form treaties of friendship, and whom likewise the British approached. This chief, the King of Kandy, however, disliked, and had the strongest suspicions of the motives of, all Europeans, and was, moreover, inflated with a sense of his own importance, so the overtures of the British Governor came to naught.

On the death of the King of Kandy in 1798, trouble arose concerning the succession to the throne, which was usurped by a stranger without any pretensions. Plots and counterplots ensued among the Kandians, and after a while one of the parties endeavoured to enlist the services of the British, to establish order. The Governor refused to interfere in the internal affairs of the Kandians, and nothing of particular importance occurred until 1802, when some native traders

---

6. Sam Rice's brother Charles was present, with the fleet, at these captures. He died in 1801, and his Ceylon prize-money was subsequently paid to his relatives.

from British territory were ill-treated and robbed by the Kandians, and redress for the outrage being refused. Governor North decided to march on Kandy.

Although Kandy was no great distance from Colombo, it lay high up in the mountains, and was most difficult of approach, the roads being bad, the jungle dense, and the passes dangerous. On the 31st January 1803, the 51st, forming part of General Macdowall's column, commenced the march, and after surmounting many difficulties, on the 19th February stormed and carried two strong posts, and put the enemy to flight. Hardships and sickness told considerably on the men, but within a week of the first brush with the enemy, the 19th and 51st Regiments marched into Kandy, which the enemy had evacuated and set on fire. The capture of the capital had been tolerably simple, but little good came of it, for the general soon found that sickness had reduced his force to less than two thousand men, barely one half of whom were Europeans, that supplies were running short, and that his communications with Colombo were cut by the enemy, who began to assume a threatening attitude on all sides of Kandy. A few skirmishes took place during March; when, learning that no reinforcements would be sent to him, Macdowall patched up a truce with the Kandians, and leaving a thousand men, two-thirds of whom were natives, to garrison Kandy, withdrew the remainder of his force, including the 51st, in safety to Colombo, which was reached on the 9th April.

During the rest of the year small detachments of the regiment were employed in repelling aggressions on the part of the Kandians, who raided British territory in many directions. Several officers and a considerable number of men died of disease, and the 51st was reduced to a mere skeleton. Nor was the health of the other troops at Colombo any better; and when it became known, in June 1803, that the garrison at Kandy, now a handful of weaklings, was being besieged by the infuriated Kandians, it was found to be impossible to send a force to its relief; and India could not spare a single man for Ceylon, as all available troops were required for the Mahratta War.

In the end, the Kandians recaptured their capital, and murdered the remnant of the British garrison in cold blood, though preserving the life of Major Davie, the commandant, whom they cast into prison, doubtless under the impression that he might be useful to them some day. The war died out in 1805, without any attempt on the part of the British to revenge their murdered compatriots, for the reason that no sufficient reinforcements were ever available, and the fate of Major

Davie is pitiful to think of. For nearly nine years he languished in a dungeon in Kandy, and died there, worn out by disease, not to be revenged until 1815, when the power of the Kandian kings was broken forever, and the whole island taken over by the British.

The 51st continued to garrison Colombo until 1807, and suffered much from the enervating climate, losing a great many officers and men, and having a number of officers invalided home—amongst them Samuel Rice, whose constitution was undermined, and who never really recovered from the effects of service in Ceylon, although he managed to fight through many subsequent campaigns. In September the remnant of the regiment landed in England, after an absence of fifteen years, the last nine of which had been passed in absolute exile. Home news lost most of its interest during the six or eight months which it took to drift through to Ceylon, and what was going on in Europe affected the exiles little, for their own petty war and its attendant hardships gave them sufficient to think about.

Yet, in Europe stirring events had been in progress, and the 51st, in going to the East, were denied the satisfaction of taking part in the reoccupation of the Mediterranean, which commenced with the capture of Minorca by a force under Sir Charles Stuart, only a month after the regiment sailed from Lisbon. They missed also the subsequent capture of Malta in 1800, and the chance of sharing in Abercromby's great victories over the French in Egypt in 1801. But they did not miss much else, for the Peace of Amiens (March 1802) brought the war to a close, and though France again declared war against England fourteen months later, no actual fighting took place on shore.

The British navy, however, continued to be actively employed, more especially in frustrating Napoleon's designs for an invasion of England, and this grand scheme was finally wrecked in October 1805, when the mighty Nelson, at the cost of his life, almost annihilated the French fleet at the Battle of Trafalgar. Napoleon being thus deprived of the means of transporting his "Army of England" across the Channel, turned and vented his wrath on Continental Europe, carried his conquests far and wide, and proclaimed one of his brothers King of Naples, and another King of Holland.

That there was plenty of fighting in prospect for the army was apparent to the officers of the 51st when they reached England, but for the moment they had no men, and the next few months were devoted to bringing the regiment up to strength, as well as to gaining an insight into the vast changes which had taken place in the army and in military methods during the past decade; for the officers, who had been absent from England for so long, soon realised that they were considerably behind the times. In Ceylon they had heard little or nothing of the great reforms in progress at home—reforms initiated by none other than their old commanding officer, Major-General John Moore, and, as will be shown in the next chapter, far-reaching in their ultimate results.

CHAPTER 6

The Reform of the Army

After such brilliant work as was done by Abercromby's army in Egypt in 1801, it may seem strange that any one should have questioned the ability of the British army to meet and defeat any numerically equal force in Europe. Fortunately for England, however, there were in the army officers whose deep study of their profession told them that the tactics of fighting were moving towards a change, and that old methods before long would have to pass away. Fortunately, again, such officers were not carried away by the glamour of the recent victories in Egypt, and the fact that they themselves participated in those victories added considerably to the weight of their counsels. It has always been the case that campaigns, however successful they may have been, have been followed by reforms in the army; for it is only from experience gained in actual warfare that it is possible to discover the shortcomings of a force, or how to set matters to rights. There was, therefore, nothing peculiar in the move which was made in 1802 towards overhauling the affairs of the army, and the prime mover in the reforms was the Commander-in-Chief, H.R.H. the Duke of York.

As was mentioned in an earlier chapter, it was common knowledge, as far back as 1792, that a long immunity from European warfare was beginning to tell on the wellbeing of the British army, and that the officers were in a measure losing touch with their profession. Still, no immediate action was taken, and the good work done in India, the West Indies, and elsewhere led the authorities to believe that there was nothing very much amiss. In 1802, however, came the opportunity. The peace patched up in that year brought about extensive reductions in the establishment of the British army, and it became necessary to place a great many officers on half pay. Moore, who, after much foreign service, was then commanding the Canterbury district, and who, as we have previously shown, had great ideas on the subject of good officers, seized the opportunity offered by these reductions to weed out such officers as he deemed undesirable.

The matter of seniority was nothing to him, and he applied, at any rate to the regiments under his immediate command, the hitherto unheard-of principle—selection, pure and simple, and made by himself His methods were somewhat severe, and he did not confine his operations to the junior officers, as is evident from his correspondence with the Adjutant-General of the Army. "Some commanding officers," he wrote in 1803, "the state of whose regiments justify it, must be told to retire from the service, the duties of which they are unequal to. The command must not be allowed to devolve upon their majors, who may be equally incapable, but be given to officers of approved talents. One or two measures of this sort generally known would excite an exertion which at present is much wanted."[1]

Moore was ably supported, not only by the commander-in-chief, but also by his old commanding officer of Corsican days, General David Dundas, who, in these early years of reform, first was Quartermaster-General of the Army, and afterwards was in command of the Southern District—and so again Moore's commanding officer. Moore's suggestions carried immense weight with the authorities, and a great number of officers who had failed to take their profession seriously found themselves retired on half pay. The result, though disastrous to the officers concerned, put new life into the commissioned ranks, and opened the way for the remodelling of the whole organisation of the army. The question of the officers having been settled, and their zeal and efficiency having been assured, Moore's work was simplified, and it was on Moore—only a major-general commanding a comparatively small district—that the military authorities leaned in carrying out their scheme for the reorganisation of the army.

This was, of course, natural enough, for Moore himself, if not the originator of the scheme, was at any rate the chosen mouthpiece of General Dundas, whose views concerning the training of troops were held in high esteem. But what is not easy to understand is the absence of opposition on the part of the older conservative officers, senior to Moore. The fact, however, remains that he was given a free hand, and when, in 1803, he determined to reform the discipline and training of the army on lines which he had been working out for many years, principally during active service in the West Indies, Holland,

1. Maurice's *Diary of Sir John Moore.*

and Egypt, he was given the command of a special brigade of selected regiments, with which he was permitted to experiment to his heart's content.

The sole purpose of his system was to convert the British army into a thoroughly sound and reliable fighting machine, suitable to the times. He had observed that Napoleon was adopting new tactics; he foresaw that the times were changing; and he realised the fact that the experiences of fighting in India, in the West Indies, in Holland, and in Egypt would be of small value to troops pitted against Napoleon's trained veterans in Europe, unless such experiences were thoroughly examined, with a view to discovering if the army had learned anything worth learning, or if it was still behind the times. Moore was perfectly con-vinced that in tactical formations in the attack and the defence the methods of the infantry of the army were out of date; but he knew, also, that the men of the British army were made of sound stuff, and that under efficient officers they could be trained to do anything. It is worthy of note, however, that the changes which Moore introduced did not arise, as is usually the case, from any improvement in firearms, but rather from a careful study of recent campaigns in various parts of the world. In short, Moore saw what was wrong, and endeavoured to set matters right, with what result will presently be shown.

In order to understand how it came about that the British infantry within a few years proved more than a match for the French in the Peninsular War, it is necessary to have some knowledge of the methods of fighting previously adopted by the armies of the two nations, and then to see how Moore altered these methods, by assimilating the good and by eliminating the bad, by pruning and by inducing fresh growth. We shall see that, in the new system of training, everything depended on the regimental officer; and we shall see that, when war came, it was the regimental officer who made the British army almost invincible.

Without entering too deeply into the history of tactics, we may say that up to the middle of the eighteenth century the fighting formation of inantry, whether in attack or defence, consisted generally of solid bodies of troops, which marched up in two massive columns, and then deployed, in the face of the opposing force, into two lines each composed of three ranks. Skirmishers were then unknown; and very great attention was paid to drill. About 1757 we find the Austrians using light troops (Croats) to harass Frederick the Great's army on the march; but these do not appear to have been properly organised, and, though always annoying, they seldom acted with real judgment. In 1774 Mesnil Durand invented a system in which skirmishers played a considerable part. Battalions were to move in double company columns at deploying intervals, two of the ten companies of each battalion acting as skirmishers to cover the whole front of the line of columns.

It was held that in this way the fire of the skirmishers would make itself felt to such an extent that it would only remain for the heavy columns behind to push in and crush the enemy by sheer weight. This was to a certain extent the system adopted by the French in 1793, and employed by the French generals in the Peninsular War, and by Napoleon until his final defeat at Waterloo, except that the columns of attack were deep and solid, and not merely single battalion columns or lines of battalion columns.

It may therefore be said that skirmishers first took their place in the organisation of Continental armies about 1774, but years before that the question of their employment had been freely discussed. As early as 1754 Comte Lancelot Turpin de Crissé had published a work on the Art of War, in which he dealt with the uses of light troops at some length, and the British army had had its bodies of trained light infantrymen certainly before 1758.[2] In all probability they originated about the year 1757, when the British generals, fighting against the French in America, found that the latter's Red Indian allies perpetually annoyed them on the march and on other occasions, and determined to meet them in their own methods of fighting.

Consequently, every regiment in America was ordered to select "the most enterprising officers and the most active of the privates with the appellation of *Rangers*." Lord Howe, then commanding the 55th Regiment, but in 1758 raised to the command of the army in the field, was immensely impressed by the Red Indian methods of warfare, and was supported by several commanding officers, who realised the absurdities of tight clothes and movements in solid formation, when engaging the enemy in the rough forest country of the New World. The success which attended the experiment of the *Rangers* led to the formation of a light company in every regiment, and the valuable services which these companies performed during the next few years fully justified their existence. And the matter was carried still

---

2. Highlanders, in whom guerrilla warfare was inherent, had been employed much in the same way as light infantrymen for a number of years, though without any systematic training.

further, for, in 1758, a whole regiment was equipped for light work, and named Gage's Light Infantry.[3] In that year, however, while leading a desperate attack on the French, Howe was shot dead, at the head of the Rangers, in the hour of victory.

At the peace of 1763 all the light companies of regiments were reduced, and the lessons learned in America for the time being were forgotten. In 1770, however, some one remembered the value of light troops, and the light companies were established afresh. In all probability that someone was Lord Howe's brother, General William Howe, who had distinguished himself as a leader of light infantry in Wolfe's Quebec campaign of 1759, for in 1774 he was allowed to take the light companies of seven regiments to Salisbury, and exercise them as a battalion in certain manoeuvres which he had invented. There was apparently little similarity between Howe's formations and those of Mesnil Durand mentioned above, for whereas the latter's flank companies were employed with their own battalion, as part and parcel of it in the fight, Howe's idea was to take these companies away from their regiments, and form them into separate battalions, for distinct and special work. In this way Sir William Howe, in chief command of the British forces, employed the flank companies of regiments during the War of American Independence, the most important and most hazardous duties being performed by battalions composed of them.

Both Viscount Howe and his brother, Sir William, gained their first knowledge of light troops from the Red Indians, and it may perhaps be remarked that, in 1880-1881, irregular war-fare with the Boers gave us the idea of mounted infantry. There is a striking analogy between the old light infantry and the modern mounted infantry: each was the outcome of a desire for greater mobility than ordinary infantry soldiers were capable of; each began in the same way; the light company and the mounted infantry company contained the picked men of the battalion, and, in war, these companies of the best men were taken away from their regiments to work, with similar compa-

---

3. Fortescue (*History of the British Army*) says that the regiment was clothed in dark brown. This would seem to have been the first regiment in the British army to be designated "Light Infantry"; it was numbered the 80th, but was disbanded within a few years. In 1759 Morgan's Light Infantry was raised, numbered the 90th, and disbanded in 1763. For the next forty years no light infantry regiments appeared in the Army List. The following are the dates of the formation of other light infantry regiments: 1803, 52nd and 43rd; 1808, 68th and 85th; 1809, 71st and 51st; 1815, 90th; 1822, 13th; 1840, 105th and 106th; 1855, Royal Marines; 1858, 32nd. There are now in the Regular Army seven light infantry regiments, each with two battalions.

nies of other regiments, as separate battalions, the merits or demerits of which it is not necessary to enter into here.

To return to the development of light troops in the British army. In 1782 the light companies of nine regiments were assembled in camp at Coxheath, Kent, and, together with two battalions of infantry and two regiments of light dragoons, were practised in what was termed the "Dundas Exercises," which were being tried for the first time. A year or two later, Dundas visited the Prussian manoeuvres, obtained some fresh ideas, and then published his monumental work, which eventually became the first drill-book authorised to be used in the British army. Dundas, however, had very little new to say about light troops, and his exercises were practically on the Continental model. In 1794 Sir Thomas Graham[4] (afterwards Lord Lynedoch) raised a regiment (which was numbered the 90th), and had it equipped and drilled as a light infantry corps, though it was not recognised officially as such for another eleven years. It was in the above year that Moore was working with Corsican troops in the field, and he always considered the Corsicans the best light infantrymen in the world, although he acknowledged that they lacked the discipline necessary for holding their own against highly-trained troops.

In 1798 Howe[5] again came to the front, and superintended the training of a brigade of all arms, assembled on the Essex coast, in his light drill. Lastly, in 1800, H.RH. the commander-in-chief ordered the assembly at Horsham of a temporary corps, for the purpose of training a body of men in the use of the rifle, fourteen regiments being called upon to furnish thirty privates and a proportion of officers and non-commissioned officers. After the summer training, these men were moved to Blatchington, and were then formed into the Rifle Corps (95th),[6] for whom Colonel Coote Manningham and Lieutenant-Colonel the Hon. W. Stewart drew up the famous *Regulations*

---

4. Thomas Graham, of Balgowan, was born in 1748, and married (1774) a daughter of Lord Cathcart. On his wife's death in 1792 he joined Lord Hood's fleet as a volunteer, but came home in 1794 and raised the 90th, or Perthshire Volunteers, being gazetted to the command of it in the same year. He was thus forty-six when he obtained his first commission, but he became a famous general, and the victor of Barrosa.

5. This was the Sir William Howe previously mentioned, subsequently (1799) 5th Viscount Howe. His eldest brother, the 3rd Viscount, killed in 1758, was succeeded, as 4th Viscount, by his brother, the famous Admiral, who again was succeeded by his brother. Sir William.

6. Afterwards the Rifle Brigade.

for the Rifle Corps, published in 1801. The methods of training these riflemen were very similar to those employed in training temporary light infantry corps composed of the light companies of regiments, except in so far as the superior range and accuracy of the rifle over the flintlock musket altered the conditions of the attack and defence.

By this time it had been discovered that Napoleon had developed the use of his *voltigeurs* enormously, and that his victories were being secured by the judicious employment of these light troops; so English books dealing with the systematic training of light troops now began to appear. The earliest of these was one based on a translation of a work by a "German officer of distinction and of much military experience," which, first produced in 1798 (reprinted in 1801 and 1803), under the title of *Regulations for the Exercise of Riflemen and Light Infantry, and Instructions for their Conduct in the Field,* was ordered to be studied by all officers of the army.

Who that German officer was is never made clear, and in 1803 there appeared another and a far more valuable work, entitled *A Treatise upon the Duties of Light Troops,* translated from the German of Colonel Von Ehwald, but there is nothing in this book to lead one to believe that Von Ehwald was the author of the earlier work. The gallant Colonel had served in the Seven Years' War, commanded a corps of Hessian *jägers,* in British pay, during the American War of Independence, and subsequently commanded a light corps of the Danish army, and his book contains a mass of useful information on the training of light troops, as well as examples of their work in the field during several campaigns.

Judging by the contents of this treatise, it is more than probable that Sir John Moore had studied it in the original, for Von Ehwald's ideas on discipline and training were identical with those upon which Moore subsequently set to work. Both Von Ehwald and Moore held the opinion that an army which could place in the field large numbers of light troops, so highly trained and disciplined as to be capable of working intelligently in extended order in more or less independent small parties, would be able to outflank, outmanoeuvre, and defeat an enemy of superior strength who adhered to close formations. Rapidity of movement, however, and the ability to make good use of ground as well as of their fire-arms, were essential to the success of light troops, and Moore knew that unless there could be produced a higher standard of discipline than was yet known in the British army, it would be impossible to create light troops of any value.

And Moore's ideas of discipline differed somewhat from those of most officers of the time, in that he did not believe in the "mechanical discipline" which made a mere automaton of the soldier, but rather in that "intelligent discipline, best illustrated, perhaps, by a pack of well-trained hounds, running in no order, but, without a straggler, each making good use of his instinct, and following the same object with the same relentless perseverance."[7] In his determination to establish this new form of discipline lay Moore's success, and he always maintained that by no other means than by inculcating the strictest habits of intelligent discipline in all ranks could self-reliance and initiative come natural to a body of troops. Whether he discovered this for himself, or whether he learned it from Von Ehwald, or whether, again, both of them were following the lead of Napoleon, whose skirmishers had already made their mark in European warfare, the fact remains that Sir John Moore was the first person to attempt to apply it to a large number of British soldiers, and he was the first person to succeed.

In the summer of 1803, therefore, Moore commenced work with his famous brigade at Shorncliffe Camp, and he decided to train his brigade as light troops, not in the usual way by extemporising battalions out of light companies detached from various regiments, but by employing whole regiments. For this purpose the 52nd and the 43rd were, in 1803, formed into light infantry regiments, and, together with the newly raised Rifle Corps (95th), handed over to Moore to train. He began at the beginning, and thoroughly overhauled the existing regimental systems; he went deeply into interior economy, and instituted many reforms—so far-reaching and excellent that they have remained almost unaltered to the present day. He insisted that discipline could only be maintained by the officers of all ranks always being in touch with their men, and ever having their welfare at heart. A hard worker himself, he saw that all the officers of his brigade worked hard also; and during the training seasons at Shorncliffe the officers were seldom off duty on weekdays, and had to brush up for the general's inspection on Sundays, for Moore did not recognise any necessity for recreation.

On one occasion the father of a young officer wrote to the general to say that he proposed to send his son a horse. Moore's reply was characteristic: "that he should be very pleased that the horse should be sent, but that it would be necessary for the father to send with it

---

7. Colonel Henderson's *Science of War.*

someone to ride it, for his son would have no time to do so."[8] His first care was to have efficient officers; he watched them carefully, and he got rid of those whom he deemed useless for his purpose, thus laying the foundation-stone of the future building. With good and reliable officers, establishing a chain of responsibility from highest to lowest, with a thorough organisation of battalions on the company system, with non-commissioned officers and men no longer ruled with a rod of iron, but respecting and relying on their officers, Moore began to see his way clear.

His next step was to practise, for a considerable time, drill and movements in close formation—a proof that he was thorough, as well as patient. An ordinary man with a new hobby to ride might have been inclined to slur over, if not scoff at, things which he considered old-fashioned. But Moore had a use for them, because he intended to make his brigade absolutely perfect, and an example to be followed by every other brigade in the British army. His brigade was to be steadier on parade and better drilled than any other, and until he was sure that it was so, he restrained himself from taking the regiments on to their training as light troops. And he had other reasons, for he felt that square drill, practised as a means to an end, was the best discipline for men who were presently to act independently and work out things for themselves. Moreover, he knew that light troops alone would not win a battle, but that they must be supported by well-disciplined bodies of men, moving in close formation and maintaining strict order, until the moment arrived for them to be thrown into the fight.

Sir David Dundas took the greatest interest in all that Moore was doing, and often visited his camp. His drill-book was still the official manual, and, as the first of its kind, was of the greatest value. "There was, however, so much that was rigid, formal, and unnecessary in Dundas's drill that it gained for him the nickname of 'Old Pivot'; while he also made the fatal mistake of distributing the whole science of military evolution into eighteen manoeuvres, which were a sad stumbling-block to slow-witted officers. 'General,' said Sir John Moore to him in 1804, 'that book of yours has done a great deal of good, and would be of great value if it were not for those damned eighteen manoeuvres.'

"'Why—ay,' answered Dundas slowly in broad Scots, 'blockheads don't understand.'"[9]

---

8. Maurice's *Diary of Sir John Moore.*
9. Fortescue's *History of the British Army*, vol. 3.

Yet Moore struggled manfully with the eighteen manoeuvres, and tried new methods of performing them, before passing on to lighter movements—extended order formations, advanced-guards, rear-guards, and outposts.

Undoubtedly, Moore's opportunity was unique, for his brigade had its place in the defence of England, and it was thought that the French intended to land somewhere near Shorncliffe. Consequently, the brigade was considered to be on active service, and at the same time was being trained for war, a state of affairs which naturally tended to make all ranks keen to acquire military knowledge. There was none of the make-believe of peace training; only a few miles of sea lay between the brigade and the enemy, and on any dark night the French might attempt to effect a landing between the Martello Towers which studded the coast-line. At night, therefore, these towers and three neighbouring forts were fully manned, and outposts covered the camp on the heights above, the sentries being provided with ball ammunition.

By day, while a lookout was still maintained by the guards, the brigade was drilled and practised at manoeuvring over the country inland; and now and again the order was given to strike camp and march, when, within an hour, the whole brigade loaded up and moved off—with everything complete and ready for active service in any quarter of the globe. All this resulted from the discipline which the general instilled into his regiments, and for three continuous years he had them in his care. So that when, in 1806, he was called away for service in Sicily, he left his brigade in the highest state of discipline, and as light troops certainly superior to any in Europe. The proof of this Moore did not live to see, but his three regiments a few years later formed the Light Division, which throughout the Peninsular War carried all before it.

Moore developed light movements enormously, producing a marvellous elasticity in comparatively large bodies of troops, and under his training whole regiments became as mobile and rapid in manoeuvre as previously no company of a regiment had been. To swiftly reach a given point, and there bring as many rifles or muskets as possible into the firing line; to make every officer and man use his own intelligence in carrying out movements; and to impress upon them the necessity for mutual support,—were the chief aims of Moore's training; and he it was who originated for the British army that self-dependent Thin Red Line which so soon was to become the destroyer of Napoleon's deep and massive columns.

For it was proved over and over again in the long war which followed, that, with opposing forces of equal numbers, the line two-deep, every man of which was so disciplined as to stand firm, and every man of which had the opportunity of using his rifle or musket, could make short work of the more condensed three-deep line, or of the column which presented a large target, and which at the same time could return the fire only from the muskets of two ranks at the contracted head of the column. It is interesting to note that Colonel Von Ehwald was a strong advocate of the two-deep line both in attack and in defence, for purposes of firing as well as for using the bayonet. "In an attack with charged bayonets," he says, "I am convinced that, if the corps drawn up in two ranks advances resolutely upon the other in three, it will not be worse off for that rank less, as the pressure of one upon the other, of which the French tacticians speak, exists only in the imagination."

Now, the outcome of all this training of light troops was a new fighting formation for the British army. In the first place, Moore had proved that whole regiments could become intelligent and reliable skirmishers, if properly taught; and he had proved, also, that companies, or smaller bodies, of skirmishers, acting independently though at the same time working towards the consummation of a "general idea," were of the highest value when the commanders of skirmishing units were allowed a free hand. Next, Moore had discovered that, with these highly trained bodies of skirmishers out in front, harassing the enemy in every direction, keeping down his fire, and shattering his *morale* massive bodies of troops in rear were no longer required.

So he instituted the attack formation as follows:—First, the skirmishers in some strength; second, a two-deep line in close order; third, a similar line; and it was with these two lines, always kept in hand, that the *coup-de-grace*—in the shape of a withering volley, followed by a bayonet charge—was given, at the moment when the enemy had begun to feel the effects of the bickerings of the skirmishers. But the secret of success in the employment of these shadowy lines against the enemy's columns lay not only in the efficiency of the skirmishers, but also in the superior discipline of the troops behind, who were brought up in line of quarter-columns to within effective range of the position, and then deployed into shoulder to shoulder lines of two ranks.

It was for these reasons that Moore drilled his regiments to become equally proficient in close order movements as in skirmishing. Simple as all this may appear nowadays, it was a revolution in fighting methods, and necessitated a vast amount of preliminary training and disciplining; but Moore's system had been carefully watched by the authorities, and so satisfied were they of its soundness, that it was applied as far as possible to all regiments of the army. It took time, but the ultimate result was good, and it was soon found that a new spirit was gradually passing into all ranks.

To sum up the nature of the reforms introduced into the army between 1802 and 1807: we find, to begin with, a marked improvement in the zeal and efficiency of the officers, produced not only by getting rid of the useless ones, but also by the introduction of new regulations relating to the grant of first commissions and subsequent promotion. Thus the minimum age for an ensign was fixed at sixteen,[10] and an officer was required to have served at least three years for promotion to the rank of captain, and seven years to that of major. Next we find the establishment of a new and high code of discipline, as well as of morals, among both officers and men, from which followed a closer union between the one and the other, and a greater regard for the welfare of the soldier on the part of the officer. Again, one uniform system of drill and manoeuvre was laid down and rigidly enforced for each arm of the service, for hitherto such matters had been left to the commanding officers of corps.

> "Such changes," wrote Lord Londonderry,[11] "together with the establishment of hospitals for the wounded and disabled soldiers, and for the education of children whose parents had fallen in the defence of their country, could not fail of producing the most beneficial effect upon the moral of the British army, which, from being an object of something like abhorrence to its own countrymen, and of contempt to the troops of other nations, rose to command, as well as to deserve, the esteem of the former, and the respect and admiration of the latter."

The above is an outline of the somewhat startling ideas connected with military reform which were thrust upon the officers of the 51st on arriving home from Ceylon in the autumn of 1807, and they were

---

10. This order appears to have been held in abeyance during the Peninsular War, as officers as young as fourteen frequently joined regiments. Its object, however, was to abolish the pernicious custom of granting ensigncies to children in the nursery, and allowing them leave of absence until they were old enough to join.

11. *Narrative of the Peninsular War*, by Lieut.-General Charles William Vane, Marquess of Londonderry, G.C.B., G.C.H., Colonel of the Tenth Hussars. 1826. He was better known as General Charles Stewart, Adjutant-General of Wellington's army.

not slow to appreciate the situation. Their men were all new to them, as they had brought few back to England, and they realised at once that it would require strenuous efforts on their part to make up the leeway. It speaks well for them that they were not found wanting, and they were fortunate in having a commanding officer [12] capable of rising to the occasion. The necessity of getting into fighting trim with all speed was apparent to everyone; for the cloud over Europe still hung low and black, and the British expedition sent to Copenhagen was at the moment destroying the Danish fleet—an act which, it was well known, would increase Napoleon's hatred of England tenfold. And so it proved, for before the end of the year a French army invaded Portugal and entered Lisbon, and Napoleon thus fulfilled his promise of humbling England's ancient ally.

The difficulties encountered by the regiment in learning its new work were increased by constant changes of station; first it was quartered at Chatham, then at Chichester, while early in 1808 it moved to Gosport, and in the spring to Guernsey. There is no doubt that the regimental officers had plenty to do, with parades morning and evening, and with a considerable amount of routine work connected with interior economy. They were up early, as a subaltern of each company had to call the company roll and inspect the rooms immediately after reveille, and they were kept busy until they had seen the men have their dinners at 1 p.m. At three o'clock the officers dined, and turned out for parade afterwards; so they had very little leisure for recreation, though what form of recreation officers and men indulged in at this period is never made very clear.

Some of the officers hunted and shot, but outdoor games, as we know them now, had not come into fashion. Cricket and football were in their infancy, and had not reached the army; nor were there any organised athletic sports; and, in all probability, the only games played by the men were skittles, and a kind of "fives" in what was termed the "ball alley." Only by marching were the soldiers kept in good condition, for it had not yet been discovered that there was a value in wholesome recreation.

By the spring of 1808 the 51st was a regiment again, but in the matter of dress quite a different regiment to that which left Lisbon for India ten years before; for the uniform of the army had undergone alterations, and the mode of dressing the hair had changed. The "queue," which had taken the place of the "club" in 1799, and which was at

12. Lieut.-Colonel (afterwards Sir Ralph) Darling.

first ten inches in length, was now shortened to seven inches, and was tied, a little below the upper part of the collar of the coat, with a black bow,[13] so that one inch of hair remained free at the end; the men's *coiffure*, however, being no longer powdered white. The officers still wore powdered hair and cocked hats of considerable size, sometimes putting them on even with the shoulders, at other times fore and aft; but for the men a new head-dress had been devised, and this took the form of a cylindrical *shako*, with a brass plate in front and above it a red and white tuft coming out of a black cockade.

The red coat had changed its shape, and was buttoned up tight to the waist, the lapels, in the case of the officers' coats, reaching right down, and being so made that they could be buttoned across to form a double-breasted coat, or thrown back to show the lining of facing cloth—something after the fashion of the front of the present lancer tunic. The officers also wore very high and roomy collars, to admit the large black neckcloth, which was now much affected. And thus turned out, the whole regiment was undoubtedly as smart as could be,—but what was better, the officers and men were efficient soldiers.

In the meanwhile, events on the Continent had gone from bad to worse, and Napoleon, not content with the occupation of Portugal, had thrown off his alliance with Spain, marched on Madrid, and transferred his brother Joseph from the throne of Naples to that of Spain. England at once rose to the occasion, decided to free Portugal and Spain from the French yoke, and forthwith launched an expedition of about 25,000 men for the purpose. The 51st, having so recently returned from foreign service, was not included in the expeditionary force, which landed, on the 1st August (1808), on the Portuguese coast, near the mouth of the Mondego River, and commenced the advance on Lisbon.

On the 16th the French were first encountered at Obidos, where a slight skirmish took place, and on the following day Sir Arthur Wellesley fought and won the battle of Roliça.[14] Without entering into the details of this the first campaign of the Peninsular War, we may mention that the British and Portuguese routed the French at Vimiera on the 21st August, and before the end of the month the enemy, by the Convention of Cintra, agreed to evacuate Portugal. After this the British army occupied Lisbon, and prepared for operations against the French in Spain.

---

13. A survival of this queue-bow is to be found in the "flash," still worn by the Royal Welsh Fusiliers.

While these events were in progress, the 51st, chafing at having been left behind, were moved from Guernsey to Chichester, and before long had the satisfaction of receiving their orders for active service.

---

14. Roliça is sometimes written Roleia; Vimiera, Vimeiro; Corunna, Coruna, &c. The spelling followed in this book is that to be found on the Colours of British regiments.

CHAPTER 7

The Corunna Campaign, and After

After the occupation of Lisbon, Sir Arthur Wellesley, deeming it improbable that the army-would resume operations for some months, went home on leave of absence; and, a little later, Sir John Moore was given command of the British forces in Portugal. In October he received despatches from Government wherein he was informed that it had been decided to send Sir David Baird, with 10,000 men, to Corunna, and Moore was instructed to take the 20,000 British troops from Lisbon, and to form a junction with him forthwith, when, together with the Spanish army, he was to attack the French and drive them out of Spain.

To carry out his orders Moore had a choice of routes; he could transport his force by sea to Corunna, or he could march through Portugal and Spain. The former plan he rejected, as being likely to cause delay; for, with sailing vessels and at such a season of the year, it was impossible to estimate the length of time that the voyage would occupy. He decided, therefore, to adopt the land route, knowing that, if necessary, he could send his ships up the coast to some port, which would then become his base, instead of Lisbon. Accordingly, he desired Baird to march south-east to meet him at a point to be afterwards named, probably either Valladolid or Burgos, but the exact spot depending on the movements of the French.

Nearly three months before this the 51st had been warned for active service, and on the 18th August marched from Chichester to Portsmouth, where the regiment embarked in three transports, to join Sir David Baird's force, then assembling at Falmouth for some undisclosed destination. The regiment, mustering six hundred bayonets, was in fine fettle, and Captain Sam Rice was in command of the light infantry company. But eager as he and his brother officers were to get to business, they were forced to possess their souls in patience, for they were kept on board their transports for upwards of two months, with little or nothing to do, except to discuss the object of the expedition, their knowledge of which was vague in the extreme. As far as the soldiers were concerned, they were jubilant, and from a cause which nowadays may seem trivial. The order had gone forth that their hair was no longer to be "tied," but cut short at the neck! At length the long weeks of waiting came to an end, and on the 8th October Baird's fleet of transports sailed from Falmouth, five days later anchoring off Corunna. But even then further delays occurred, as the Spanish officials objected to the landing of the force, and it was another fortnight before the disembarkation was completed.

To return to Moore. Before the end of October he had set his troops in motion, but his arrangements were much upset by the reports of the state of the roads which he wished to utilise for his march. So bad were they said to be, that he considered it advisable to divide his force and move by two routes; and before long he had reason to be anxious about the safety of his detached columns, for the situation was under-going a change. At the time of his departure from Lisbon, Moore had every reason to believe that the Spanish troops, aided by the British forces under himself and Baird, would be able to deal a heavy blow to the French invaders, and in this belief he was supported by the knowledge that King Joseph, fearful of the impending attack, had withdrawn from Madrid to the neighbourhood of Vittoria, where he concentrated the French army on the Ebro. But Moore did know that at this very time Napoleon was pouring reinforcements over the Pyrenees in such quantities as to bring the strength of the French in Spain up to some 250,000 men.

Napoleon had determined to secure Spain and Portugal at all costs; and, placing himself at the head of the reinforcements, early in November defeated a Spanish force which attempted to bar his way, and advanced rapidly to Burgos. Thence he pushed a corps to the Carrion river, to protect his right flank from the British, while he moved on Madrid. In the meantime, Moore's main body was marching, *via* Ciudad Rodrigo, on Salamanca; while Hope, with the cavalry, artillery, and ammunition, had been sent by the circuitous route, Badajoz, Talavera, Madrid, Escorial Pass, to rejoin Moore at Salamanca, Valladolid, Burgos, or elsewhere, according to orders to be issued to him later.

On the 15th November Moore reached Salamanca, and learned that the French had already occupied Valladolid. Consequently he decided to wait at Salamanca until Baird and Hope could join him. But the two latter had met with great difficulties in the matter of transport, and had been delayed beyond all expectations, so that on the 26th November the head of Baird's column had got no farther than Astorga, five marches north-west of Salamanca, and Hope was at the Escorial Pass, six marches south-east of Salamanca. On that same day Lefebre's French Corps, of 30,000 men, was approaching Valladolid, barely three marches north-east of Salamanca, while Napoleon himself, marching on Madrid, was at Arauda, some sixty miles as the crow flies due east of Valladolid. Fortunately for the divided British forces. Napoleon was in ignorance of their whereabouts; neither, on the other hand, was Moore aware of the exact situation of the French, until two days later, when both he and Hope were informed of Napoleon's proximity.

Hope realised at once that he must risk everything in the attempt to take his artillery and ammunition to Moore at Salamanca; while the latter, after sending orders to Baird to retire on Corunna or Vigo, decided to wait as long as possible for Hope, and then, retracing his steps into Portugal, defend the frontier and cover Lisbon. Fortune favoured Hope, who, making a desperate cross-country march, successfully formed a junction with Moore at Salamanca, whereupon Moore changed his plans. He had heard that the Spaniards intended to defend Madrid to the last, and, in order to assist them in their endeavour, he determined on a bold stroke. He saw that Napoleon's vast army was, like some beast of prey, sprawled out over the provinces of Spain and crawling forward with open jaws within measurable distance of Madrid; he saw the hopelessness of trying conclusions with a beast ten times his own strength, but he knew that if he suddenly dealt a furious blow on the beast's tail the beast would spring round and attempt to rend him.

This, then, was Sir John Moore's idea when, at the beginning of December, he made up his mind to strike at Napoleon's line of communications, which stretched back to the Pyrenees. He calculated that Napoleon would immediately turn upon him with all his strength, and the Spanish and Portuguese forces would thus be given time to collect for the defence of their respective capitals. His own subsequent line of action he had also worked out carefully: having dealt his blow, and having succeeded in bringing the bulk of the French army against him, he would draw off his little force to Corunna or Vigo, and at one or the other place embark and sail to Lisbon or Cadiz.

Fresh orders were therefore despatched to Baird, who had meanwhile retired from Astorga, three marches to Villafranca. In these he was instructed to advance towards Valladolid, and on the 11th December Moore moved towards the same place, reaching the river Douro on the 13th. Here a French despatch was intercepted, and from it Moore discovered the true state of affairs. Napoleon had captured Madrid nine days before, had despatched Lefebre towards Lisbon and his other corps in various directions, and now ordered Soult to move his corps from the Carrion river westward into Galicia. It was also evident, from this French despatch, that Napoleon had no know-ledge of the movements of the British, and that Soult's corps was without support and of no great strength. So Moore decided to strike at Soult forthwith, and, with this object, arranged with Baird to join forces at Mayorga, instead of at Valladolid, at the same time instructing his ships at Lisbon to proceed up the coast to Vigo, and giving orders for the establishment of supply depots along the route by which he intended eventually to withdraw to the ships.

Upon receipt of these orders Baird advanced again to Astorga and, on the 20th December, joined Moore at Mayorga. He took with him all available battalions, but some were still in rear, since the Spanish authorities had been unable to provide transport or provisions on the road for any but small bodies of troops moving at intervals of some days. The 51st Regiment, forming part of Leith's Brigade, was still far behind, and did not come into the zone of operations until the eventual retreat was in full swing Moore, however, now had sufficient men for his purpose, for he knew that Soult's force was in numbers inferior to his own; and the operations at once commenced by a brilliant cavalry action, in which Paget, with 400 British sabres, routed 600 of the French cavalry at Sahagun. Soult was now known to be at Saldanha and Carrion, and Moore decided to halt his force for forty-eight hours in order to allow the rear divisions to close up, and then to attack at dawn on the 24th December.

On the night of the 23rd-24th the troops set out on the march which was to bring them at daylight before the bridge of Carrion, but they had not marched far before they received the unwelcome order to retrace their steps and return to their bivouacs at Sahagun. Moore had received information which upset all his calculations; the scheme which he had devised for drawing Napoleon's armies after him had worked only too successfully, for he learned that Napoleon was already in full march upon him, and that within a few hours the situation of the British army might become critical. He determined, therefore, to abandon the attack on Soult and endeavour to carry out his original programme by withdrawing to his ships before Napoleon's masses should fall upon him. That Christmas day was spent by the disappointed army in making the second march of the long and arduous retreat to Corunna.

Napoleon, as was his wont when once his mind was made up, came like a thunderbolt. On the 21st December, at the head of 40,000 men and 150 guns, he left Madrid, and, although he had to negotiate high mountain passes, often blocked with snow, he marched a hundred miles in less than five days, reaching Tordesillas, on the Douro, on the 25th December, and having his advanced cavalry well ahead of him on the way to Benevente. He firmly believed that he and Soult had now ringed-in Moore's force, which he imagined to be still at Sahagun. But Moore, leaving only his cavalry and the two light brigades of infantry at that place, had slipped away in the nick of time and had crossed the Esla by the 26th without serious molestation. On the following day the British cavalry fought long and gallantly and completely checked the pursuit; on the 28th Craufurd's light, or flank, brigade covered the withdrawal of the cavalry over the Esla by the bridge of Castro Gonzalo and then blew up the bridge; and on the 29th the cavalry again covered themselves with glory by defeating a strong body of French horsemen who had succeeded in fording the river.

On that day Moore's columns, which had been marching by two different routes, reunited at Astorga, and there the soldiers felt convinced that they would be called upon to halt and fight, since they knew that Moore had told the Spanish general that he would make a stand at Astorga, and they saw 10,000 Spaniards come into the place. But Moore had given up all idea of offering battle until he had reached the coast and was within sight of his ships. His men had already suffered from the hard marching in pouring rain and in snow, and along bad roads ankle-deep in mud; provisions were becoming scanty, and the general considered it advisable to push on with all speed to Villafranca and Lugo, where large supply *depôts* had been formed. On the 30th December he rested his troops at Astorga, and by the 31st both British and Spaniards were clear of the place, which was entered within thirty-six hours by the infantry of Napoleon and Soult, coming from La Baneza, where they had joined hands in the closing hours of 1808.

The new year opened on 25,000 dispirited, and even sullen, British soldiers marching through the snow-laden passes, and unable to understand why they should not turn and fight. Discipline became lax; the men broke the ranks in search of plunder and drink; and the stragglers were only kept on the move by the exertions of the cavalry of the rearguard.

Yet Moore had outwitted Napoleon, who, in sheer disgust at having failed to cut off his adversary, halted two days at Benevente, handed over the pursuit to Soult, and himself returned to Paris—not again to encounter British troops in the field until the eventful day when his fate was sealed at Waterloo. His deputy, however, took up the work with zeal and alacrity, and pressed forward to Astorga as rapidly as possible.

The horrors of the retreat of the British army after leaving Astorga have been so often described that it is needless to refer to them further than to say that, with the exception of some dozen regiments, the troops were completely demoralised and out of hand. Moore's feelings of bitterness can be well understood, for here, almost at the first trial, the discipline which he had assiduously-preached throughout his service had completely broken down. But this condition of affairs existed only among the troops of the main body, for the regiments forming the rearguard (which included the three which he had personally trained at Shorncliffe) behaved throughout with conspicuous gallantry and prevented Soult's pursuing force from overwhelming the disorganised army.

Passing through Bembibre and Villafranca, Moore reached Lugo after forced marching from which the men were worn out, and here he decided to halt in order to enable the stragglers to come up, and, if necessary, give battle. This, in a measure, raised the spirits of the army, as the men far preferred the prospects of a fierce fight to those of an immediate continuance of retreat. But, perhaps, the greatest check to the demoralisation which had set in was the fact that, at Lugo, Moore had the satisfaction of finding a most welcome addition to his force in Leith's Brigade of 1800 fresh men, who had not been harassed by the arduous marches of the past week, and with Leith's Brigade, as has been already mentioned, was the 51st Regiment and Captain Sam Rice.

At Lugo, therefore, on the 6th January 1809, Moore took up a strong position, and all ranks, full of hopes of being speedily attacked, fell into their places with evident delight. That same evening the rearguard came into Lugo, and on the following morning Soult appeared. But he felt his way with caution, and soon learned that the force opposed to him was not merely the rearguard, which had always been keeping him back, but Moore's whole army. Making a feint attack on the Guards' Brigade on the right of the position, he moved a division against the left, which was held by Leith's Brigade. The fight soon began in earnest; Soult's guns opened on the advanced piquets of the 76th Regiment, which then fell back on the 51st, when the two regiments began to use their muskets with vigour.

At this moment Moore himself was an eyewitness of what was taking place, and realising that Leith's men were greatly outnumbered by their assailants, yet knowing that he could spare no troops to reinforce them, galloped up to the 51st, and, appealing to his old regiment to stand firm, placed himself at their head. The response was immediate and unanimous. With a wild cheer the men emptied their muskets at the enemy, then, without hesitation, charged home, and drove the French before them at the point of the bayonet. The day was saved, and the enemy, with a loss of some three hundred men, drew off.

But this gallant action, which received the well-merited praise of the general, produced a state of affairs such as Moore least desired; for Soult feared to attack the position again until he should receive reinforcements from the rear. Throughout the 8th January the British army remained in its position, expectant and ready, with its officers and soldiers prepared to stake everything on the issue of the hoped-for battle. Yet the day passed without a sign of a French advance, and towards evening Moore's spirits fell, for he guessed that Soult was waiting for reinforcements. At first he thought of turning on his adversary while he was still weak, but he came to the conclusion that the risk was too great; on the other hand, to remain where he was until Soult should consider himself strong enough to renew the attack would be suicidal.

Therefore, he saw but one way open to him—*viz.*, to slip away from the position and continue the retreat to the coast; and, his mind made up, he issued his orders for the march. Destroying such stores and horses as would hinder their progress, and leaving their bivouac fires burning in order to deceive the enemy, the disheartened troops evacuated the position in the dead of night. Fortune was against them all through the night; rain fell in torrents, and the inky darkness made it impossible for them to see their way, so that, by dawn, instead of having put fifteen miles between themselves and the enemy, many benighted battalions, after marching all night, found themselves but five miles from their starting-point, and yet thoroughly exhausted.

But Soult did not discover that his enemy had gone until late next morning, and even then he appears to have been unwilling to push the pursuit as rapidly as he might have done.

Continuing the retreat in wretched weather, Moore's troops suffered every manner of hardship and privation, but on reaching Betanzos, on the morning of the 10th January, matters began to improve. The columns were still well covered by the rearguard, who kept the French at a distance; the sea was within sight, and the climate and weather improved considerably. Moreover, provisions had been sent forward from Corunna to Betanzos, and the half-starved men received ample food; so that, seeing all their troubles at an end, they made the last march to Corunna, on the 11th, with light hearts.

But Moore had no such feelings, for he had received the depressing news that his ships, which he had ordered to come round from Vigo to Corunna, and which he had expected to find in the harbour, had been delayed by stress of weather. Doubtful for how long he would have to wait, and within how short a time Soult would be able to bring overwhelming force against him, the general prepared for the worst, making all arrangements to fight, as well as for the immediate embarkation of his army so soon as the ships should arrive. The bridges outside Corunna were blown up, and all stores, munitions of war, and horses, which he would not be able to remove, Moore caused to be destroyed.

On the 14th January the ships entered the harbour, and the embarkation of the sick and wounded, guns, cavalry horses, and transport animals was proceeded with as quickly as possible. Meanwhile Soult began to press in, and Moore, seeing that he could not expect to embark all his troops without a fight, selected a defensive position some two miles outside Corunna. The four days' rest, with good food, had had a wonderful effect on his men; the stragglers had come in; fresh arms and ammunition had been supplied from the ample stores at Corunna; the sickly men had been sent to the ships; and the general found that he still had 15,000 determined infantry-soldiers and nine guns wherewith to withstand Soult's onslaught. All the morning of the 16th the French were seen to be massing in front of the position, but Soult apparently still feared to attack, and Moore, thinking that he would not do so, gave orders for the embarkation to continue.

Yet, an hour later, Soult's guns suddenly opened, and his columns dashed forward. Moore, overjoyed at the sight, and sure of victory, saw before him a great and glorious finale to the painful scenes which he had witnessed during the previous weeks, and rode from point to point of the field, giving his orders with calmness, and inspiring confidence in all directions. For some time the battle raged furiously; the French were as eager for the fray as were the British; here and there the latter were forced to give way, but re-forming rapidly, turned again, and recovered the lost ground.

At length, the issue of the fight was no longer doubtful; the French were driven back on all sides; the order for a general advance of the victorious British line was given, and was being carried out, when Moore fell mortally wounded, and Baird was also struck. Confusion followed, further orders remained unissued, and when Hope, the next senior, took command, it was too late to continue the struggle. Prudence demanded that he should withdraw the army and embark before the French could recover and return to the attack, and under cover of darkness the whole of the British force, save only the outposts, were withdrawn from the position, and embarked. That night and the following day were spent in getting everyone on board, and by the 18th January the last of the troops covering the embarkation quitted Corunna for England, Soult's guns opening on the ships as they put to sea.

Thus ended Moore's last campaign, and those who knew nothing of the general's original plan considered the retreat to have been a disastrous flight, yet Moore's plan succeeded completely. He drew Napoleon and 70,000 men away from the south and saved Lisbon from a French occupation, which was the most that he ever expected to do. The amount of hardship which his troops would have to endure in the withdrawal to the coast, perhaps he had not anticipated; but, had he lived, doubtless he would have claimed that the result was well worth the sacrifice, and if, moreover, the victory over Soult at Corunna had been completed, few would have been found to cavil at his plans and operations.

The part played by the 51st in the battle of Corunna, though small, was not unimportant. The regiment stood in second line to the left rear of Elvina, opposite to which village the fiercest of the fighting took place, and where Moore received his death-wound. Considering its position, its losses were not heavy, only amounting to some five-and-twenty men—mostly wounded. Neither did the regiment suffer to such an extent in casualties during the actual retreat as did most other regiments of Baird's original force; and if, as has been maintained, want of discipline was accountable for heavy losses during the retreat, then the officers of the 51st had good reason to be proud of the discipline of their corps.

Their three months' absence from England, however, had lowered their numbers by 107 men, and many gallant officers and soldiers suffered from the effects of the hardships of this campaign to the end of their days. Sam Rice, although he came out of it unscathed, was an invalid for some months afterwards, and was unable to pass the doctors when his regiment was next sent on active service. Yet, for this he must have remained ever thankful, for the expedition in which the 51st took part in the autumn of 1809 was, as will be shown, productive of nothing except death and disease.

On disembarking in England after Corunna, the regiment was assembled at Sandown Barracks, and in April marched into Devonshire, being quartered first at Kingsbridge and then at Berryhead. In May it received the honour of the title of Light Infantry, probably as a reward for its good services in the Corunna campaign, and probably also as a memorial to Sir John Moore, the exponent of everything pertaining to light infantry, and the former commanding officer of the regiment. The 71st was made a light infantry regiment about the same time, but previous to that there had only been four regiments in the British army so designated, and as light infantry they considered themselves superior to all other regiments of the line. As such they wore a distinctive uniform, which was much like that of the old light infantry company; and their special duties on active service were to be always in front of the army, gaining and keeping touch with the enemy, fighting advanced- or rear-guard actions when on the march, and forming a chain of outposts round the army when halted.

The spring and early summer of 1809 were spent by the 51st in recruiting the regiment up to fighting strength, for when, in April, Sir Arthur Wellesley returned to Portugal to continue the war, it was not sufficiently strong to form part of the expedition. By July, however, this difficulty had been overcome, for the stories told of the Corunna campaign had roused the fighting spirit of the country, and vast numbers of militia-men volunteered into the line. But when, in this month, the 51st received a fresh call to arms, it was not for Portugal, but for Holland, an expedition having been fitted out for the purpose of destroying the French fleet and arsenals in the Scheldt. Sam Rice, who had just given up the command of his company on promotion to Major, did not accompany the regiment on this service, but remained in command of the depot at Berry-head Barracks.

The Walcheren Expedition, as it was called, proved a complete failure. Operations commenced satisfactorily, and Flushing was bombarded and captured in August; but, owing to misunderstanding between the military and naval commanders (the Earl of Chatham and Sir Richard Strachan), the enemy was not pursued with energy, and the troops (some 40,000 in number) were kept idle on the island of Walcheren, until fever decimated their ranks. In September the greater part of the misdirected expedition returned to England, and for several months afterwards the men continued to die from Walcheren fever. The unfortunate circumstances gave rise to the following caustic epigram:—

Lord Chatham, with his sabre drawn,
Stood waiting for Sir Richard Strachan;
Sir Richard, longing to be at 'em,
Stood waiting for the Earl of Chatham.

So far the regiment's experiences of European warfare had not been pleasant. Within a year it had taken part in two campaigns, in each of which, although it had acquitted itself honourably, it had sustained weighty losses. Unlike many other regiments, the 51st had no second battalion upon which to draw to replace casualties, and consequently it was not fit to proceed on active service in the Peninsula until the end of 1810.

Meanwhile, Sir Arthur Wellesley, in supreme command of the allied armies, had been actively engaged with the enemy from month to month, and had won several hard-fought battles. He successfully frustrated Soult's invasion of Portugal by defeating him on the Douro, in May 1809, and driving him out of Oporto. He gained a signal victory over Marshal Victor at Talavera, in July; and thence retreated for the winter to the banks of the Agueda River, between Almeida and Ciudad Rodrigo. In 1810 Lord Wellington (as he now was) had for his opponent Marshal Massena, who had been ordered to invade Portugal (while Soult directed his attentions to Badajoz), and who, in June, commenced operations by investing Ciudad Rodrigo, then held by a Spanish garrison.

Capturing that fortress in July, Massena advanced on the neighbouring Portuguese fortress of Almeida, which also fell into his hands, Wellington's advanced troops—the Light Division—being forced back behind the Coa River after a desperate combat. In September, however, Wellington encountered his adversary at Busaco, thoroughly defeated him, and then withdrew rapidly to the impregnable lines of Torres Vedras, which, with great foresight, he had caused to be thrown up in front of Lisbon. Massena, ignorant of their existence, and imagining that Wellington was retreating for immediate embarkation, pressed forward for the capture of the Portuguese capital, but only to find his way barred by a series of strong fortifications. Behind these defences the British army remained unmolested throughout the winter, while the French, withdrawing to a safe distance, sat down to await the coming of spring. This, then, was the situation in Portugal when the 51st Regiment, quartered at Steyning Barracks, received orders to join Wellington's army in the Peninsula; and by this time Major Sam Rice was ready to be up and doing.

CHAPTER 8

Campaigns of 1811 in the Peninsula

In January 1811 the 51st embarked at Portsmouth for Lisbon in three of His Majesty's ships, one of which (the *Danemark*), having on board three companies under Major Rice, separated from the fleet during a heavy gale, but eventually reached its destination on the 19th February. Lieut.-Colonel Mainwaring was in command of the regiment, which left Lisbon early in March to join Wellington's army, then advancing from the lines of Torres Vedras in pursuit of Massena, who, with the breakup of the winter, had secretly' withdrawn from his cantonments about Santarem, leaving dummy sentries on outpost duty, in order to deceive the British. But the *ruse* succeeded for only a few hours, for the officers of the Light Division, who, from across the Rio Mayor, had been watching the enemy throughout the winter, detected the men of straw through their "spy-glasses," reported that the French were in full retreat, and immediately took up the pursuit. Almost at once they were on the heels of Ney's rearguard, engaged it at Pombal on the 11th March, and at Redinha on the 12th, and fought again at Cazal Novo and Foz de Aronce[1] on the 14th and 15th; but Ney, who knew his business only too well, never suffered himself to become seriously embarrassed, his force always melting away at the opportune moment, much to the disgust of his pursuers.

The young soldiers, of whom the 51st was now largely composed, made an early acquaintance with the horrors of war, for a very few marches brought them into the country through which the French army had recently retreated, and signs of cruelty to the Portuguese inhabitants and of wanton destruction of property were visible everywhere. Villagers, deprived of all that they possessed, were left to die

---

1. Other spellings, Casal Novo, and Foz d'Arouce (or Foz do Arouce).

of starvation; and towns and villages were ruthlessly set on fire. Leyria was still in flames when the 51st passed through it, and the road onwards was "broadly marked by the putrefying carcases of dead French soldiers stretched beside the wreck accumulated by their wanton, shameful outrages."

The regiment joined Wellington's army at the village of Carripinar, and on the 19th March the whole force, except the two divisions still in close pursuit of the enemy, assembled at Moita, where a halt of some days was made, in order to obtain supplies from Lisbon. On the 28th March a forward movement brought the troops to Celorico, when the 51st took its place in the 7th Division (Major-General Houston), and on the following day marched out with the centre column for the attack on Guarda. The enemy, however, made no attempt to defend the town, but withdrew at once, with the loss of a considerable number of prisoners.

Still retreating rapidly, Massena took up a position behind the Coa, and at Sabugal, on the 3rd April, Wellington attacked him with great success, utterly defeating him, and two days later forcing him to cross the frontier into Spain. Wellington then commenced the investment of Almeida, a Portuguese frontier fortress in possession of the French, while Massena, unable to feed his army on the country, retired to Salamanca. All April was spent by the British force in the vicinity of Almeida, and the following extract from a letter written by Major Rice on the 16th of the month, from "*Villa Mayor, upon a branch of the Coa, and near Almeida*" will help to show how the situation appeared to the regimental officer:—

As you will have heard of all our operations since Massena's flight, which was tolerably rapid, it would be useless for me to attempt a recapitulation, whose only merit would consist in incorrectness and stupidity. You will see by the public documents that no general action has taken place, though much skirmishing with the advance, which has always been to its credit and gallantry. Had the gentlemen—I mean the French—not been so very swift of foot, the business would have been most decisive and glorious for those concerned, as well as for the nation at large. The chase has been given these several days. It is indeed even reported they have quitted Salamanca. The whole of our army is now concentrated between Almeida and Ciudad Rodrigo—fortresses in possession of the enemy which still hold out. How they are to be disposed of is all a secret, but of this and all other matters of real importance you will be better informed at home than I am here.

The whole tract of country passed by us since we left Lisbon is completely devastated—scarce a village or town that has not been fired by the French. The beautiful city of Leyria, with its convents and churches, has been made a dreadful example of—immense and valuable libraries all committed to the flames. For a collector of old and mutilated manuscripts and parchments there was a fine field, for they were kicking and blowing about in all directions. The poor, half-famished inhabitants literally vegetate in the fields,—a sight more distressing than any I have yet witnessed, and I thought till then that I had been pretty familiar with every species of human misery.

It does not do to moralise, for such things are the consequence of warfare, but I do verily believe that never before was it conducted with so much barbarism—*au part des Français*,—the bare details of which shock the most obdurate and unfeeling heart. Lord Wellington and staff have just passed us. He is going to the side of Badajoz. Something, I conclude, of importance has transpired that calls his attention in the Alentejo. What is now to be done is mere matter of speculation; time, as in everything, will discover. We are horribly fed, sometimes three or four days without bread.

Again, on the 23rd April, he wrote from the same place:—

Still stationary; nothing whatever has transpired of any moment in this quarter since my last advice. Almeida continues invested; what is to be the result, as I said before, I am ignorant of It is, however, pretty clear that no operations have as yet begun as to indicate the intention of a siege. One would suppose that something must shortly be attempted, unless Lord Wellington is informed as to the positive provisionment of the garrison, by which the trouble and the loss of heads may be spared. The French are friendly, and give us no trouble. They occupy a position on the Agueda with a corps of 4000 men—merely, I conclude, as a reconnaissance from the main body of the army, which is at Salamanca and in cantonments in the neighbourhood, or it may be further, from what I know, so little do we hear.

His lordship we have heard nothing of since his departure for the Alentejo. Some serious errors have been committed, to the full extent of which we remain in the dark. Much anxiety is, of course, expressed. I trust things will not prove so bad as report makes them, as any little reverse gives encouragement to *our friends*. A squadron of the 13th was surprised and taken near Badajoz lately; it was acting as a picket to a division of our army; the consequence was so far serious that the French cavalry pushed through the cantonments of the infantry, who, supposing themselves in security, were totally unprepared, and gaped (wide enough, I daresay) at the sight.

A loss of a few ears, arms, old hats, &c., I conclude, took place, though as yet no details of the reverse have arrived. It is a d——d bad business, and won't bear telling. What a gallant business at Cadiz! Is it not a pity so much good blood should be spilled for those dastardly Spaniards? Ought not now those zealous English fools in the cause of Spain to be sickened, or do they want another bloody fight, by way of ascertaining if British soldiers will fight? The game of Spain must be up. Of this country (Portugal) I shall not yet talk, though its ultimate fate cannot but be foreseen. But I must not discuss politics. The weather is here dreadfully cold and unpleasant, though you will scarce believe it from our geographical situation. Guarda, from which we are distant but five leagues, is supposed to be one of the highest cities in Europe, so of our atmosphere I leave you to judge. Hunger, misery, and grumbling is the order of the day.

Wellington's departure for the Alentejo and the events in the neighbourhood of Badajoz, to which Rice refers in the above letters, had been occasioned by the fact that while the pursuit of Massena was being carried out, Soult, who had assembled a powerful army in the south of Spain, advanced rapidly, and after defeating the Spaniards, detached Mortier to besiege the fortress of Badajoz, held by a Spanish garrison. On the 11th March the latter ignominiously surrendered, and the French, having secured Badajoz, moved on and captured Campo Mayor. A week later, Wellington, seeing no chance of drawing Massena into a general engagement, and thus feeling confident that he could spare a portion of his force, despatched Marshal Beresford with two divisions of infantry and some cavalry and artillery towards Campo Mayor. That fortress was reached on the 25th March, but the enemy did not await the arrival of the British, who, seeing the French in full retreat towards Badajoz, pushed on, and after a brilliant cavalry charge captured the enemy's convoy, only, however, to lose it again by rashly pursuing too far and coming under the fire of the guns of the fortress.

Early in April, Beresford began the investment of Badajoz, but so many difficulties, real or imaginary, lay in his way that before the investment could be completed the French had ample time to provision the place and repair its defences. It was on the 7th April that the incident of the capture of a squadron of the 13th occurred, and Napier says of it that the French general, with 3000 infantry, 500 cavalry, and four guns, "surprised a squadron of the 13th, which was in front, and then came so close up to the main body as to exchange shots; yet he was permitted to retire unmolested, in the face of more than 20,000 men!" Napier attaches no blame to the 13th Light Dragoons for what occurred, but rather extols their gallantry. Of the supineness and inactivity of Beresford in all these operations he has, however, much to say; and Rice's remarks point to the fact that camp rumours were for once tolerably accurate.

With Wellington's arrival in front of Badajoz on the 21st April new life was put into the operations, for he gave orders to prosecute the siege with all vigour before Soult could come to the succour of the garrison. Requisites for the siege, however, were not forthcoming in sufficient quantities, for although guns, ammunition, and entrenching tools had been ordered up from Lisbon, the transport for their conveyance was hopelessly inadequate. Yet the engineer officers set to work to mark out the trenches, and were preparing to break ground, when Wellington received information from his northern army which necessitated his immediate return to the neighbourhood of Almeida. Leaving instructions, therefore, with Beresford to delay the siege of Badajoz for the time being, he hurried north, to find, on his arrival, that Massena's activity was causing considerable anxiety, for it was known that the French marshal was advancing in strength to raise the blockade of Almeida.

By the 28th April Wellington was back with his army, and taking in the situation at once, decided to give battle between the Agueda and the Coa. Massena conducted his operations much as his adversary had foreseen that he would do, and within the week was fought the battle of Fuentes d'Onor,[2] on ground midway between Ciudad Rodrigo

2. This is the spelling of the name of the village as borne on the colours of the regiments present at the battle. Napier calls it Fuentes Onoro, other writers Fuentes d' Honor, Fuentes d'Honoro, &c. The correct local spelling is, however, Fuentes de Oñoro.

and Almeida.

Hereabouts the river system is somewhat intricate, no fewer than five considerable streams flowing, in almost parallel channels, from south to north. On the east the Agueda flows close by the walls of Ciudad Rodrigo; westward of the Agueda are its tributaries, the Azava, the Duas Casas, and the Turon; and a little to the west of Almeida is the Coa—all within a space of thirty miles, and for the most part unfordable. As early as the 24th April Massena had pushed forward his advanced troops from Ciudad Rodrigo, with the object of seizing the crossings of the Azava, but the British outposts on that river drove them back, and continued to hold the river line, until Wellington arrived and selected a position behind the Duas Casas, when the outposts gradually fell back and allowed the French to advance. This they did on the 2nd May, and, on the 3rd, succeeded in crossing the Duas Casas at one point and capturing the village of Fuentes. They did not, however, remain long in possession, for after a fierce fight the British drove them out and forced them back across the Duas Casas.

Next day, Massena moved forward with 5000 cavalry and 40,000 infantry, and Wellington made some alterations in his dispositions, so that his front now extended for a distance of some seven miles. By this new arrangement, the 7th Division (to which the 51st belonged) was placed on the extreme right, near the hill of Nava de Avel, opposite to which the French appeared to be massing in strength. On the morning of the 5th May Massena pushed on, and simultaneously at-tacked the village of Fuentes and the right of the British position. The 7th Division, outnumbered, were forced back, but the Light Division and the cavalry hastened to its support, and restored the fight. Wellington, now observing that his right was in imminent danger of being turned, ordered the 7th Division to draw in, and the Light Division covered the withdrawal in a magnificent manner.

The enemy's strong force of cavalry made strenuous efforts to crush this portion of the line, and what immediately occurred is best described in the words of Napier. "The Light Division," he says, "was thrown into squares; the Seventh Division, which was more advanced, endeavoured to do the same, but the horsemen were too quick upon them, and some were cut down; the remainder stood firm, and the *Chasseurs Britannique* ranged behind a loose stone wall poured such a fire that the French recoiled and seemed bewildered."

According to all accounts, the battle scene at this phase of the fight was a most picturesque one. The vast plain was covered with charging bodies of horsemen, who once and again endeavoured to break the squares, which, nothing daunted, met the onslaught, and leisurely retired.

But the grandest sight of all on that memorable day was perhaps that presented by Norman Ramsay's two-horse artillery guns, which, hemmed in and cut off by the enemy's cavalry, saved themselves, not by their fire, but by cleaving their way at full gallop through the astonished French horsemen. This was, however, but one incident of many in a day of great deeds, and for a long while the issue of the fight hung in the balance. Failing to effect his purpose on the British right, Massena directed his attention to the capture of the village of Fuentes; but at this point also his troops were eventually beaten back, and at night-fall the British and French sentries, separated only by the breadth of the Duas Casas, agreed to take water from the river without molestation—a tacit agreement which always existed in Peninsular war-fare between the veterans of the opposing armies.

Considering the critical situation in which the 7th Division was for so long placed, the casualties in the 51st on this day were remarkably few—only half a dozen wounded. In the briefest of letters Sam Rice described the events in which he had taken part as senior major of the regiment.

"We have suffered little," he wrote, "though the first attack was made on our regiment by a body of cavalry, who came up to the charge, but were soon convinced that we were not to be trifled with. I am well and safe. I had an 'all-but,' having my cap whisked off by a three-pounder, but received no other injury than a temporary stunning from the concussion. The French again menaced us this morning, but it has since proved a mere manoeuvre, and they are off, and we prepared to follow. I literally have not time to say more."

This was written on the day after the battle, and it is possible that the writer was too sick at heart to say more; for something had occurred, as will be disclosed a little later on, which must have caused endless regret to every officer of the regiment who came out of action. They were not, however, given much time to brood over their misfortune, for on the 10th May Massena gave up the attempt to reach Almeida, and withdrew his army beyond the Agueda, when he was relieved of his command by Marmont. That same night, Brenier, in command of Almeida, seeing that there was now no hope of succour reaching him, resolved on a bold stroke. Having destroyed the guns of the fortress, he marshalled the garrison, and, in one solid mass, at dead of night, broke through the blockading force, almost before any one was aware of what was taking place, and eventually made his escape with only a few casualties. Wellington, disgusted at the escape of the garrison, vented his wrath on his lax troops in no measured terms, and leaving Sir Brent Spencer with a sufficient force to watch Marmont, despatched the remainder of the army to Badajoz, the siege of which he proposed to renew at once.

While Wellington was fighting Massena at Fuentes d'Onor, much had been going on in the neighbourhood of Badajoz, and Wellington, although seemingly so fully occupied in the north, was at the same time planning for the overthrow of Soult in the south. It will be remembered that when he hurriedly left Badajoz, at the end of April, to attend to Massena, he instructed Beresford to prosecute the siege leisurely. Certainly Beresford could do no more, since, as has been said, he lacked all the requisites for a regular siege, but he attempted more, and failed ignominiously.

From the 5th to the 12th May the first siege of Badajoz was carried on without sufficient organisation, and assaults were directed on various points before they had been properly breached, with the result that within the week Beresford had lost nearly a thousand men, and had made no impression on the fortress. Then came the news that Soult was moving to the relief of the garrison, when Beresford at once raised the siege, marched south, and prepared to give battle. On the 16th May was fought the memorable and bloody battle of Albuhera (or Albuera), where, more by good luck than good management, Beresford, with a loss of four thousand of his eight thousand men, succeeded in defeating his adversary, whose losses were still heavier. The investment of Badajoz was now resumed, and Wellington was soon on the spot, making arrangements for a second siege. Badajoz at this time was probably the strongest fortress on the Spanish frontier. It was situated on the south bank of the Guadiana, a broad and deep river, which was of itself considered to be sufficient protection from an attack from the north.

On that side, therefore, the defences of the fortress consisted only of a simple rampart. On all other sides the fortifications were formidable, having regular bastioned fronts, with solid masonry parapets, encircled by a ditch in places thirty feet deep. Within the north-east angle of the fortress stood the ancient castle, built on a hillock one hundred feet in height, and overlooking the Guadiana; yet, in its turn, overlooked by the high ground (barely five hundred yards distant) to the north of the river. In order to guard against the possibility of an enemy's artillery occupying these heights and demolishing the castle, a detached fort, known as St Christoval (or San Christobal), had been built on them; while, on the opposite side of Badajoz, there were two detached works—Pardeleras on the south, and Picurina on the south-east.

In the first siege, Beresford had attempted to attack from the north, capture St Christoval, and, after establishing batteries, breach and assault the castle. St Christoval, however, proved too strong for the assailants, and thus Beresford was forced to leave his work undone. When Wellington came on the scene to prepare for the second siege, he decided to follow Beresford's plan, and accordingly, on the 24th May, the 7th Division invested St Christoval. Trenches were now commenced towards the castle and towards St Christoval, and batteries were soon erected. During the first few days of June the trench-work made rapid progress, and the guns fired continuously on the castle and on the fort. On the 6th June, a practicable breach in St Christoval was reported, and the assault was ordered to take place forthwith.

On the night of the 6th-7th, the assault was launched, Major Macintosh, of the 85th, commanding the Stormers, and Ensign Dyas, of the 51st, the Forlorn Hope. The advanced party succeeded in dropping into the ditch undiscovered, and the Stormers with their escalading ladders followed close behind, but on reaching the breach it was found that the defenders had succeeded in repairing it, and had added to its summit a high perpendicular wall—so high that the ladders would not nearly reach the top. Then the enemy's musket-fire fell upon the unfortunate Stormers, and shells, rolled from the ramparts, bursting amongst them, played havoc in the ranks. Retreat was inevitable, and upwards of a hundred dead and wounded were left in the ditch.

Next day the guns reopened fire on St Christoval, and on the 9th June a second assault was ordered. Ensign Dyas again led the Forlorn Hope, and Major M'Geechy, of the 11th, the Stormers. The ladders carried were much longer than those used on the previous occasion, yet they did not prove long enough; for the defenders had removed the debris from the foot of the breach and thus rendered the place safe from escalade. Shot and shell now rained on the baffled assailants, but, nothing daunted, they reared their ladders and pressed up them, in the attempt to reach the rampart—only, however, to be bayoneted at the top, or to be hurled backwards into the ditch as the defenders pushed the ladders away. The disaster was complete. M'Geechy was killed, and ere the troops could extricate themselves from the ditch hundreds had fallen. Of the 51st alone there fell in these two desperate assaults one officer killed and three officers wounded, twenty-six men killed and seventy wounded; but Dyas, the hero of two Forlorn Hopes, escaped unharmed, and was personally complimented by Wellington for his gallantry.

Major Sam Rice, who had taken an active part in these assaults, wrote, in his usual laconic way, from Camp before Badajoz, 16th June 1811:—

> The siege of this place, which began under such favourable auspices, I am sorry to say, is not likely to terminate yet awhile, and, if at all, only by starvation, for it is most ably defended, beyond, I believe, the calculations of the scientifics. We opened fire from our batteries on the 2nd June, and proceeded to batter and destroy, but without much effect, for the guns and all apparatus are withdrawn within these last three days. The cause is said to be that Marshal Soult is again coming forward with a determination to dispute the point, and afford relief to the garrison; but before this a general action must be fought, and a bloody one it will be, for on this depends the fate of Badajoz and of the frontier—at any rate for a time. The place still continues invested, but all expect to move directly to the army in front. We have been most cruelly harassed day and night, and totally uncovered, as well as exposed to a most scorching sun. Our Regiment has suffered much in two unsuccessful attempts to storm a fort—100 men killed and wounded, and several officers. I have escaped wonderfully, though never under a hotter fire in all my life. I am writing from the bare ground, on which I have taken up my abode this last month entirely. Mainwaring is sick; I command the Regiment, reduced already to 300—so much for honour and glory!

Almost immediately after this letter was written, Wellington, learning that Marmont had come down and united with Soult, raised the siege, and withdrew his force rapidly, a few miles, to the Cay a river, and on the 19th June the French armies entered Badajoz. The combination against Wellington was now weighty. Soult and Marmont could put sixty thousand men into the field, whereas the Allies on the Caya could not muster half that number. But the French marshals failed to discover this weakness, and Wellington found the ground about the Caya so favourable that he was able to present a bold front and deceive his opponents as to his actual strength, which, even after Spencer joined him with the force left in the neighbourhood of Almeida, stood at no more than twenty-eight thousand fighting men. Unwilling to risk a battle without knowing the actual strength of their adversary, Soult and Marmont made no attempt to advance, but shortly afterwards retired and separated, to commence a new plan of campaign.

The following letter from Major Rice gives his views on the situation about this time:—

Campo Mayor, 19th July 1811.
Since my last we have been tolerably quiet; scarce even alarms, which have their advantages in keeping the body and soul in that activity so essential to the military character. It seems now pretty well ascertained that the French army is broken up for the present. Soult, with a corps, reoccupies Seville. Marmont, with the remaining force, Plasencia and its neighbourhood. By an intercepted letter from Marmont, and which is said to be authentic, he complains much of the disorganisation of his army, and want of resources of every kind, and particularly money, without which he can anticipate no future good. I suppose the gentlemen soldiers begin to grumble—pay or plunder is the cry. For my part, I've heard so much of armies being annihilated, want of pay, food, and clothing, &c., &c., and cowed at even the sight of British troops, all which statements have proved so incorrect by pretty fair experience, that I now give ear to nothing that is said, however apparently good the authority.

Whatever may be their motives, one thing is pretty certain and known to both parties—that no active warfare can be carried on at this season of the year in the Alentejo without mutual destruction. The campaign may probably open again early in the autumn. On what point the attack is likely to be made, I as little care as I am able to form an opinion, but wherever it is, they will certainly get cursedly licked. So much for presumption! The whole of our army, which has been bivouacking in this vicinity, is now nearly in motion, standing by divisions along the frontier, to Castello Branco and beyond.

We march tomorrow for Nissa (or Niza), a town this side the Tagus, and near one of the principal fords, Villa Velha. The weather is most dreadfully hot. Crowded, and stenched out by all sorts of agreeables—dead animals, &c.—our situation is not the most delectable one. Withal, bad fare, and every article exorbitantly dear. Mainaring has got a staff appointment, and an officer from half-pay has been brought in. What satisfaction is there in serving if it has not its reward! I am fairly sick of the business. I have had nothing but losses of late. A valuable horse broke from me while at Badajoz, swam the Guadiana, and I believe is now in the French lines. Poor Harry's[3] pistol, which I had in my sash the night of the storm (St Christoval), dropped out, and I lost also my poor dear Mary's[4] snuff-box, which I considered almost as my guardian angel, it having been my companion in every affair.

The latter part of this letter helps to throw light on Sam Rice's character, and it is evident from it that he was a man who bore no ill-will to anyone. He mentions casually that "an officer from half-pay has been brought in," and he immediately dismisses the subject with, "I am fairly sick of the business," and never refers to it again. Yet he, the senior major of the 51st, had been passed over for the command of the regiment, and Lieut.-Colonel Mitchell, who had had no previous connection with the regiment, had been brought in over his head. Under such circumstances an ordinary man might have been excused if he had given vent to his feelings by filling two or three sheets of paper with abuse of every one in authority. Major Rice was the victim of circumstances; by no fault of his own he had lost the command of his regiment; but he was above all things loyal, and he refused to give away his commanding officer, Colonel Mainwaring. He says nothing whatever of any trouble.

On the 16th June he writes, "Mainwaring is sick; I command the Regiment"; and on the 19th July, "Mainwaring has got a staff appointment." It would have been easy for him to have told the whole story, and thus excused himself, as certainly nine out of ten people would have done. He, however, chose the better part, and left unsaid anything that might have detracted from the conduct of his commanding officer, and anything that might have been seized upon by gossip-mongers as affecting the good name of the Regiment.

In later years Sir John Colborne related what took place in the

3. His brother, Lieut. Henry Rice, R.N., who died 1808.
4. His sister, Mary Rice, who died 1810.

following words:[5]—

> Colonel Mainwaring, of the 51st, was placed in a position [Battle of Fuentes de Oñoro] in which he thought he was sure to be surrounded by the French. So he called his officers and said, 'we are sure of being taken or killed; therefore we 'll burn the colours.' Accordingly, they brought the colours and burnt them with all funeral pomp, and buried the ashes, or kept them, I believe. It so happened that the French never came near them. Lord Wellington was exceedingly angry when he heard of it, as he knew well enough where he had placed the regiment. So he ordered Mainwaring under arrest and tried him by court-martial. An old colonel, who undertook his defence, said, 'I believe it was something to do with religious principles.' 'Oh,' said Lord Wellington, 'if it was a matter of religious principles, I have nothing more to do with it. You may take him out of arrest; but send him to Lisbon.' So he went to Lisbon, and was never allowed to command his regiment again; he was sent home.

Such is the story, and there is little doubt that when Sam Rice wrote, on the 16th June, that he was in temporary command, as Mainwaring was sick, he knew perfectly well that his commanding officer, although he certainly had been invalided to Lisbon, had been virtually relieved of his command. But the authorities, evidently unwilling to be too severe on an officer who had performed good services for his country, but who had erred through excess of zeal, so arranged matters that, on the 13th June 1811, Lieut.-Colonel Mainwaring exchanged to the half-pay of the 26th Foot (with Lieut.-Colonel Mitchell) and was appointed commandant of Hilsea Barracks in England. The matter, of course, had to be referred home, and so took some time, and in the meanwhile Colonel Mainwaring had taken his regiment to the camp before Badajoz, and had been hurt in the trenches.

Now, as a matter of fact, Sir John Colborne was wrong in saying that "the French never came near them," for it is perfectly certain that the 7th Division was posted in a most perilous position, and was very seriously attacked, although certainly the 51st was not so desperately engaged as were some of the other regiments. The division, numbering some four thousand infantry (of whom the 51st and 85th were the only British regiments), and supported by fourteen hundred cavalry, was detached two miles from the main position, on practically open

---

5. *Life of John Colborne, Field-Marshal Lord Seaton.* By G. C. Moore-Smith, M.A.

ground, and everyone in the division knew that since Wellington's left flank was impregnable, Massena would, of necessity, direct his attack on the right flank. Wellington himself was well aware of this, but either he did not anticipate so vast a turning movement as his adversary eventually launched, or he had intended that the 7th Division should only hold the out-lying position assigned to it long enough to induce Massena to develop his attack against it.

Be that as it may, the fact remains that, at one time, the 7th Division was threatened by twenty thousand of Massena's infantry and nearly the whole of his masses of cavalry, and for a while was in imminent danger of being cut off and annihilated. Wellington, of course, set matters right as soon as he realised that the situation was becoming critical, but there were some who imagined that he was intensely annoyed at having made faulty dispositions in the first instance, and that he endeavoured to justify himself in the eyes of the 7th Division by venting his wrath on the colonel of the 51st.

At the same time the burning of the colours was an extraordinary procedure on the part of the colonel, and it is not easy to understand how it was that the other senior officers of the regiment acquiesced in it, if, indeed, they did so. When the circumstances became known to Wellington, he was bound to take notice of what had occurred; but apparently the officers of the 51st considered that he was unduly severe in treating their colonel's action as anything more than an error of judgment, for which a reprimand might have been sufficient. As it was, they always maintained that the commander-in-chief had been harsh and unjust, because it had been represented to him that Colonel Mainwaring had doubted the wisdom of his dispositions.

Years afterwards his nephew, Frederick Mainwaring,[6] who, when only fourteen years of age, fought as an ensign of the 51st at Fuentes d'Onor and elsewhere, wrote very strongly on the subject, and referred to the incident of the burning of the colours, though without actually mentioning what had occurred, in the following words:—

An action, in which this officer took the greatest responsibility upon himself, and which ought to have reflected credit upon him rather than annoyance, was misrepresented to the great Duke, who, with all his bright qualities, is said (if report does not greatly belie him) never to alter an opinion or a resolution once formed.[7]

6. Frederick Mainwaring served with the 51st throughout the Peninsular War and in the Waterloo campaign. Before he had reached (continued next page.)

Colonel Mainwaring was not the only commanding officer in the Peninsula who was troubled by the presence of his regimental colours in the field, for there were occasions upon which the colours hampered the movements of a regiment very considerably. In action they could never be neglected, since they were held to contain, as it were, the soul of the regiment. Originally used as the rallying-point, they had gradually come to be regarded as what nowadays would be termed the mascot of the regiment, so that their loss in battle was thought likely to lead to the most dire consequences. The officers who carried them knew that they were in honour bound to defend them to the last, and when a whole regiment was ordered to skirmish to the front, it was often necessary to leave a company behind to guard the colours.

As the war in the Peninsula went on, light infantry regiments realised that their colours were an encumbrance, and observing that rifle regiments were not provided with colours, some of them got permission to place theirs in store. But this was exceptional, and most regiments continued to carry their colours into action. At Waterloo they were everywhere conspicuous, and even in modern times their defence in the field has led to fierce fighting and the performance of signal acts of gallantry. Now, however, the extended battlefield has made their presence an impossibility, and they are no longer taken on active service. Perhaps, in this way, the sentiment attached to the "flag that bore the battle and the breeze" has been rudely crushed; yet the colours of today, emblazoned with numerous battle honours, are useful in reminding the young soldiers of a regiment of the victories won by their ancestors.

Whether, as a result of this trouble over the 51st colours at Fuentes d'Onor, Rice suffered to any great extent by being passed over for the command of the regiment is questionable. He certainly did not succeed to the command for another six years; but, if nothing had occurred. Colonel Mainwaring could have continued to hold it for that length of time, or for even longer. The fact of another officer having been brought in over his head did not reflect on Rice's character as an officer, for it always has been well known to everyone in the service that an out-side officer must take the place of a commanding officer relieved of his command; and it will readily be understood that such

his nineteenth year he had been present at the battles of Fuentes d'Onor, Salamanca, Vittoria, Pyrenees, Nivelle, and Waterloo, besides many minor actions.

7. *Four Years of a Soldier's Life*, in Colburn's *United Service Magazine*, August 1844.

an arrangement is a necessity. As we shall see, the authorities made it up to Rice in more ways than one, and he eventually received as many decorations and honours as he would have received if he had succeeded Colonel Mainwaring[8] in the command of the 51st.

Having failed to reduce Badajoz, Wellington decided to invest Ciudad Rodrigo, and towards that place his troops were now moving. The 51st marched from Campo Mayor to Sabugal, and thence proceeded to Alfayates and Villa Mayor, at which latter place the regiment remained throughout the greater part of August and September, as will be seen from the two following letters from Major Rice, who during this time was in temporary command of the regiment:—

Camp, or Bivouac, near Peña Macor,
August 9th, 1811.

My last (from Campo Mayor, I believe) in-formed you that, the foe being no longer to be dreaded in that quarter, the army was moving into cantonments along the frontier, and that we (that is, the 7th Division) were to occupy Nissa, or Niza. Such did take place, and all indulged in the fond hope that we should enjoy a little *otium* for a month or so; but, alas, it is willed otherwise, for we are once more in motion, and are so far advanced northwards, retracing our footsteps to the Coa. What is to be done, or the cause of this sudden movement, is a mystery, and I believe only known to the Lord of Lords—*in this country*, N.B.! I do not myself think any serious attack will again be made by Monsieur François, and in my opinion it is only a little ruse of Baron Douro's to distract him—harass—or what you will, and causing a 'diversion in the south,' as we say in Greek, &c., &c. Whatever may be the cause, it is no little annoyance to be so constantly on the march in this hot weather, and in a country more wretched than you can possibly imagine. Not an article of any description is to be purchased, and were it not for our rations we should be literally starved. We have not been under a roof for this some time; every day we take up fresh ground, and

---

8. Colonel John Montague Mainwaring, previous to having incurred Lord Wellington's displeasure, had had a most distinguished career. Entering the army in 1784, he served with the 67th Regiment at the capture of several of the West India islands; was with the 51st in the Corunna campaign, and in the Walcheren expedition; and took the regiment to the Peninsula in 1811. On retiring from the 51st he was given the command of Hilsea Barracks; was promoted colonel, 1813; major-general, 1819; lieut.-general, 1837; and died in 1842.

seek shelter in the woods, which luckily abound, or we should actually be grilled alive. As yet I have held out tolerably well, being unwilling to give in while there is a prospect of anything going on. How long I shall last I cannot say, for we are all getting sickly. The Regiment has no more than 300 men. When his lordship sends dispatches, it is said that he stops private letters; he probably dipped into mine and saw their brilliancy, so fearing to be eclipsed he arrested their progress. This may account for their non-receipt!

Villa Mayor, upon the Coa,
19th August 1811.

I wish I could convey to you anything new and interesting relative to this country, or what is likely to be the result of such apparently protracted operations. I am most positively in the utmost obscurity; mystery is the order of the day, really I believe because no one but the lord of lords is enlightened, and I sometimes doubt whether he is always so, such is the fluctuating state of Spain, and probably the difficulty of gaining intelligence of the real movements of the foe. The whole army still remains cantoned upon this frontier; the advance upon the Agueda, with pickets probably as far as Ciudad Rodrigo. They talk of a siege, but I do not hear of the arrival of the battering train, which may possibly be *en route* from Oporto. You will hardly suppose us to be in such ignorance, but true it is, for one division scarce knows how the other is posted; but as there is one tolerable fair directing head, it is of no moment of what materials are composed those who act in so confined a sphere.

The French don't appear to have made any movement, still occupying Plasencia and the contiguous country. Ciudad Rodrigo has but a garrison of 1500 men. A considerable body at Salamanca, but nothing to oppose us if we choose to invest that place or make an advance, which is not, I think, likely. The French to do anything here must assemble in great force and bring forward their supplies, which you know is difficult in any country, much more so in such a barren desert as this is. The grand puzzle now is, what has been the cause of this rapid and unexpected movement from the Tagus to the Coa, when everyone supposed we should be resting till the autumn? Be sure to send the fishing-rod. I'm longing to whip the Coa.

From this letter, as well as from many other letters, one sees how very little was known, even to senior officers of regiments, as to what was going on, or what was likely to happen. This is a matter which is often forgotten by the layman, who is apt to think, when reading the history of a campaign, that the regimental officers failed on certain occasions to appreciate the situation, and therefore failed to do the right thing at the right moment. Whereas, in nine cases out of ten, in all probability the regimental officers were completely in the dark as to the intentions of the commander of the forces; and if the officers knew little of the operations in progress, or of the reason for movements, the men in the ranks knew still less.

Thus we constantly find in the Peninsular letters and journals of regimental officers and soldiers—at any rate at the beginning of the war—expressions of distrust in the generals, grumblings at having to perform forced marches for no apparent reason, and disgust at being ordered to retreat at the moment when they expected to give battle. But, as the war progressed, the men learned to take things as they came, and made no attempt to reason out the whys and the wherefores of strategical movements. The discipline which had been drilled into the soldiers taught them that it was not necessary for them to exercise their reasoning powers until they were in actual touch with the enemy, and the officers seldom thought ahead of the immediate tactical situation.

It must be remembered that a century ago few of the rank and file could read or write, and few of the regimental officers were students of the theory of the art of war. It was not possible, therefore, for these officers and men to work out any great strategical scheme, especially as they had no means of learning anything of the enemy's movements going on at a distance. Hints and rumours filtered through from the staff officers, and were greedily seized upon for discussion in the bivouacs, but in the generality of cases they were quite erroneous and frequently misleading. So the regimental officers contented themselves with living in the present, without troubling about problems of strategy, and they were quite unable to fathom the mystery of the part played by politics in the war. It will be noticed that Sam Rice, at the time a senior regimental officer, in his letters declines to discuss politics, and says little about strategy.

In the vast store of literature dealing with the Peninsular War, there are many volumes of officers' letters and journals, principally of officers who served on the staff, and so to a certain extent behind the scenes. Moreover, the majority of these books were written up and edited years after the war had come to an end, and after every movement in the various campaigns had been thoroughly discussed. There are few books by regimental officers containing their views written down at the time and not altered before publication, and in such as there are we find questions of strategy either avoided or dismissed in a few words, and even questions of tactics only vaguely referred to. For but vaguely did these regimental officers ever know whither they were going, or for what purpose, from one month's end to the next. It was enough for them to be told that their regiment would march at a certain hour in a certain direction, and that what would happen afterwards would depend on circumstances.

As soon as touch was gained with the enemy, the regimental officers and the men were given a general idea of the existing tactical situation and what it was intended that they should do. But even then they were not told all, and as often as not they went into action knowing no more about the dispositions of the enemy than they could see with their own eyes. Consequently there were occasions when, with a little more information—a slight dispersal of the "fog of war"—they might have crushed their enemy beyond recovery, instead of merely crippling him.

Why information about the enemy should have been withheld it is difficult to understand, and it must have been most irritating. Of the intentions of their great chief, officers and men never expected to be informed, and they had neither the desire nor the ability to probe into them. To Wellington himself this inability on the part of his army to forecast his plans was probably an immense satisfaction, for, he must have argued, if his own troops could not see through the veil, it was not likely that the enemy would be able to do so. And, naturally, for a general to be sure that his plans are kept secret, with a possibility of his being able to blind and deceive his adversary, is a great asset in war. On the other hand, it is an undoubted fact that Wellington carried this matter of reticence to extremes; he seldom took even his staff into his confidence; any information which he collected he kept to himself; and only on rare occasions did he discuss his plans with anyone.

The wisdom of such an attitude on the part of a commander-in-chief may, of course, be questioned, on the grounds that if he were unfortunate enough to be killed at the critical moment, the next senior officer would be in the awkward predicament of having to formulate a plan of his own on the spur of the moment. It may be argued that

Wellington's plans were so thoroughly worked out in every detail that there was no loophole for failure, and no doubt as to what was intended. That may have been so; but there is no proof, for fortunately it was never put to the test, and the great man saw all his plans brought to a finish. Still, it is well known that Wellington realised to the full the danger of his policy of reticence; and it is on record that he himself expressed the opinion that had he been placed *hors de combat* by the shot which passed over his head and wounded Lord Uxbridge at Waterloo, the British and their Allies would have suffered defeat. His generals may have chafed under such an autocratic rule, yet they, as well as the whole army, had absolute confidence in their leader—at any rate after the first year or two.

But the "grand puzzle" about which Rice wrote on the 19th August was not so intricate as he seems to have thought; for Wellington had made up his mind all along to attempt the capture of Ciudad Rodrigo, and had only cantoned his troops about the Tagus in order to deceive the enemy as to his intentions. He was now moving his army up towards the fortress with all speed, hoping to reduce it before it could be re-victualled for a siege. But in this he failed, for a convoy of stores of all kinds had reached the place while Wellington's troops were still at a distance from it. The 51st had remained at Villa Mayor until the 22nd September, had then marched to Guinaldo, and on 25th to Albergueria. Rice by this time had been forced to go to hospital, and on the 26th September he wrote from Aldea da Ribeira:

> I have been confined to my bed for these eight days with a violent attack of dysentery, accompanied by a good deal of fever. I think the former is in some measure conquered. Am taking bark, for I am most terribly low and hipped—all alone in a most miserable village. How I shall get on I know not. The task is arduous for an invalid in this most horrid of countries. The regiment is a league in advance; a retreat or an action must take place within twenty-four hours, for the French are only distant five leagues from our outposts. Our army is in a wretched state; they say 30,000, with an immensity of officers, sick; in short, you see nothing from morning to night but misery. You must not consider my case desperate, so I beg of you not to alarm Fanny.[9]

His next letter was from Celorico, upon the Mondego, 12th Oc-

9. His sister.

tober 1811—

I gave you a few hasty lines, I think, on the 26th September. As I predicted that a retreat or an action would take place within twenty-four hours, so it happened. The French pushed forward in great force, and would gladly have brought on an action, but a wise head said nay, and we retrograded. The 3rd Division was pressed hard by the cavalry, but retired in good order by squares, so suffered not so much as might have been expected. The French have again taken themselves off, Marmont by the pass of Banos to Plasencia, and the Comte d'Orsini[10] (or some such name), with the remaining force, is gone into cantonments in the vicinity of Salamanca. What will be the end of all this kicking about and expense of shoe leather I cannot say. Our advanced posts extend nearly as far as before, though several divisions are on this side of the Coa, where I think they will remain for the winter, or until some fresh alarm calls us again into motion. I have been very unwell since my last, but am now considerably better, and have to complain principally of weakness. Another fortnight will, I hope, put the old horse once more on his legs. The best of them cannot go for ever. His lordship is just coming in to inspect the hospitals.

Shortly after this the 51st went into winter quarters at Peña Macor, while Wellington perfected his arrangement for converting the blockade of Ciudad Rodrigo into a siege. That the regimental officers did not take a very bright view of the situation is evident from the following letter from Major Rice:—

> Pena Macor,
> 4th December 1811.
>
> We have got papers down to the 15th November. Grand news was expected, such as Northern Coalition—the old joke! I wish we could get those Russian bears on foot; nothing can be done here but by something of the sort. Bony, I fear, is too deep, and John Bull such a cursed fool that I am no longer sanguine in the cause and the issue of the glorious struggle. The army has again been on the *qui vive*, but nothing done. A convoy of provisions was attempted to be thrown into Ciudad Rodrigo, but our lord was too deep. He has good intelligence and certain requisites. General Renaud passed some days here with us.

10. Dorsenne.

He likes good living and plenty of wine—a tolerable sort of Frenchman. He was taken by Don Julian, the famous guerrilla partisan. He thinks Bony will never forgive him, and is alarmed. I shall struggle on a little longer before I give in—take another round or two—the odds against me. My poor brother major [11] died the other day—a short illness, which terminated with a melancholy disease—what the wigs call *timor orsi*—otherwise, fear of hell.

So 1811 closed, and was followed by a year of strenuous work for the British troops—a year of great victories, yet one also of arduous marches, vast hardships, and heavy casualties. And Major Sam Rice managed to "struggle on" to the end of it.

---

11. Frederick Sparks.

CHAPTER 9

Ciudad Rodrigo and Badajoz

While resting in cantonments when no operations were in immediate prospect, the army in the Peninsula forgot its hardships, and indulged in such recreations and amusements as it was found possible to organise. Everything was done by the officers to keep up the spirits of the men, though, since the age of playing games had not yet come, there was little for them to do, beyond repairing their clothing and shoes preparatory to the next campaign. The officers, however, were able to amuse themselves in a variety of ways; when not on short rations most regiments kept a certain number of pointers and greyhounds, and many of the officers shot and coursed regularly; fishing was also to be had in the rivers and streams; and each division usually kept a scratch pack of hounds. Wellington himself throughout the war hunted a pack which he had got out from England, and in many parts of the country provided excellent sport for his headquarter staff and any officers who cared to join in.

Nor were balls and other social entertainments forgotten, and whenever a portion of the army was in the neighbourhood of a town the Spanish ladies showed no unwillingness to enjoy gaieties offered to them. But perhaps the greatest amusement was that provided by private theatricals, which were held on every possible occasion for the entertainment of the men. Several divisions had their own theatres, the parts of both sexes being played by the officers, and everything being done well—even to printed programmes. With such recreations, and with periodical race meetings, the idle time passed pleasantly enough; and when the men were again called upon to take up arms, they did so cheerfully and with renewed vigour.

During this winter of 1811-12, however, the officers of the 51st had few opportunities of hunting, for, until the first week of January, they were kept at Peña Macor on the look-out for the enemy, in daily expectation of receiving orders to march. Still, they managed to enjoy themselves, as is vouched for by one of the ensigns.

"We led a most agreeable life," says young Mainwaring; "the neighbourhood abounding in game, our days were spent in coursing and shooting. In the evening there was always a party at someone's quarters, where cigars, egg-wine, and good-humour generally sent half of us tipsy to bed. Three times a-week a division club, formed by the German Light Brigade in an empty convent, added to our amusements, and brought us all together. Here was dancing, music, and cards; a *faro* bank for those who were disposed to lose their money; two military bands for the youngsters to dance to: and a sutler's room, where was every species of refreshment at most moderate prices. Many a wild mad scene have I been witness to, and perhaps partaker in, at this club, but all was in perfect good-humour; no arguments or strife; nothing but the ebullition of health and youth. Our generals and our superior officers joined in and added to all our pleasures and amusements, as in the field they shared all our privations and hardships."

On the 9th January Major Rice wrote hastily—

We are once more on the *qui vive*; the siege of Ciudad Rodrigo has commenced. What will be the issue must depend on circumstances. Marmont, it is supposed, has gone to the relief of Count Suchet in Catalonia. Our lord, I conclude, thinks it a fair opportunity of doing somewhat, all of which you will hear in due time, and in an official shape—much better than through private hand, at all events such an one as mine. We have (I mean our division) no orders as yet to quit our present position; possibly relief, support, or succour may be required. If so, we heroes, tried and valiant, shall fly.

On the following day came the long-awaited orders to move, and the 7th Division, marching through Sabugal and Alfayates, reached Guinaldo on the 13th January, and thence pushed on towards Ciudad Rodrigo. The division, however, was not destined to take part in the actual siege operations, or in the terrific assault which terminated them, its special duty being to stand off and cover the siege of the fortress by guarding the passes of the Sierra de Gaeta against an inroad by the enemy from that direction. The 51st, with their headquarters at the village of Pajo, furnished four officers' piquets on the mountains in front of the two principal passes, in situations fully exposed to the rigours of winter, the ground covered with several feet of snow, and wolves howling round the sentries throughout the night. Yet in after years the officers looked back on this unpleasant duty almost with pleasure, remembering only that, when not on piquet, they enjoyed excellent woodcock shooting!

Meanwhile Wellington had pushed on the siege works with astounding rapidity, had effected practicable breaches several days earlier than he expected, and on the evening of the 19th January assaulted and carried Ciudad Rodrigo. Then the 7th Division, no longer required at the passes, was withdrawn to the vicinity of the fortress. In a letter, written from Fuente de Guinaldo on the 27th January 1812, Major Rice says—

> We quitted our Alpine abode yesterday, and have approximated a little to Rodrigo. It was conjectured that, upon the fall of that place, the army would make some forward movement—Salamanca at least; and some were so sanguine as to have flattered themselves to have spent the remainder of the winter at Madrid. Such an *événement* would be rather agreeable than otherwise, particularly to me, who am such an admirer of the Spanish *signoras*. We heard yesterday of the sad reverses of the Spanish patriots under that obstinate old fool Blake—complete defeat and himself taken prisoner. Valencia is also fallen—to complete the tale of woe. The taking of Rodrigo will not compensate for so much disaster, as it is impossible, unless the Spaniards gain some ground, that our small aid can be of ultimate use. Rodrigo is fast being put into a state of defence. How it is to be garrisoned, or by what troops, I do not know—Spaniards, I presume. Our loss at Rodrigo has been rather severe, as you will see by the *Gazette*. Two generals out of pocket, and poor Craufurd[1] has died. He was wounded in the vitals, mostly fatal in such cases. Who would not be a soldier when so pleasant a fate is in store for him? We are all now pretty tranquil, and I suppose shall remain so for a short time—until Marmont, with his hordes, gets in motion.

Early in February the 51st moved to its old quarters at Peña Macor,

---

1. Major-General Robert Craufurd, of the Light Division. He was mortally wounded in the assault on the lesser breach, and was subsequently buried there.

and thence, a little later, commenced the march towards Badajoz, the reduction of which fortress Wellington had determined to attempt at once. The 7th Division was again detailed for covering duty, and, with the 6th Division, was placed under the command of General Graham. Crossing the Tagus at Villa Velha, the two divisions reached Elvaz, and bivouacked close to Fort La Lippe until the arrival of the army destined for the investment and siege of Badajoz.[2] Then Graham crossed the Guadiana by the bridge of boats above that place, and moved into position to the south-east. A short letter from Major Rice, dated Puebla, two miles from Zafra, 19th March 1812, describes what was taking place:—

> Our lord continues to dash, having undertaken once more the siege of Badajoz. The better to insure success and prevent molestation two *corps d'armée* have been formed and advanced into Spain—Hill on the side of Merida, and Graham of Balgowan in this direction, for which you must turn to maps. Our corps is respectable, comprising three divisions of infantry, two brigades of cavalry, two troops of horse artillery, with lots of heavy field-pieces. We crossed the Guadiana on pontoons on the morning of the 16th, and passed Valverde and Santa Martha. At the latter place we had near surprised a body of French, but had the mortification of seeing them in the distance retiring in squares, flanked by cavalry. We took one solitary dragoon. The French evacuated Zafra last night. We continue to pursue, but how far I am not in the secret—various reports, but only the wigs of course know. We are greeted in all the towns by acclamations of *Viva los Inglezes*—how charming and flattering! We suffer a few privations; long marches; and in the evening we generally turn in under the trees without any other covering than the 'grand canopy.' I hope we shall do something brilliant. Prepare yourself to hear of gallant exploits. I trust the siege of Badajoz will go on well. We, the 7th Division, luckily for us, were thought too good for the spade and shovel duty.
>
> P.S.—I have just heard that we shall march again tonight. I suppose to put a little salt on Mr Frenchman's tail!

Nothing very brilliant, however, was done by Graham's corps, although it certainly carried out its *rôle*, and prevented any attempt

---

2. Napier gives the following figures: troops (British and Portuguese) employed at the siege, 21,784; Hill's covering force, 9674; Graham's covering force, 19,567.

of the enemy to raise the siege. Nor was this an easy task, for Graham displayed considerable activity, and endeavoured to do something more than merely to hold the French in check. Discovering that a small body of the enemy was occupying Llerena, eight leagues distant from his headquarters, the general ordered the 51st and 100 German riflemen to make a forced march and surprise the place. The garrison, however, had received information of the threatened attack, and evacuated Llerena, which was immediately occupied by the 51st.

Yet, within a few hours, the regiment learned that Soult was making a night march on the town with 5000 men, and the small British force, in its turn, was obliged to beat a hasty retreat. Graham waited a day or two, and then determined to turn the tables on Soult. He issued sudden orders for his whole corps to march on Llerena and surprise Soult's force, and the 51st again took part in the enterprise. Everything went well throughout the long march, and just before dawn the troops approached the town. The surprise was thought to be complete, and success seemed certain, when, of a sudden, there arose a panic, which had the most dire consequences. General Graham and his staff had ridden, unknown to the troops, on ahead of the columns to reconnoitre, and were fired upon by a single *vedette*. They immediately galloped back to the columns, with the unfortunate result that they were mistaken for the enemy's cavalry. Major Rice, writing a week afterwards, thus describes the affair:—

> In one of our night rambles, when the whole force of our corps, 12,000 in number, was advancing upon Llerena, the heads of columns were thrown into confusion by alarm of cavalry. A firing unfortunately began. Friends, and not foes, were shot. We[3] expended two officers and a private. It had like to have proved a business of the most serious nature. The Hero of Barrosa rowed us all most terribly for unsteadiness. The real fact is he himself was in fault, having been in front with a parcel of A.D.C.'s and staff, and other tom-fools; not being in their places, and gaping about, they came suddenly in contact with a French cavalry picket, upon which D.I.O.[4] was the word full speed. Our advance gave them a fire and frightened their animals, who ran furiously between our columns. We mistook the business for a charge of cavalry, and unfortunately a fire ensued. Several generals were spilt and run down. The affair was ludicrous enough.

3. *I.e.*, the 51st.

4. "D—n it, I'm off"—a common expression of the period.

I was at the head of the column, but escaped by my horse tumbling head and heels into a ditch—a species of good luck, for I was running the gauntlet.

All this firing, of course, put an end to surprise, and by the time that order was restored and the advance resumed, Soult and his five thousand had slipped away. After a short stay at Llerena, Graham moved on to the ground upon which had been fought the battle of Albuhera; and while there the troops heard in the distance the desperate firing which resulted in the capture of Badajoz.

It will be remembered that, twice during the previous year, the fortress had been besieged and unsuccessfully assailed. On each of those occasions Wellington had directed his attack from the north, intending first to capture the detached work of St Christoval, in order to establish batteries there preparatory to an assault on the castle. For his third attempt he adopted a new plan, and decided to attack from the south, capturing the Picurina outwork, breaching the bastions opposite to it, and then delivering the assault. The trenches were pushed rapidly forward; Picurina was carried by assault on the night of the 25th March, and the breaching batteries were immediately established.

For ten days they battered the walls of the fortress, until the necessary breaches were effected, when Wellington gave immediate orders for the assault to take place; and on the night of the 6th-7th April 1812 occurred one of the most bloody struggles in the annals of war—a struggle the horrors of which lived in the memories of the surviving assailants for ever afterwards. The breaches defied all attempts; time after time assaults were delivered and beaten back; and the ditch became filled with dead and wounded. Elsewhere, however, fortune favoured the assailants, the 3rd Division entering the place by the San Vincente bastion. Thus Wellington captured his second fortress in 1812, but at the cost of 5000 men out of the 21,000 engaged.

The scenes which followed the fall of the place are indescribable; the victorious troops gave themselves up to plunder and licentiousness of every description. Drink drove them mad, and no one could control them. There is no denying the fact that fearful crimes were committed by the British soldiers in Badajoz that night, for each man carried his loaded musket and his bayonet, and brooked no interference with his revels. Yet these men were not hardened criminals, for in their sober moments they would have shuddered at the very mention of such crimes as, under the influence of drink, they themselves committed. They started to enjoy themselves—to hold high carnival—

but they were drunk with success at the outset, and, even before the wine-vaults had been sacked, the carnival became the wildest and most lawless ever held. But with this great tragedy scraps of comedy occasionally mingled, and some of the scenes would, at any other time, have been considered highly entertaining. Dressed as monks and nuns, or wearing the gay clothes of Spanish ladies, grizzled and begrimed veterans danced and sang through the streets; and when eventually they were driven out of the town, they wended their way to their bivouacs, wearing these same garments, and staggering under the weight of such plunder as they had collected.

Quartermaster Surtees, who had an opportunity of seeing for himself many of the horrors of this night and of the next day, tells the hideous tale, in his *Twenty-five Years in the Rifle Brigade*, sufficiently fully to enable one to realise how utterly demoralised a well-disciplined army can become almost at a moment's notice. His remarks on the reason for this are of particular value, because he had risen from the ranks and was intimately acquainted with human nature as represented by the private soldier, and because he was a man who thought deeply. He concludes his account of the sacking of Badajoz in the following words:—

An English army is, perhaps, generally speaking, under stricter discipline than any other in the world; but in proportion as they are held tight while they are in hand, if circumstances occur to give them liberty I know of no army more difficult to restrain when once broke loose. A reason may perhaps be assigned for it in part. On such occasions as this siege, where they were long and much exposed to fatigue almost insupportable, to the most trying scenes of difficulty and danger, which were generally borne with cheerfulness and alacrity, they perhaps reasoned with themselves and one another in this manner,—that, as they had borne so much and so patiently to get possession of the place, it was but fair that they should have some indulgence when their work and trials were crowned with success, especially as the armies of other powers make it a rule generally to give an assaulted fortress up to plunder.

They had also become quite reckless of life from so long exposure to death; but an English army cannot plunder like the French. The latter keep themselves more sober and look more to the solid and substantial benefit to be derived from it, while the former sacrifice everything to drink, and when once in a state of intoxication, with all the bad passions set loose at the same time, I know not what they will hesitate to perpetrate. The reader will judge of the state of our soldiers who had been engaged in the siege when Lord Wellington found it absolutely necessary to order in a Portuguese brigade to force the stragglers out of the town at the point of the bayonet.

Major Rice's next letter was written on the 10th April 1812, from Camp in front of the Albuhera River, Beresford's position of the late bloody fight—

Since we crossed the Guadiana on the 16th March, of which I hastily apprised you, this *Corps d'armée* has been, I may almost say unceasingly, in motion, having made nearly the circuit of Southern Estramadura, the object of which was to force the French from the towns and positions they occupied, and to throw every impediment in the way of concentration. In our numerous night marches, with a view to surprise, we have in general failed, owing to the very superior intelligence of our active enemy. Some good, however, may have resulted, though they very speedily retraced their steps, and yesterday they appeared in force within a league of this, but I believe nothing more than a strong reconnaissance of cavalry.

Report now says they are off and our dragoons advancing, but it is of little consequence, since they could not relieve Badajoz. This, I hope, will go by the packet which takes the intelligence of the capture of Badajoz by assault. The particulars of the gallant but bloody business you will have in a better shape than I can give you. It was the most awful and tremendous firing I ever heard. We have had the good luck to escape, though our labour and anxiety for this last twenty days has been such as to claim attention as assisting in the glorious cause.

I have just been reconnoitring the ground of the battle of Albuhera, and have been conceited enough to think that even I could have managed it better. The blundering was great,[5] and terrible the sacrifice. Boots, caps, jackets, *et cetera*, are still kicking about—in short, it is the richest 'bed of honour' I have seen

---

5. "Marshal Beresford had fixed upon and studied his own field of battle above a month before the action took place, and yet occupied it in such a manner as to render defeat almost certain; his infantry was not held in hand, and his inferiority in guns and cavalry was not compensated for by entrenchments."—Napier's *History of the Peninsular War*.

for a long while. If the French come on we are to act the farce over again on the same boards. I am scribbling this upon my knees amidst the greatest confusion of noises you ever heard— Babel a joke! Marmont, we hear, is not idle, and has invested Rodrigo. If so, we must again trot up to the north. No end to our labour. I am a good deal done up, but still hold on. I have not yet been into Badajoz. The confusion terrible, as you may suppose, after an assault, and given up to plunder. An order has this moment arrived to move to our front, I suppose to give chase. Soult has heard of our success, and I believe has thought it advisable to face about.

On the 19th April he wrote again, from Niza:—

The morning after I last wrote to you we broke up from the position of Albuhera and made an advance movement on Santa Martha. Soult was within two leagues with 30,000. He made a little show with cavalry, but thought proper to retire with his infantry, having heard of the fall of Badajoz. Had it not fallen it is thought that a general action must have taken place, which was to have been tried again upon the same ground—but this, I think, I before stated. I, and we all, thought of a chase; but no, for suddenly operations were changed. Our lord had heard that Marmont was playing the devil in the north, and had pushed to Castello Branco and Villa Velha to destroy the bridge of boats. The latter was not actually done *by the enemy*, but in the general panic it was cut adrift, which has occasioned some trouble in restoring. The plain truth and matter of fact is that a deep game has been playing, for had not Badajoz *miraculously* fallen the siege must have been raised, we not having force to contend and resist the two divisions. We are now going all hands pell-mell north as hard as we can. Several divisions have crossed the Tagus—our turn tomorrow, God knows what is going to be done, as reports are so various.

One thing is pretty clear: Marmont and his Goths have behaved with their usual barbarity, having destroyed and sacked most of the unfortunate towns which had previously escaped. Never in this world was so cruel and distressing warfare waged. It cannot last; the misery is too great to be endured, and all for what? Our army, pretty well jaded to death by one thing or other, cannot stand the incessant fatigue. The sickness is alarming, and every

131

regiment worked to nothing. No energy whatever on the part of the Spaniards—at least not that I have seen. We shall in a few days pass the Coa, if Mr Frenchman will permit.

I expect opposition; at all events he will annoy, and destroy the bridges. When we have arrived at Rodrigo, Soult will again show himself before Badajoz and down we shall come again, and so on until we are done up. You see I am not more sanguine as to general results than yourself I am sorry to see so little hope. You can form no idea of the scene at Badajoz; no place was ever so sacked—and a variety of other things—*nameless!* The weather is horrible; constantly wet, and little covering.

The somewhat desponding tone of this letter is perhaps an indication of the writer's weariness of soul—a weariness produced by constant marching about without any apparent prospect of doing any good. The senior regimental officers, who had the welfare of their men at heart, and who understood, from long experience, that the soldiers' powers of endurance had limits, ever dreaded a breakdown, and their fears grew greater when they saw their regiment being harassed for no clear purpose. This is evident from their letters, as is also the fact that when once they knew that they were marching for the definite object of meeting the enemy and of giving battle, they cast aside their fears and prepared their men for the coming struggle. But let us get behind the scenes and see what was really happening at this particular time.

After the capture of Badajoz Wellington spent no time in inaction. General Graham was placed in command of the fallen fortress, and was given sufficient men to repair its defences and prevent its recapture by the enemy; while the bulk of the army marched away. Soult, who had been hastening from the south to the relief of the French garrison, and who had been held in check by the covering troops, on hearing that all was over, turned about and withdrew towards Seville. Marmont, however, had succeeded, while the siege was in progress, in invading Portugal and penetrating to Castello Branco. Wellington now advanced against him; but the French general, forbidden by Napoleon to attempt to form a junction with Soult, saw that little was to be gained by advancing farther. His first impulse was to fight, but he remembered that the rivers in his rear were in flood and would impede his withdrawal in the event of defeat, so he deemed it more prudent to retire behind the line of the Agueda River, and there await developments.

Meanwhile Wellington was straining every nerve to meet the heavy combinations which the French were bringing against him. King Joseph, in supreme command of the French in the Peninsula, was in occupation of Madrid, and thence issued orders to his subordinate generals, who, however, lacked confidence in the military plans of their chief—a fact which proved of the greatest advantage to Wellington. United action on the part of the French generals would have placed the Allies in a grave situation; but fortunately the three French armies were at this time widely separated, and Wellington contrived so to deceive his adversaries that they were quite unable to say against which force he intended to operate. Soult in Andalusia felt certain that the Allies would invade that province; King Joseph imagined that the Spanish capital would be the immediate objective; while Marmont, away to the north, had every reason to believe that Wellington was bringing all his strength against him. As a matter of fact, the original intention of the British commander had been to carry the war into Andalusia, but, abandoning the idea (for political and military reasons), he determined to attack Marmont. Yet, by means of false reports and ostentatious movements, he contrived to continue to deceive Soult as to his real plans.

Before following Marmont, however, Wellington deemed it necessary to prevent Soult and the army of Andalusia from reinforcing him. Soult, south of the Tagus, would have to cross that river before marching to the assistance of Marmont; his pontoon trains had been captured in Badajoz, and the only means of crossing the river was by the bridge of boats which Marmont had constructed at Almaraz. The importance of this crossing was well known to the French, who had consequently thrown up three strong forts and a bridge-head to protect it; but the destruction of Almaraz, with its bridge and its stores, was essential to Wellington's plans, and, though doubtful of the possibility of its being carried out, he ordered General Hill to make the attempt. As events turned out, the surprise of Almaraz was one of the boldest enterprises of the war, and by the 18th May Hill had done all that was required of him. But until the work had been completed, whither Hill had taken his force and for what purpose were things known only to Wellington, who had halted the remainder of his army to await news of the result of Hill's mission.

Writing from Castello Branco, 22nd May 1812, Major Rice describes what was going on—

Hill's corps has marched upon Almaraz, to destroy the bridge across the Tagus. The object, it may be conjectured, is to prevent Marmont or anybody else crossing. I venture not to speculate further. What our lord is about I know not. Guinaldo is his headquarters. I suppose he is planning something great and glorious. Touching ourselves—the 7th Division—no talk of moves; an unusually long respite from toil, and much in favour of boots, shoes, and horseflesh. Our assizes have been going on since our arrival, and likely to continue. Much business on hand. I am on the jury. We generally hang or shoot half a dozen fellows, notwithstanding every soldier is a gentleman and a man of honour, and receives votes of thanks from both Houses of Parliament, which he does not value so much as a pot of Whitbread's Entire.

From the latter part of this letter it is evident that Wellington had taken the opportunity of some leisure time to overhaul the discipline of his army, and his methods were drastic in the extreme. Even before he had witnessed the outrages committed by his men at Ciudad Rodrigo and Badajoz, he had been appalled by the indiscipline of his troops in disregarding orders concerning marauding. The British army was operating in a friendly country, and it was therefore all the more important that the inhabitants and their property should be treated with due respect. The French, on the other hand, were at war with Spain, and if, therefore, they pillaged and laid waste as they went along, it was perhaps no more than the inhabitants expected, though it is only fair to the French generals to state that, as a rule, they did all in their power to suppress marauding and pillage.

It must be admitted that it was most difficult to impress upon the British soldiers, marching on the heels of the French through a country already pillaged, that it was a sin to take the goods of the people, and doubtless at an early stage of the war the men got into the habit of taking from the inhabitants of the villages any food or provisions of which they were in want. As time passed matters went from bad to worse, and the men did not stop at food, but began to plunder the inhabitants of their money and valuables. Wine-cellars were discovered and entered, with the result that drunkenness and outrages of every description became common. Wellington, alive to the gravity of the situation, issued stringent orders which, had they been carried out, would have put an end to these evils; but there were no means of carrying them out, and all this he represented from time to time to the home authorities.

He pointed out that under existing circumstances it was impossible to bring home to the offenders the offences which they had committed, and he recommended wider powers to courts-martial and the formation of military police. He did not complain of the discipline of regiments as a whole, but he wrote in the strongest terms about the absence of discipline to be found in detachments, which, of necessity, were always out in various parts of the country; and he drew particular attention to the number of malingerers who filled the hospitals principally for the purpose of plundering when on the march.

"The disorders which these soldiers have," wrote Wellington to Lord Liverpool, "are of a very trifling description; they are considered to render them incapable of serving with their regiments; but they certainly do not incapacitate them from committing outrages of all descriptions on their passage through the country, and in the last movements of the hospitals, the soldiers have not only plundered the inhabitants of their property, but the hospital stores which moved with the hospitals, and have sold the plunder. And all these outrages are committed with impunity; no proof can be brought, on oath, before a court-martial that any individual has committed an outrage, and the soldiers of the army are becoming little better than a band of robbers."

On the top of all this came the wild orgies which accompanied the sacking of Badajoz; and Wellington determined to adopt the strongest measures in order to restore the discipline of his army. We may say here, and without in any way belittling the military genius of England's greatest soldier, that Wellington knew nothing of the finer processes of producing and maintaining discipline among British soldiers. He was not of the school of Sir John Moore. He had no sympathy with the soldier, or indeed with the officer. He spoke of the men who won his victories for him as the scum of the earth and as the sweepings of the jails, and he treated them always with coldness, amounting almost to contempt. Probably he was the hardest master under whom men ever served, for at all times he governed by the lash, and he never hesitated to shoot or hang an unfortunate soldier, if he deemed it necessary to make an example.

That these executions were not sometimes necessary we do not pretend to say, but the method of carrying them out, in the face of the whole army, served only to brutalise it. Officers and men became callous even of the capital punishment, and judging by the letter quoted above. Major Rice thought little of condemning to death half a dozen men for possibly trivial offences. Several of Wellington's generals, taking their cue from their chief, flogged and hanged freely, with the result that there was no love lost between them and their men; but, like the dog who licks the hand that beat him, these soldiers would follow their commanders without questioning, and perform for them prodigious acts of valour. Few of the Peninsular generals were really popular with their men, but Graham and Hill were exceptions. The latter, though a brilliant leader, was always sympathetic, and endeared himself to all ranks, who spoke of him among themselves as "Daddy Hill," though he was barely old enough to have been the father of any of them.

The feelings which the soldiers had towards Wellington ("Old Douro," as they called him) are well described by an officer of the 51st[6]:—

> Where is the British soldier who ever saw him on the field of battle that felt not within himself, though ten times his number stood in his front opposed to him, that that field must be one of victory? Wherever he was, with his calm countenance, on those occasions always with a smile upon it, the soldiers would say, 'Ay, there he goes, boys. All's right.' And forward they rushed, careless of danger or numbers, and thus driving the French out of the strongest and most impregnable positions—such was their confidence in his talents and good fortune. And these were not the sentiments of the private soldier alone, but the deep-rooted feeling of every individual in that army. We followed, we fought for him, but though he won our confidence, he never gained our love."

These words were written after the Peninsular War and after Waterloo, and scores of Wellington's officers wrote of their chief in a similar strain. But in earlier Peninsular days, before the regimental officers and the men had discovered their commander's greatness, they had no great confidence in him, and they were wont to grumble at his orders and to criticise his actions. Many of his earlier subordinate generals, although quite ignorant of war, saw something wrong in everything that Wellington did, and their removal to a less active sphere in England gave these detractors the opportunity of spreading calumnies

---

6. Ensign Mainwaring.

about the only capable head which the army then possessed. Wellington, however, survived all this and much more, and as the war went on, the voice of the army changed, until, in the end, there were few officers conceited enough to venture to doubt the wisdom of his plans, and few of the rank and file who had not absolute faith in everything that he did.

He established among both officers and men a reputation for infallibility, and he convinced them of his instinctive genius for war. That he lacked the ability to gain their affections was nothing to them, and it is certain that, in spite of those who maintain that popularity with the troops is essential to military genius, if any of his Peninsular or Waterloo veterans were alive today, they would still hold Wellington to be the greatest of British generals, even though they might admit that he was a hard master, and one who never forgot and seldom forgave.

Long after he had fought his last battle—even to the end of his days, Wellington upheld his harsh code of punishment, and he resisted strenuously, with all the weight of his opinion, every attempt to diminish flogging in the army in times of peace. Not until twelve years after his death was this put an end to, and not until 1882 was flogging on active service finally swept away by the Army Discipline Act. Old and tried officers held views similar to those of the great Duke,—by the lash alone could the discipline of the army be maintained; and no greater supporter of corporal punishment can be found than that high-minded leader of men, Sir William Napier, the historian of the Peninsular War.

He was a man acknowledged to have been beloved—even worshipped by all ranks, as the epitome of all that was just and sympathetic, a man who wrote of British soldiers, as a class, as the most noble of men; yet, in 1846, he put all his vast powers of reasoning into a letter to *The Times*, in order to inveigh against what he considered the sentimental spirit of modern times which desired the abolition, or reduction, of flogging in the army. He firmly believed in the lash for certain offences as a deterrent of crime, and no one knew and understood the British soldier of his time better than did Sir William Napier. We can only conclude, therefore, that the times have changed, and the men with them; for thirty years' immunity from the lash has resulted in no harm to the British army.

CHAPTER 10

Salamanca and Madrid

In June 1812 Wellington was ready to attack Marmont, whose army he had now succeeded in isolating. By destroying the bridge at Almaraz the commander-in-chief had made it practically impossible for Drouet and Soult to reinforce Marmont; King Joseph's army was out of hand, and not likely to take the field; and the only other French army of any importance was kept busy in the neighbourhood of Corunna, where small bodies of British troops were landed from time to time to harass the Frenchmen. Marmont was at this time near Salamanca, where he had strong fortifications, and it was known that he intended to hold first the line of the Tormes River, and then, if forced to retire, the line of the Douro.

On the 13th June, Wellington's army, consisting of nearly forty thousand British and Portuguese troops, advanced to the Tormes, and on the 17th was in front of Salamanca, from which the French withdrew without offering battle, though they left some eight hundred men in occupation of the forts. Major Rice wrote, on the 18th June, from Camp, left bank of the Tormes, half a mile from Salamanca—

> My latest from the Azava will have told you of our forward movement. We arrived before Salamanca on the 16th with little opposition; skirmishing, principally with cavalry; their advance posts all driven in. The military *coup d'œil* was fine, as the whole operations and effect could at once be seen. Marmont made some show of defence in the evening, but thought it prudent in the night to retire with his principal force. He has, however, left two works in the town garrisoned, which defend the passage of the bridge, and which cause, therefore, a temporary inconvenience, as all supplies for the army have to be carried round

by the ford. One division of the army is in the town, and not-withstanding all the firing that is going on, the shops are open, and every one walking about as in times of the most profound tranquillity. The apathy of these people is beyond description; death or danger seems not to cause a sensation.

What is extraordinary enough is that tonight there is to be a ball given by General Graham. They will dance to the sound of the cannon. We are now constructing batteries; by tomor-row morning we hope they will be pounded out of their dens. Salamanca has been a fine town, the public buildings beauti-ful in the extreme, but most miserably dilapidated by the soft and gentle hand of war. I am just going to take a review of the ladies; yesterday they did not show. The cannon is roaring most tremendously. Our labours and fatigues have been very great; march always at one o'clock; now are continually on the alert, men remaining accoutred day and night. The enemy have fallen back upon Toro; whether we follow, or they retrograde, at present *je n'en sais rien*.

You talk of Philippon and his defence. The fellow showed genius in his mode of defence; but I cannot say much for his defend-ers; nothing that skill could devise was left untried; the place[7] was taken at last at the strongest point—so much for what I have said. We have been enjoying the 'canopy' since quitting our cantonments; the weather is scorching by day, and cold by night—pleasing variations. I still hold out. The Tormes is in winter a river of military importance, being extremely rapid. It has apparently a magnificent bridge of thirty arches. I am just going reconnoitring, but it will be a reconnaissance confined solely to the sweet *signoras*.

But the Frenchmen were not "pounded out of their dens" as quickly as the major had hoped, for the forts held out for another week or more, during which time Marmont made every endeavour to drive the British away and relieve the garrisons. he 51st were engaged almost daily in assisting to frustrate Marmont's designs, though they came in for no serious fighting until the 22nd. On that morning the regiment came off twenty-four hours' outpost duty, but no sooner was the brigade bivouac reached than an order was received to advance. Moving forward for about a mile, the brigade deployed into line, and

---

7. Badajoz.

then continued the advance up the slope of a hill, beyond the crest of which nothing could be seen. That the enemy was at hand, however, was soon made evident, as musket shots were heard, and a few stray bullets passed over the men's heads.

Presently balls came over the hill in showers, and some, grazing the hill slope, began to make havoc in the ranks. But the 51st and 68th, now aware that the enemy was within measurable distance, moved steadily forward, unable to fire since no mark was visible, and intent only on closing with the foe. At length the hill was surmounted, when, not ten yards away, the assailants saw the line of Frenchmen, and, with a wild cheer, dashed in. Yet they were too late; the enemy's advanced post had played its part, and, breaking, the men who composed it fled to the village, about one hundred yards away, where a large force, lying concealed, immediately opened fire and checked the British advance. The gallant brigade had carried out its orders and cleared the hill, so falling back a few yards it sheltered itself behind the crest, until the enemy's fire slackened and then ceased. It had been a brisk skirmish, and the 51st had suffered a good deal as they advanced up the hill. Captain Smellie and some twenty men having been wounded, and two or three men killed. A week afterwards. Major Rice, in a short note, dated Between Toro and Salamanca, 30th June 1812, described the affair—

The gallant 7th Division forced a post, left of the enemy. Wellington, our lord, was pleased to say that we run into them handsomely. The burst was sharp—the hottest I have ever experienced; we lost two or three and twenty. I escaped with only the loss of my favourite horse, which was shot under me. Marmont is expected to defend the passage of the Douro. We are dreadfully harassed; have not been under cover for a month. Much haste.

John Green, [8] who, as a private of the 68th, was present on this occasion, refers to the fight in the following words:

The 51st Regiment suffered considerably, having several killed and wounded. Major Rice's horse was shot from under him. Some men belonging to the *Chasseurs Britanniques* skinned the horse, and sold the flesh to their own men and to the Portuguese at three *vints*, or four-pence halfpenny per lb.

---

8. *Vicissitudes of a Soldier's Life*. By John Green, late of the Durham Light Infantry. 1827.

Major Rice had been unfortunate in his horses. One, it will be remembered, broke away and deserted to the enemy at Badajoz. The second was fated to be eaten by the allied troops. Probably the owner considered the end of his second horse no more dreadful than that of the first; and it is to be hoped that Government compensated him for the loss of his two chargers, though it is not probable that any such generosity was shown to the British officer, who, at that time, was even required to provide at his own expense beasts of burden to carry his baggage in the field.

Five days after these events the Salamanca forts fell, and Marmont beat a retreat towards Valladolid. Wellington followed leisurely, keeping touch with the enemy's rearguard, and engaging it slightly at the bridge of Tordesillas on the 2nd July. But neither side yet felt inclined to give battle; and the British were by no means hopeful that their labours were going to be rewarded with a fight. Major Rice certainly took a gloomy view of the future when he wrote, on the 6th July, from Camp near Medina del Campo—

Our lord, I am just told, is making up his dispatches, and we scrubs are graciously permitted to avail ourselves of the opportunity. Since I last communicated, nothing of importance has transpired. The army appears to have come to a *check*—rather, I think, than a *fault*. Marmont has earthed himself safe on the left bank of the Douro, and secured the bridge in front of Tordesillas. The fords are not good and are always precarious, but about these I know nothing, so I ought not to presume to give an opinion as to what is intended, or what can be done with safety to the army. His lordship only can know, as he must necessarily possess the best information as to the strength and resources of the enemy.

For my part, I am not a bit more sanguine in this glorious cause than ever, and though we have dashed a few leagues in this patriotic ground among the *vivas* of the mob, manoeuvring seems to be the game that both parties are inclined to, and, if I may judge, both are equally shy as to general action. We have been wretchedly off for this some time; scanty fare, bad biscuit, &c. The weather dreadfully hot by day and cold by night—beyond what I ever experienced. We are lying in cornfields without the smallest covering. How the men stand this severe work is to me astonishing. A few days must soon bring to light our lord's gigantic plan for annihilating the foe. If we take water or form bridge, it will be a second Lodi. My brains are baking into a paste. It is just rumoured that the brutes won't fight; if so, the game must be up in this favourite peninsula.

Marmont was now reinforced by Bonet's division, and, with this addition to his strength, the French general was able to turn on Wellington and force him to retire. Though at times Marmont pressed his adversary hard, day succeeded day without any decided advantage being gained by either side. Throughout the 19th, 20th, and 21st July, the hostile armies manoeuvred in presence of each other, at the end of which time both armies had passed to the left bank of the Tormes River. On the 22nd, Marmont, by rapidly extending his left, attempted to cut Wellington's communications with Portugal, but the wide extension proved his ruin, for the British commander saw the opportunity for which he had been waiting so long, and immediately seized it. He hurled one division against the French left with such vigour as to roll it back in complete disorder, and, simultaneously, with two other divisions he assailed the centre with like results. Then bethinking himself of making victory doubly sure, he despatched the Light Division post-haste to the Huerta ford, in the hope of barring the passage of the Tonnes to the disorganised masses of the enemy. This movement, however, failed, as the French crossed higher up stream, and made good their escape towards the Douro.

Such, briefly, was the battle of Salamanca, in which Marmont was severely wounded and twelve thousand Frenchmen placed *hors de combat*, while the Allies suffered a loss of six thousand.

The pursuit was taken up at once, and Clausel, who had succeeded Marmont in command of the French army, collected his forces and withdrew rapidly to Valladolid, which place, however, he was obliged to evacuate on Wellington's arrival near the town on the 30th July. Deciding to profit to the full by his almost unexpected success, the latter then turned south and marched straight for the Spanish capital. King Joseph fled, and on the 12th August the victorious Allies entered 1 Madrid amidst the acclamations of the populace.

Major Rice found no time to write of these events, but one of the subalterns of the 51st thus describes the entry into Madrid:

The next day, the 12th August, the anniversary of the Prince Regent's birthday, we entered the capital of Spain, and never in my life did I witness such a scene. No quiet John Bull can conceive the enthusiasm the people of Madrid displayed on that day. If we had been angels instead of men, we could not have been better received. Our division was the first British one that entered, and our regiment, being the head of the column, had the good fortune to lead. The crowds gathered round us so quickly that we could scarce move on; they seemed frantic with joy; every balcony, every window was filled with beautiful women, who showered down flowers upon our heads as we passed, and the air was rent with acclamations of 'Long live the brave scarlet fellows (*colorados*), our deliverers!' 'George forever!' 'Wellington, the brave Wellington, forever!' But when Wellington himself came, no language can describe their feelings or enthusiasm. They fell on their knees to kiss the ground his horse's hoofs had pressed, and they deemed themselves fortunate if they could only touch his clothes. Never shall I forget our entrance.

The French still held the Retiro, a fortified post in the centre of the city, and on the following evening, while the officers of the 51st were preparing to go to a ball given by the citizens to Wellington and his officers, orders were received for the regiment and the 68th to invest the place forthwith. Some few shots were exchanged with the French sentries that night, but a cordon was drawn rapidly round the Retiro, and next morning, when the fort was on the point of being stormed, the garrison surrendered—amongst the captures on this occasion being, strange to relate, the eagle of the 51st French Regiment, which, with others, was sent to England and eventually deposited in Chelsea Hospital. And there were some of the British 51st who regarded this eagle in the light of a phoenix rising from the ashes of the colours burned on the eve of the Battle of Fuentes d'Onor.

Madrid now gave itself up to gaiety—balls, bull-fights, illuminations, and *fêtes* of every description, and a week later the 51st marched to the Escorial, where it was quartered until the 1st September. On that day Wellington, leaving two divisions under General Hill at Madrid, took the remainder of his army with him and marched north, for the purpose of driving back the enemy from the Douro to Burgos.

"Our march," says Ensign Mainwaring of the 51st, "though rapid, was by no means disagreeable; for traversing a rich wine-country, our route lay through vast plains covered with vineyards, and at this season, autumn, just before the vintage, the vines were laden with clusters of ripe grapes, tempting to the appetite and beautiful to the eye. In this manner we travelled on, without anything occurring worthy of note till we came within sight of the castle of Burgos, and we began to anticipate, not with much pleasure, all the inglorious toils and arduous and fatiguing business of a siege—the most disagreeable military duty a soldier has on service, digging and delving in dust and dirt like ploughmen, to shelter ourselves, ere morning's dawn, from shot and shell whizzing about our ears at each moment, killing or mutilating our next neighbour. No excitement, as in a general action, by the immediate prospect of getting at the foe, your only hope that you may get through your twenty-four hours in the trenches unscathed, back to your bivouac, to eat, drink, and sleep till your turn in the batteries comes round again, varied by the storm of an outwork or a sortie of the enemy, to either of which occurrences the soldier looks forward as something to enliven and break in upon the routine of his daily labours."

Clausel had withdrawn slowly from the Douro as Wellington advanced, and on the 18th September passed through Burgos, leaving a garrison of eighteen hundred men in the castle. To invest and reduce this Wellington set to work immediately, twelve thousand men being detailed for the siege and twenty thousand for the covering force. So strong, however, was the castle, and so determined the garrison, that after an investment of thirty-three days, during which time five separate assaults were delivered and repulsed, and several desperate sallies of the garrison were met and beaten back, Wellington was obliged to abandon the enterprise and raise the siege, when he learned, in the middle of October, that Clausel, having received a reinforcement of twelve thousand fresh troops from France, was marching down upon him with some forty-four thousand men. During these operations the 51st, with the remainder of the 7th Division, formed part of the covering army, watching the country between Burgos and Vittoria, and spending some days near the village of Monasterio, but never called upon to do more than check reconnaissances pushed out by the enemy.

On the 21st October began the memorable retreat from Burgos—a retreat which proved almost as arduous as that to Corunna, nearly four years before. The weather was generally severe, and the enemy pressed the pursuit vigorously, ever engaging the cavalry of the rearguard and sometimes making captures. The rivers were in flood and seldom passable save at the bridges, facts which gave the advantage to Wellington, whose engineers, now adepts at mines and explosions, blew up each bridge as it was crossed, and thus from time to time checked the French onslaught. In this way, by the 26th October, Wellington was behind the Pisuerga River, with the mined bridge at Cabezon between him and the enemy, and thence he despatched parties to secure the bridges in his rear—*viz.*, at Tudela and Tordesillas on the Douro, and at Valladolid and Simancas on the Pisuerga. The 7th Division was employed in holding the three last-named bridges, the 51st being responsible for that at Valladolid. The French came on swiftly, and leaving a division in front of Wellington's main body, threw out their right and swept down on the post held by the 51st.

Opening from the high ground on the opposite bank with cannon and musketry, the enemy soon rendered the bridge untenable; but the company of the 51st defending it, even after the lieutenant in command had been borne to the rear with his right arm shattered, gallantly held on until the mine was ready. Then, having lost three men killed and fourteen wounded, the company withdrew rapidly as the bridge was blown up. The bridge at Simancas, being similarly menaced, was also destroyed, as was that at Tordesillas, on the 28th, by a party of the Brunswick *Oels* Corps detached for the purpose. But the destruction of the latter bridge was of little avail, for it was followed by an act of daring gallantry on the part of the French, perhaps without parallel in the history of war. Riding up to the broken bridge, the Frenchmen, annoyed at finding it impassable, hesitated for a moment, but then, dismounting, they set to work to form a small raft, upon which they placed their arms and clothes. Napier tells the story of what followed, and it is worth repeating:

> "Sixty officers and non-commissioned officers," he says, "then plunged into the water with their swords between their teeth, swimming, and pushing the raft before them. Under the protection of a cannonade they thus crossed this great river, though it was in full and strong water and the weather very cold, and having reached the other side, naked as they were, stormed the tower, whereupon the Brunswickers, amazed at the action, abandoned their ground, leaving the gallant Frenchmen masters of the passage."

The French restored the bridge as quickly as possible, but in the meanwhile Wellington had withdrawn to the left bank of the Douro by the Tudela bridge and by the Puente de Douro, and on the 30th October he marched towards Tordesillas in such strength as to prevent the enemy mailing use of the bridge which they had so nobly won. On this very spot Major Rice wrote his last letter of the year:—

> Camp before the Bridge op Tordesillas,
> left bank of the Douro,
> 5th November 1812.

You will not fail to perceive, as per date, that our movements of late have been retrograde—I won't call it in this place *retreating*, because it is possibly only a little run on the part of our Most Noble and Gallant Marquis, whose judgment and military abilities are inferior *nulli*—not even Bony the Great. You will, however, see all in public print, and then you may call it what you like, and I think we shall be perfectly *d'accord*. My last short and hasty, though brilliant, display of matter was from Monasterio. The following day we were pushed in very gallantly (by *superior force* understood); our loss not great, and we committed some havoc among the legions—hats and wigs cheap enough. The great superiority of the enemy in all the arms of war, I suppose, upon reconnaissance, decided his lordship on raising the siege of Burgos and falling back. The fact of the matter is, we were doing too much for our means, and, *entre nous*, are lucky in getting clear off. Our movements have been rapid, and not a little pressed; fine destruction of bridges, &c.; in fact, all the agreeables attending retrograde movements, or, as Soult calls them, *to the flank*.

Our division defended the front of Valladolid, to retard the enemy. Our regiment lost a few men; a poor woman, singularly enough, was killed by the first cannon ball fired, and an officer minus an arm. Two officers of ours have also died this week. Our sufferings have not been a little; the weather horridly cold and wet; not once under cover for these last two months. The poor soldiers dreadfully off; but I must not depict all the miseries; the truth must not be told at all times. And why tell you, or talk on subjects which you cannot understand? I often think how ridiculous one of my compositions would appear in print, under the head of 'Intercepted Correspondence from Spain!'

The whole army is now encamped in an immense vineyard—as far as the eye can reach, and the river between us and Mr Frenchman. Our people chat across, while going for water or washing. War is a strange business, and I am most heartily tired of the novelty. Hill's army has quitted the Tagus, and is moving upon us. The game, I think, is pretty well up. It is labour in vain, while poor John Bull only suffers and bleeds, as you will see by those who caught the bubble against the walls of Burgos. How lucky we are to get out of the digging business! So excellent a corps must always be in front, for the general safety of the whole. The unfortunate country people are being driven to desperation; what between friend and foe, their situation is deplorable; everything is taken from them, either by force or on requisition.

The scenes of warfare are too shocking to witness. Sick and wounded men, in want of every comfort, add to the horrors which words cannot describe. But one must not reflect. Some French wag wrote up upon a wall: *un bon soldat faut avoir la force d'un cheva, le coeur d'un lion, l'appétit d'un souris, l'humanité d'un bête*—a true bill enough, and expressive of the Peninsular and Favourite War. The army must have repose; it is naked, jaded, and done up. If the lord gets hold of this, I shall certainly be hanged. You shall hear soon of further operations and all agreeables.

Officers writing from the seat of war seldom told the whole bare tale; possibly they had the feeling that their letters were overhauled in transit, or they may have been disinclined to mention incidents which their friends at home, knowing nothing of war or of human weakness under trying circumstances, would regard as outrages. But these things left unsaid came out afterwards, and what Major Rice thought that his brother (to whom the above letter was written) would not understand was the extraordinary incident which took place at the very commencement of the retreat from Burgos. Arriving late in camp, after a heavy day of marching, near the town of Duenas, between Burgos and Valladolid, the men heard that the wine-vaults were full of the recent vintage, and with one accord they broke loose and sacked the vaults.

Some of them were found dead, literally drowned in wine, it having overflowed in the cellars and suffocated the poor wretches who were too drunk to escape. Next morning, at daybreak, when we stood to our arms to recommence the march, the scene was one, perhaps, without parallel in the annals of military history; for I scarcely exaggerate when I say that, with the exception of the officers, the whole army was drunk."

Thus wrote Ensign Mainwaring of the 51st, and Napier bears him out in saying that at one time "twelve thousand men were in a state of helpless inebriety." Fortunately the rearguard was well away from the neighbourhood of the wine, though, as the historian points out, there was at the moment little to fear from the enemy, "since the French drunkards were even more numerous that those of the British army." Small wonder that the major thought that his civilian brother would not understand such things. He himself realised, as probably did Wellington also, that fatigue had produced so great a craving for drink as to drive the men mad. To punish twelve thousand men equally implicated was, of course, out of the question, and fortunately there was no further opportunity of obtaining drink during the retreat. The incident, however, showed the temper of the troops, and, though many bore their hardships with extraordinary fortitude, and though all fought valiantly when called upon to do so, there is no disguising the fact that the discipline of the army as a whole was bad.

The woman who Major Rice says, was killed by the first shot at the Valladolid bridge, was the wife of a soldier of the regiment, and at the moment when the unfortunate shot struck her she was sitting by the side of her husband, eating her breakfast in fancied shelter. One wonders what the women of those days were made of, for numbers of them accompanied the army throughout the Peninsular War, and shared all the trials and troubles of their husbands. Numerous are the stories told of the heroism of these women, but why they were permitted to take the field is never made clear. With every regiment there marched several of them; children were born to them on the line of march; they died of fatigue; they saw their husbands killed in action, and sometimes they married again, while still on active service.

Green, in his *Vicissitudes*, mentions the case of a regimental woman (of the 68th) who married no fewer than four husbands during the war, each one dying or being killed almost before her eyes. One marvels at the indomitable courage possessed by these women of a century ago; and there were officers' wives who at times were present with the army, one notable case being that of Mrs Dalbiac, who, throughout the battle of Salamanca, seated on her horse, and often exposed to the enemy's fire, calmly watched her husband's performances in the fight. Nor was this courage restricted to British women, for everyone knows the romantic story of the young Spanish lady who became the wife of Major (afterwards Sir Harry) Smith, after Badajoz, and thenceforward followed the fortunes of her husband in bivouac and camp until the end of the war.[9]

The army remained in the Tordesillas camp only a day after Major Rice despatched the above letter, when it marched to Salamanca, and there, on the 10th November, it was joined by Hill's force from Madrid. It will be remembered that when Wellington marched north on the 1st September, he left two divisions (under Hill) in occupation of the Spanish capital. After a while the armies of Soult and King Joseph began to display considerable activity, and towards the end of October were reported to be marching on Madrid in overwhelming strength. Whether Hill could have held his own is doubtful; perhaps, fortunately, he was not required to make the attempt, even if he had any intention of doing so, for Wellington, so soon as he had decided on withdrawing from before Burgos, ordered Hill to abandon Madrid and join him, if possible, by way of the Guadarama Pass. On the last day of October, therefore. Hill, having blown up the Retiro and destroyed the stores in Madrid, retreated by the Guadarama, and was never seriously pressed by the French.

The united army then marched out of Salamanca on the way to Ciudad Rodrigo, and during the following week the rearguard was almost continuously at bay. The main body plodded on, generally in pelting rain, always on muddy roads, short of food, and otherwise distressed beyond measure. As on the retreat to Corunna, the soldiers grew sullen for want of a battle, and at length the sight of vast herds of swine in the forests proved too much for them. They wanted food, and here it was at hand; so they quitted the ranks by hundreds to shoot the pigs, until Wellington, hearing the heavy firing, thought that the enemy was pushing an attack. For a time the army was at the mercy of the French, had they but known it; but order was presently restored, though not before two of the marauders had been hanged, by Wellington's command, as an example to the rest, and not before two thousand British stragglers had been captured by the enemy.

At San Muños the 51st came in for a sharp skirmish, and had

---

9. *The Autobiography of Lieutenant-General Sir Harry Smith, Baronet of Aliwal on the Sutlej, G.C.B.* Edited, with the addition of some supplementary chapters, by G. G. Moore-Smith, M.A. Sir Harry saw much service in the Peninsula and at Waterloo; made a name for himself as victor of Aliwal (India); and was subsequently Commander-in-Chief at the Cape of Good Hope. The memory of Sir Harry is kept alive by the name of two towns in South Africa—Aliwal North, and Harrismith; while that of his wife is preserved in the name of Ladysmith.

Captain McCabe killed and eight men wounded; at the passage of the Huebra, the Light Division, covering the rear, had some heavy fighting, for the enemy's pursuit was vigorous, and his artillery fire often heavy. Stragglers were cut off, and a good deal of baggage was captured, but at length the troops saw the friendly walls of Ciudad Rodrigo, and knew that their troubles were at an end. The retreat had lasted for nearly a month; the weather throughout was inclement; the sick and wounded suffered severely; the whole army was hungry as well as footsore; and consequently the bulk of the men were out of hand, and even insubordinate. The pig-raiding prevailed up to the last day's march, for no punishment could stop it; and had the retreat continued a little longer, Wellington's army must have suffered some terrible disaster.

Once back on their old ground, and supplied with ample provisions from Rodrigo, the men's spirits were restored, and getting into dry quarters in the villages surrounding the fortress, the soldiers settled down for the winter, and put the weary retreat out of their minds. They were worn out; for almost a year they had marched continuously, and fought frequently; they had placed to their credit the capture of Ciudad Rodrigo and Badajoz, the victory at Salamanca, the triumphant entry into Madrid, and numerous minor successes. Only the retreat from Burgos tarnished their laurels; for when their losses, during this last phase of the year's operations, came to be reckoned up, they were found to be heavy. Including the siege of Burgos, Wellington's army suffered to the extent of some nine thousand men, not counting a vast number of officers and soldiers subsequently invalided from the effects of the unfortunate retreat.

Major Rice, probably to his own astonishment, succeeded in struggling on to the end of the year's campaigning, and then, having seen his regiment settled in tolerable comfort in cantonments, was forced to give in. He was immediately invalided home, and his brother, who had received his Tordesillas letter only on the 26th December, was no little surprised at the arrival, on the 15th January (1813), of the following hurriedly written note, bearing the Falmouth postmark:—

You will be surprised, but I trust agreeably, that I am landed on British ground. I made my escape with some difficulty, though honourably, from the Favourite Peninsula. I ventured my carcass in the packet as the safest conveyance, but it was like to have proved most woeful. Never did I, nor probably ever shall I, suffer such distress. Dreadful weather, and all but lost by bad reckoning on the part of the marine tribe. We got on the breakers off Ushant—blowing a gale of wind; nothing but a miracle saved us from a watery grave. I never felt till then *Danger*—in its most pitiable state. I've been in contact with my friend *Death* often, and rather familiar, but he appeared at that moment more grim than usual. I will recount my manifold adventures when we meet, which I hope will be in a few days. I touch on my way at Morshead's and my friend Kelly's near Launceston. You shall hear on what day I can be with you.

Falmouth, 11 o'clock, 13th January 1813.—Just landed from the packet—fatigued and jaded beyond description.

Such was the homecoming of one of many gallant men, who, broken down by the hardships which they had endured while fighting for the honour and glory of their country, arrived to find their stay-at-home fellow-countrymen playing the part of arm-chair critics, and decrying Wellington's great work. These critics forgot the splendid victories which the commander-in-chief had won, and the fame which he had been building up for England, and they remembered only what had happened latest—the retreat from Burgos, which they regarded, seemingly with joy, as a disaster to British arms. Yet is it ever so.

CHAPTER 11

Driving the French out of Spain, 1813

Major Rice was not fit to take the field again for some months; Colonel Mitchell was also invalided early in the year; and the junior major (Major Roberts), therefore, had the good fortune to command the 51st during the early part of the campaign of 1813. The winter had been spent pleasantly enough in cantonments, the officers hunting, shooting, and holding race meetings; and although sickness, resulting from the hardships of the past year, was prevalent amongst the troops for some time, the long rest completely restored the health of the army.

In the early spring Wellington began to get his divisions into fighting form for the coming campaign. The retreat from Burgos showed him the necessity of paying attention to discipline, in order to get the men in hand again; exercise was also required to enable them to cope with the physical exertions to which he knew they would shortly be subjected; and so, from February to April, regiments paraded almost daily for brigade and divisional manoeuvres, and were constantly reviewed by their generals, as well as by the commander-in-chief. By the middle of May all was ready for the great forward movement, which, within a few weeks, resulted in driving the enemy to the Pyrenees, and, before the end of the year, into France.

At first sight it seems extraordinary that such great success should have been in store for the Allies, only recently suffering from what can but be regarded as a somewhat ignominious handling by the enemy, for it was all that they could do to hold their own against him during the retreat to Ciudad Rodrigo. The winter, however, had brought about a change in the situation, and the complexion of affairs was entirely altered, not only in the Peninsula itself, but also in other parts of Europe. Napoleon had met with disaster in Russia, and, for the time being, the retreat from Moscow had hipped him, yet with no crushing effect. He required a leaven of seasoned troops wherewith to stiffen his vast army of hastily-raised recruits, and he therefore drew away from the Peninsula thousands of his best officers and men. With joy Wellington became aware of these events, and he realised that at last his opportunity had come.

The Spanish and Portuguese Governments rose to the occasion, and Wellington was given the supreme command of the allied troops, numbering in all parts of the Peninsula some 200,000 men (including the British). But for his immediate operations he could not reckon on more than 90,000; while the French still had in Spain 230,000, of whom, however, only 120,000, with 100 guns, were available to meet the Allies on the northern line of invasion. "Yet this," says Napier, "was a great power, of one nation, one spirit, one discipline"—as opposed to the heterogeneous force of the three nations. Had Napoleon been in personal command of his army in Spain, Wellington's task would have been no light one, for the Emperor grasped the situation even from afar, and instructed his brother Joseph accordingly, enjoining on him to act promptly and to concentrate every available man in the north.

El Rey Joseph, however, was not the man for the work; he preferred being a king to being a commander-in-chief; he quarrelled with his generals; he was slow and vacillating; and he failed signally, so much so that when Wellington opened the campaign Joseph's army was still scattered. All this was much to Wellington's advantage, and furthermore, he had the comfortable feeling that, advancing with his left practically in touch with the sea, the command of which his fleet held, he could shift his base as occasion demanded, and thus avoid the necessity of maintaining a lengthy line of communications as his army moved forward. In May 1813, therefore, when Wellington had matured his plans, he felt confident that he held Joseph Bonaparte in the hollow of his hand; and he made certain that there should be no loophole for failure.

Ordering Graham, with 40,000 men, to push through the Portuguese province of Tras os Montes to the Esla River, and thence outflank the French line on the Douro, Wellington himself, with 30,000, intended to march direct on Valladolid, where King Joseph had his headquarters, and force the enemy back from the Douro. That accomplished, and General Castaños with 20,000 Galicians having joined, a new front was to be formed, when the 90,000 Allies were to make a general advance and, assailing the French all along the line, drive them to the Pyrenees.

The 51st, in the 1st Brigade of the 7th Division (General Lord Dalhousie), marched from its cantonments on the 14th May, with Sir Thomas Graham's force, to the north-west. On the 18th it crossed the Douro, near Villa Nova, but not without difficulty, the crossing being effected in boats, and occupying twelve hours. Thence the direction of the march was north-east, across the country lying in the bend of the river, and on the 20th Miranda de Douro was reached. After a halt of five days, the 7th Division moved on to the Esla River, and encamped on its banks from the 27th to the 30th May. Wellington now came across to see how Graham was progressing, and after a careful reconnaissance of the Esla, he ordered the troops to cross by a ford at daybreak on the 31st; but, since the enemy was known to be in some strength on the opposite bank, it was decided to push a covering party of all arms across the river during the dark hours of the night. This party consisted of the hussar brigade, some artillery, the 51st, and 400 Brunswick light infantry, and at 1 a.m. on the 31st they moved down to the river.

Here the water was found to be deeper and the current more rapid than had been anticipated, an unexpected spate having come down during the previous few hours, but it was all-important that the covering force should cross to the other side before daybreak. Accordingly, the infantry were instructed to hold on to the stirrup-leathers of the hussars, and the passage began. For a time the greatest confusion occurred; the rush of the water caused the horses to plunge and rear; several soldiers were swept off their feet, lost their hold of the stirrup-leathers, and were drowned. The bulk of the party, however, reached the opposite bank in safety, though with their ammunition saturated, shortly after dawn, and found, to their relief, that the enemy had hastily withdrawn, leaving only a cavalry piquet of forty men to watch the ford. The Frenchmen retired before the advancing hussars, who pursued at top speed, and after a sharp skirmish captured nearly all of them.

On the 1st June the 51st marched to Toro, and on the following day pitched camp on its old ground at Tordesillas. Here Wellington reviewed the 6th and 7th Divisions, and having been joined by the Galicians, was now ready, with his 90,000 men and 100 guns, for the great forward movement, which he set going on the 4th June. King Joseph, unable to obtain the reinforcements which he had called up, thought first of making a stand at Burgos, then withdrew to Pancorbo, and subsequently to Vittoria. Wellington, following swiftly, gave him no breathing space, but pressing on his flanks on all occasions, forced him to give way. Yet the king still regarded the retirement of his army as merely a temporary expedient, and fully believed that as soon as his reinforcements should join him he could turn the tables on his adversary. But he was ignorant alike of Wellington's strength and of the fact that the Allies' base had been transferred from Lisbon to the ports of the Biscay coast.

The Ebro was crossed on the 16th June, and on the 20th the 51st, little thinking that the morrow would bring forth a decisive battle, was within a march of Vittoria. Wellington knew that King Joseph intended to take up a position to cover the place, which, with its vast accumulation of war material and stores, besides a convoy of treasure recently arrived from France for the payment of the troops, could not readily be abandoned. And Wellington was confident of a great victory.

Vittoria stood—as indeed it stands today—compactly built on an eminence, rising up at the end of a plain, or rather basin, some ten miles long by eight miles broad. To the north of the town the River Zadorra flows east and west for some miles, until, on approaching the Morillas range, it takes a sudden bend, almost at right angles, to the south. Then, through the Pass of Pueblas, it finds its way to the Ebro. Parallel to the main course of the Zadorra, and at a distance of some three miles to the north, runs a range of hills; on the opposite bank, and five miles to its south, is another parallel range; while the western edge of the basin consists of the Morillas mountains, pierced at one point—namely, the Pueblas defile.

It was behind this latter range that Wellington, on the 20th June, had assembled his army. The French defending Vittoria were holding the line of the Zadorra, intending to bar its passage at all points. Seven bridges spanned the river, which, though narrow, was deep, and in most parts flowed between precipitous banks. Reille's corps, forming the right of the French line, was posted to the north of the town, with orders to hold the two bridges at Gamara Mayor and Ariaga; Maransin's brigade, on the extreme left, occupied the southern range of hills, with the object of guarding that flank and preventing the passage of the Pueblas defile; while the centre of the enemy's line of battle extended along the Hermandad ridge. Midway between this ridge and the Morillas mountains flowed the Zadorra, with four bridges at no great distance apart. Wellington's plan was soon formed. Graham, with twenty thousand men, was ordered to march to the flank and attack Reille; Hill, with another twenty thousand, was to force the passage of the Pueblas defile, push back Maransin, and seize the bridge of Nanclares. To the remainder of the army, under the great commander himself, was allotted the task of pouring over the Morillas mountains on to the four bridges which lay below, and of assaulting the enemy's centre.

Dawn of the 21st June was ushered in by showers of rain and steamy heat. Hill moved forward to attack Maransin, and met with considerable opposition; but he succeeded in gaining the heights, in passing his division through the Pueblas defile, and in seizing the village of Subijana de Alava. Meanwhile Graham had moved wide away to the left, and the troops of Wellington's main attack had crossed the Morillas mountains and were nearing the bridges over the Zadorra— namely, from left to right, Mendoza, Tres Puentes, Villodas, and Nanclares. All this had taken time, and it was past noon before the 51st, in the 1st Brigade of the 7th Division, moved forward for the general assault on the enemy's centre. Picton was in chief command of this (the left) portion of the attack, and moved the 3rd and 7th Division rapidly down to the Mendoza bridge, the passage of which was contested by the enemy's cavalry and infantry, aided by his artillery.

The British had, however, already gained a footing on the left bank of the river, as, finding that Tres Puentes was unguarded, Wellington had hurried across it Kempt's brigade of the Light Division and some hussars. This cleared the way for Picton, for the riflemen of Kempt's brigade made a spirited attack on the enemy opposite the Mendoza bridge, which was immediately crossed by a brigade of the 3rd Division, the remainder of that division and the 7th Division fording the river a little higher up.

The fighting now became severe, as the Frenchmen held tenaciously to their position on the Hermandad ridge, and raked the assailants with artillery fire from the village of Margarita, until the 52nd Light Infantry coming up, charged the enemy out of the village. The 3rd and Light Divisions then pressed southwards and carried the village of Ariñez, from which the defenders rapidly withdrew. Thence the victorious Allies swept east, and followed the French, now ordered to retire upon Vittoria. Hill had worked his way forward on the right;

the far-distant sounds of Graham's attack on the left could be distinctly heard through the din of battle; and Wellington knew that all was going well.

At this juncture King Joseph began to realise the situation; that his flanks were in imminent danger, and that his centre, still six miles in front of Vittoria, ran the risk of being cut off and annihilated; so, unwillingly, he ordered a retirement. And his men, magnificent soldiers that they were, gave an object-lesson in the art of defending and retiring from successive positions. The six miles of country over which the ensuing running fight took place was undulating, rough, and broken; and the enemy, knowing each ridge, hillock, and fold in the ground, made every use of such knowledge, so that resistance was constant. Successive positions were taken up, and defended with gun and musket, until their defence seemed hopeless; and each position abandoned told its tale of destruction—of dead and wounded Frenchmen, and of captured guns.

Hour after hour the battle raged, and at about six o'clock in the evening the enemy made his last stand on a low ridge, barely a mile from Vittoria, refusing to acknowledge even then that he was beaten. Here stood eighty guns, pouring grape and round shot on the assailants, while amongst the guns and on their flanks the infantry used their muskets with deadly effect. For the moment the Allies were unable to face the storm, and the French general, noticing the recoil of the 3rd Division, and under the impression that he was fighting a rearguard action, commenced to withdraw the troops on his left flank. But the 4th Division, observing the movement, rushed headlong on the retiring body, and carried the position.

Then, and not till then, did King Joseph, watching events from the town, understand that the day was lost. Up till that moment he had imagined his centre to be impregnable, his left flank to be secure, and Reille still holding his ground on the right. Yet there were few of the inhabitants of Vittoria so sanguine as the king, and early in the afternoon the roads running east from the town were already blocked with carriages, carts, and fugitives on foot. Then, when the centre gave way, panic prevailed; the king ordered the guns to take the road to Salvatierra; the allied cavalry swept through and round Vittoria, and the infantry followed with all speed.

Vittoria, not fortified in any way, was evacuated; but Reille still maintained his position, which he now found to be most dangerous. Desperate fighting had been going on all day in this part of the field;

Graham's men stormed the two bridges, and carried them, but only to be driven from them again, and kept at bay by Reille's guns and infantry soldiers. A deadlock ensued; neither side could make headway. Then Reille suddenly became aware of the fact that Wellington's troops were pouring between his rear and the town, and that the victorious cavalry were threatening to destroy him. In the nick of time he saw the danger, skilfully disposed his troops, and with great gallantry fought his way to Metauco, on the Salvatierra road, where he attempted to form a rearguard to the fugitive French army. Darkness alone saved him, for the Allies, flushed with victory, pursued until they could no longer distinguish friend from foe.

In this long battle, fought in the heat of a Spanish summer, almost six thousand officers and men fell on each side; but the rout of the enemy was complete, and the French army in the Peninsula had never experienced a more crushing defeat. All their guns, their depots of stores and ammunition, their treasure chest, their wagons, their records, and in fact everything that they possessed, fell into the hands of the victors; and the army that fled was a disorganised rabble, having nothing but the clothes on their backs and the muskets in their hands.

The 51st, which had been in the thick of the fight all through, losing some forty-five officers and men, bivouacked that night two miles from Vittoria, and on the following day joined in the pursuit of the enemy towards Pampeluna. The Frenchmen were well on the run, and a rapid pursuit would probably have resulted in their complete dispersal, and in Wellington's immediate invasion of France. But a rapid pursuit was found to be impossible, for the reason that, as so often had been the case before, victory had proved too much for the Allies. "The night of the battle," wrote Wellington, "instead of being passed in getting rest and food to prepare the soldiers for pursuit the following day, was passed by them in looking for plunder.

The consequence was that they were incapable of marching in pursuit of the enemy and were totally knocked up." Two days later, he stated that no fewer than eight thousand British soldiers were absent, and scattered all over the country marauding, and that the majority of those who remained with their regiments were under the influence of drink, so that "when marches of over twelve miles were attempted, the line of route was crowded with stragglers and men seeking admittance to hospital."

In spite of all this, Wellington started, on the morning of the 22nd

June, with six divisions and the light cavalry, for Salvatierra, and on the 25th reached Pampeluna, which he immediately blockaded. After much marching about during the following few weeks, in the endeavour to clear the whole country of the enemy, the 51st assisted in driving the fugitives out of the valley of the Bastan, and then followed towards the Pyrenees, taking up a position at Echallar. During the last week of July and the first week of August the regiment came in for some sharp fighting, more especially on the heights above Ostiz, where it suffered the loss of thirty men, and again at the pass of Dona Maria. From that time until the end of August the 7th Division was occupied in watching the passes of Echallar and Zagaramurdi; but on the 30th it received sudden orders to strike tents and march to the bridge of Lesaca, for the purpose of covering the operations now in active progress against San Sebastian.

Previous to this, Marshal Soult, who had relieved King Joseph in supreme command of the French army in the Pyrenees, had reorganised his forces, and, towards the end of July, had made a bold but unsuccessful attempt to relieve the garrison of Pampeluna, being very severely handled in withdrawing to the Pyrenees, and it was in his overthrow that the 51st assisted at Ostiz, Dona Maria, and elsewhere, as mentioned above. The French marshal then took up a line of defence along the right bank of the Bidassoa, from its mouth up-stream to the village of Vera (situated at the point where the river bends almost at right angles), and onwards across the foothills and ridges of the Pyrenees to St Jean Pied de Port. In the meantime, Wellington, having disposed his troops so as to watch Soult all along the line, proceeded with the siege of San Sebastian, the great fortress standing on the seacoast, some fifteen miles (as the crow flies) from Vera.

The place was strong, well-provisioned and well-garrisoned, and Wellington was insufficiently equipped to reduce it quickly; moreover, Soult's activity necessitated the employment of large bodies of the allied army at a distance from the fortress. So much, in fact, was this the case that, towards the end of July, Wellington was obliged to utilise the services of so many of the besieging troops elsewhere that he found it necessary to convert the siege into a simple blockade. When, however, he had got rid of all these difficulties, and when Soult had been forced back, Wellington found it possible to renew the siege of San Sebastian. The heavy guns and other siege necessaries, for which he had waited for so long, having arrived from England in the middle of August, the British commander returned to the charge with all the determination for which he was ever noted.

For ten days the great guns battered the walls, during which period the besiegers suffered severely from the fire of the enemy's artillery, and were constantly called upon to repel with the bayonet the sallies of the garrison. To the men in the trenches it seemed as if the capture of the place was still far off, but Wellington thought otherwise, and on the 30th August he issued orders for the assault to take place a little before noon next day, at the same time instructing the troops covering the siege to be prepared to frustrate any attempt by Soult to interfere with the operations. It was for that purpose that the 51st was despatched with all haste to the Lesaca bridge, and thence sent forward, with the rest of Inglis's brigade, to support a Portuguese brigade on the slopes of the Peña de Haya (known to the French as Mount Aya, or Les Trois Couronnes).

The 31st August was a busy day, not only at San Sebastian itself, but also with the covering troops, for, as Wellington had anticipated, Soult made a strenuous effort to interrupt the siege. The country lying within the bend of the Bidassoa, between Vera and San Sebastian, was wild and mountainous, with few roads; and within that bend the covering troops were in position facing approximately east. Three bridges spanned the river—Behobia, close to its mouth, Vera, a little above that village, and Lesaca, some three miles higher up stream. These, therefore, were the principal permanent crossings available for an attack on the Allies' position from the east, except that the Behobia bridge was broken and required to be repaired. The river also, when low, could be forded at two or three points between Vera and Behobia; and since Soult possessed a pontoon train, he could throw bridges across the river at other points. Thus the Bidassoa, in its lower course, presented but a slight obstacle to an advance, though its passage might cause delay.

Soult's design was to pass some forty thousand across the river at two different points, each body fighting its way through the mountains until Oyarzun was reached, when, the whole force having concentrated, a fresh advance was to be made towards San Sebastian, some six miles distant. Wellington had foreseen all this, and had made his dispositions accordingly, watching the lower crossings from the heights of San Marcial, and the fords and bridges about Vera from the Peña de Haya—both strong and commanding positions.

Before daylight, Reille, with eighteen thousand men, forded the river near Behobia, and attacked the Spanish force posted about San Marcial. Wellington himself arrived on the scene at the critical moment, and so inspired were the Spaniards by his presence and ex-hortations that they fought with the greatest valour, and succeeded in repulsing the attack—even to driving the French into the river. While this was in progress, Clausel, with twenty thousand Frenchmen, crossed by the fords near Vera and assailed the slopes of the Peña de Hay a, held by the 9th Portuguese Brigade, supported by General Inglis's brigade, with which was the 51st, now commanded by Colonel Mitchell. Here the French were too strong for the defenders, who, resisting gallantly, were forced back up the slopes until they reached the 4th Division, at the foundry of San Antonio.

The fight which ensued was long and bickering, and it was not until two in the afternoon that Clausel's skirmishers reached San Antonio. Meanwhile Wellington directed a portion of the Light Division from Santa Barbara across the Upper Bidassoa, to move by the Lesaca bridge, and, taking some Spanish troops with them, to reinforce Inglis. Clausel observing these movements, and fearing for the safety of his left flank and rear, halted his force and sent to Soult for orders.

The 51st lost heavily in its retirement up the slopes to San Antonio, having one officer killed and eleven officers wounded, and upwards of seventy men killed or wounded. Nor was it possible for the regiment, when forced back out of San Antonio, to take all their wounded with them, and in connection with this the following appears in the records of the 51st: "Some of the wounded had to be left behind, and they, falling into the hands of the French, discovered that the regiment with which they had been engaged was the French 51st. Pointing to the common number, the English soldiers were then received by their captors rather as distressed comrades than prisoners. Their wants were immediately attended to, their wounds dressed, and every article of their personal property carefully preserved for them.

In the morning the French commenced their retreat, and left their grateful prisoners to be reclaimed by their regiment, which listened with joy to the universal story of the kindness they had experienced. 'This is the real chivalry of modern warfare, and robs it of half its horrors.'" At the time probably neither regiment knew, or remembered, that just a year before they had been in conflict at the Retiro, in Madrid, when the eagle of the French 51st had been captured. But this meeting of the British 51st with the French 51st is not without parallel in the annals of the Peninsular War, for there are other instances of the freemasonry of regimental numbers. In the *Historical Records of the 43rd Light Infantry*, the following incident is related:

In the evening (December 12, 1813), on calling the roll of the regiment, a dozen men were reported missing, whereupon Colonel Napier despatched an officer with a sergeant and patrol in quest. The men were found in a small house filled with apples, on most amicable terms with about as many French soldiers—oddly enough, belonging to the Imperial 43rd. The same object, that of securing the tempting fruit, had impelled both parties to the spot, and all had gone on the apple raid unarmed. The French, on observing that the English bore '43' on their breastplates, examined them attentively, cordially shook hands, and expressed much pleasure in the accidental *rencontre*, asking many-questions as to rations and allowances; and assured them that if they would accompany them to a post a little way off they would give them some first-rate brandy. Upon the appearance of the officer, the Frenchmen, believing themselves prisoners, brought forth the whole of their spoil as a peace-offering: but he merely pointed to the door, whence they effected their escape, while the English truants, with crammed haversacks, were escorted back to their quarters.

In those days the British soldier gloried in the number of his regiment, and doubtless the French soldier did so also. Under such circumstances one can easily understand that the number should have become a bond of union, even between men who when on duty were ready to bayonet one another. There is no doubt that, apart from such *entente cordiale* incidents as the above, the power of the regimental number was great; the traditions of the regiment were built up round its number, and when, in 1881, a civilian Secretary of State for War thought fit to substitute county titles for the old numbers, he introduced the most unpopular army reform ever devised by a War Minister. In the eyes of a civilian it may have been a small matter, but it was a bid to destroy the *esprit de corps* of half the army. That it did not seriously affect regiments was due to the fact that they steered a middle course, styling themselves officially by their new county titles, and unofficially retaining their ancient numbers.

But to return to the events of the 30th August 1813: while Clausel awaited Soult's orders at San Antonio, Reille had renewed the attack on San Marcial. For some hours the Spaniards continued to hold their own, but it is doubtful if they could have done so much longer, when fortunately the elements came to their aid. At about 3 p.m. there fell on the combatants one of the most violent storms ever experienced even in these lofty mountains, and the tempest of wind and rain raged for two or three hours, pinning the assailants to the ground and making further progress absolutely impossible.

As darkness came on Reille succeeded in withdrawing his force across the river, but Clausel, who had now been ordered by Soult to retire from San Antonio, was less fortunate, for although he himself with two brigades succeeded in fording the Bidassoa near Vera, his lieutenant, General Vandermaesen, with the remainder of the troops, was cut off by the rising waters. His sole prospect of escape from this perilous situation was by forcing the passage of the guarded bridge a little above Vera, and this, during the dark and stormy night, he was successful in doing, though at the cost of his own life, and with the loss of nearly three hundred of his men. Soult's attempt, therefore, to interrupt the operations against San Sebastian had proved a dismal failure, and while the covering force had been employed in thus holding the French in check, the great fortress had fallen, after an assault as desperate and as bloody as that which had won Badajoz in the previous year.

But Wellington had now cleared up the situation, for, save the garrison of the castle within San Sebastian, which held out for a few days longer, and that of Pampeluna, which was kept locked up until its capitulation in November, no Frenchmen (other than those of Suchet's corps in Catalonia) tarried beyond the Spanish slopes of the Pyrenees. It remained for the Allies to drive them through the mountains into France, and there was still heavy fighting in front of them.

CHAPTER 12

The Close of the Peninsular War

Anyone who has read a great number of letters from the Peninsula must often have been struck by the marked difference between those written by young officers and those by their seniors. The older men were often despondent in times of hard-ship, and were generally critical of the actions of those in command; while the subalterns and younger captains seem to have been ever in high spirits, and bubbling over with youth and gaiety. There is no doubt that, as far as regimental officers were concerned, this matter of youth put an immense amount of dash into all the operations undertaken, and inspired the soldiers with courage as well as with confidence. And it is not too much to say that an army officered by a preponderance of middle-aged men would have taken twice as long to rid northern Spain of the French. The human factor in warfare is usually overlooked by the casual reader of military history; he knows the characteristics of the chief commanders in a campaign; he knows such well-worn theories as Napoleon's presence on a battlefield being equivalent to forty thousand men; but otherwise he regards battalions as composed of officers and men all turned out of the same mould—of like temperament, of like age, and of like physique.

Now, if a study were made of the average ages of British regimental officers in the several campaigns of the hundred years ending 1908, it would probably be found that they varied very considerably, and it might be interesting to discover whether the ages of the officers affected the "go" of the campaign one way or the other. But, as concerns the Peninsular army, it is an undoubted fact that regimental officers were far younger than they have ever been since. As a rule, an officer was a captain within six years of joining his regiment, and, unless unfortunate, a major within another six years, while, with any luck, he obtained the command of his regiment before he was much over thirty years of age. Napier gives many instances: Lieut.-Colonel Charles Macleod, who was killed at the head of the 43rd in the breach at Badajoz, had not reached his 27th year; Lieut.-Colonel Thomas Lloyd fell leading the 94th at the Battle of Nivelle, at the age of thirty; Sir William Napier himself was only twenty-nine when he finished his last campaign, and his brother. Sir George, was but a year older at the close of the Peninsular War; Sir John Colborne (Lord Seaton) considered himself a most unlucky man in not having obtained the command of a regiment until he was thirty-two; and many other cases might be cited of the youth of the senior officers of regiments.

These were the men who led their battalions to victory after victory, and their subordinates were for the most part mere boys. Many fought through the Peninsular War while still in their teens, and Colborne affirmed that, when he was commanding the 66th, he was the only officer of the regiment over twenty-five years of age. We know that young Mainwaring, of the 51st, aged fourteen, was leading the veterans of the regiment at Fuentes d'Onor, and we have his own word for it, that when he entered Madrid with the victorious army he was so young that the gaieties of the city failed to amuse him, and that he preferred to spend his evenings quietly with the old Spanish couple upon whom he was billeted. And most regiments, doubtless, had ensigns as young as Mainwaring.

We of today naturally question the value of such youthful officers—lads who nowadays would be in the ranks of their school cadet corps. Yet it is an extraordinary fact that these boys commanded men often old enough to be their fathers, and were followed by them with the greatest devotion. Sir William Napier writes of one of his subalterns, Edward Freer, killed at the battle of the Nivelle, that, though only a lieutenant, he:

. . . .was rich in honour, for he bore many scars and was young of days. He was only nineteen, but had seen more combats and sieges than he could count years. Slight in person, and of such surpassing and delicate beauty that the Spaniards often thought him a girl disguised in man's clothing, he was yet so vigorous, so active, so brave, that the most daring and experienced veterans watched his looks on the field of battle, and would obey his slightest sign in the most difficult situations. . . . He was pierced with three balls at the first storming of the Rhune rocks, and the sternest soldiers in the regiment wept even in the middle of the fight when they heard of his fate.

There is no shadow of doubt that, young as they were, the regimental officers of this period, taken as a whole, knew their business thoroughly; that is to say, the commanding officer could handle his regiment with skill, and the captains and subalterns were expert company officers both in the field and in quarters. The majority of them possessed initiative, and in the fight seldom made a mistake or missed an opportunity. Their school was war, and in that rough-and-ready school they picked up all that they knew, for few of them, except those who had been trained under Sir John Moore at Shornliffe, had learned anything of soldiering before they landed in the Peninsula. Even the most hypercritical of modern writers must admit that the officer of a hundred years ago performed the duties of the rank for which he drew pay well and truly and to the best of his ability.

And what more, it may be asked, can be expected of any one? Certainly the State had no cause for complaint that it was not getting good value for its money, for it paid its infantry captains no more than ten shillings and sixpence a-day, and its ensigns half that sum, for doing their duty nobly, for under-mining their constitutions through exposure, privation, and hardships, and for risking their lives for days, weeks, months, and years on end. They were practical, fighting soldiers; but there have arisen modern critics who say of them that their minds were small and undeveloped, because they were not students of the military art, because they had not read military history and therefore did not realise that history is always repeating itself, and because such things as strategy and grand tactics were outside their sphere of thought.

We do not deny that if these officers were aiming at something higher than regimental soldiering, there is a measure of sense in these criticisms; but we would point out that, except in the case of one or two senior officers in each regiment, there had been no time for the study of books; for if we accept the statement that captains and subalterns were under twenty-five years of age at the close of the Peninsular War, and that most of them had been on active service practically from the day they joined, we fail to see when they could have read military history. And, even if they had had leisure to read such works on military history as were available a hundred years ago, there is no reason to suppose that their duties, as simple regimental officers, would have been performed the better. Afterwards many of them went to High Wycombe (Staff College) to continue their study of the art of war, the practical part of which they had already learned, and it was not found that their experience of war had in any way impaired their reasoning powers.

But in the Peninsula, youth and ignorance of military history do not appear to have interfered with successful leading, and he who delights to read of gallant deeds will find, in the accounts of the various fights, scores of episodes in which boy officers set brilliant examples to their men, and by their valour at a critical moment often saved the day. Such were the leaders of Forlorn Hopes and of similar desperate enterprises, and it would seem as if these lads must have matured much more rapidly than do the boys of the present age. Yet it may be that the rank and file were so magnificent that, at ordinary times, they were capable of being driven with a silken thread. That the soldiers, in spite of Wellington's *dictum* as to their being "the scum of the earth," were magnificent, is certain, and it is equally certain that they were devoted to their officers. There is scarcely a regiment in the army whose history does not record some gallant act performed by a soldier to save the life of an officer; and these rugged veterans went out of their way to show kindness to the boy subalterns in times of sickness or of hardship.

It may be thought that, with older officers, the frequent outbreaks of indiscipline which sullied the good name of Wellington's soldiers might have been avoided. But who can say whether the great captain would have benefited in the long-run? Occasionally his operations were delayed by the marauding and drunkenness of his troops, but there is no proof that his plans ever broke down owing to the youth of his regimental officers, and he never appears to have complained that they were too young, though he may have hinted that a few of his generals were too old, for some of them were ten years older than himself.[1]

But it may seem extraordinary that officers of the army as a whole should have been so young towards the end of the Peninsular War, for one has always imagined that, under the Purchase System, promotion was remarkably slow. Still, the wastage produced by the long war was enormous; deaths, wounds, and disease ploughed deep into the commissioned ranks; and to keep up the supply of officers was no easy matter.

Officers, captains as well as subalterns, were transferred from the

---

1. In 1813, Wellington was 44; Paget (Anglesey), 45; Beresford, 45; Hope, 48; Picton, 55; Graham (Lynedoch), 65; while Hill was only 41.

militia to the regular army; [2] from time to time non-commissioned officers were promoted ensigns, for good service in the field; but the majority of commissions were given to cadets of the Royal Military College,[3] at the average age of fifteen, or to boys, equally young, appointed direct to regiments.

The loss of twelve officers and seventy-two men (killed or wounded), in the fighting of the 31st August, reduced the strength of the 51st woefully, and it was one of the regiments which could least afford such a depletion, since it was in the unfortunate situation of having no second battalion in England upon which to fall back for reinforcements of officers and men. Most regiments in the field had a second battalion at home, ready to make good the casualties in the foreign battalion as they occurred, but the fate of the 51st had been against its ever having been able to recruit a second battalion. The 68th, also, with which the 51st had been brigaded for the greater part of the war, was suffering from the same cause, and so reduced in numbers were the two regiments that it became a great question what to do with them.

The regiments themselves were for linking up and forming themselves into what was termed a "provisional battalion," and Wellington agreed to the proposal; but the authorities at home, refusing to sanction anything of the kind, informed Wellington that, if he deemed it necessary, he could send the regiments home to recruit up to strength. But the commander-in-chief had no intention of parting with any of his tried soldiers, and he preferred weak battalions of veterans to full ones of recruits, so the 51st and 68th remained with Inglis's brigade of the 7th Division, to fight the war to a finish.

After the fall of San Sebastian, the 51st recrossed to the right bank of the Bidassoa and occupied its former position near Santa Barbara, facing Vera. Here it remained throughout the month of September, and early in October moved to Echallar, to await the development of Wellington's plans. Major Rice, who had been kept in England after the expiration of his sick leave, because the authorities thought that Wellington would send the regiment home, now rejoined, in the best

---

2. Later in this year (December 1813), Samuel Rice's younger brother, Frederick, a militia officer, was given a company in the 51st, but was placed on half pay in the following year. In 1815, when travelling on the Continent, he heard of the coming struggle, and hastened to Brussels, in order to offer his services as a volunteer. Although too late to take part in the battle of Waterloo, he accompanied the 51st (unofficially) on the march to Paris, and was present at the storming of Cambray. He died at Geneva in 1823.

3. At High Wycombe until 1812, when it moved to Sandhurst.

of health and spirits, though disappointed at having missed the three months' fighting in which his regiment had taken part. He saw, however, that he was still in time to take his share of plenty of rough work; and so it proved.

Wellington, having driven the French out of northern Spain into the Pyrenees, at first had no intention of following them into France, his reasons being that Napoleon might at any moment send reinforcements to Soult, and that a French army (under Suchet) was still in possession of the Mediterranean province of Catalonia, in eastern Spain. With Suchet in his rear, his position was insecure; and if large reinforcements were despatched to Soult, the allied army might fare badly, although the proximity of the sea-base rendered disaster impossible. When, therefore, San Sebastian fell, Wellington inclined to transfer the war to Catalonia, but political pressure from home and the news of Napoleon's misfortunes in Germany combined to cause him to change his plans, when, as Napier says, he "matured an offensive movement as daring as any undertaken during the whole war"—in short, an assault on Soult's whole line of fortifications in the Pyrenees, and the invasion of France.

Between the opposing armies the Bidassoa flowed from Vera to the sea; but to the north and north-east of Vera there was no such well-marked dividing line—only the labyrinth of rocky spurs and ravines which seamed the mountain-slopes. Wellington's plan was to advance simultaneously on the right and on the left, the troops on the right storming Soult's fortified posts among the mountains, while those on the left forced the passage of the Lower Bidassoa. These operations were to have commenced in the middle of September, but, owing to faulty arrangements in the matter of pontoons and subsequently to bad weather, they were deferred until the 6th October. That night everything was got ready, and at daybreak next morning Wellington's carefully laid plans were set going, their extraordinary boldness altogether deceiving Soult.

Under the protection of a heavy cannonade from San Marcial and the neighbourhood, the divisions on the left forded the Lower Bidassoa at several points almost before the French had fired a shot, and, turning the enemy out of his positions, crossed the frontier into France. At the same time, the Light Division advancing on Vera, and thence up the mountain-slopes, carried position after position with astounding impetuosity; while, farther away on the right, the 7th Division and others guarded the Echallar pass and various roads and tracks through the mountains. Desultory fighting went on upon the crests of the Pyrenees during the next two days, after which Wellington called a halt, and from his headquarters at Vera reorganised the commands of his army. Hill was given the right, from Roncesvalles to the Bastan; Beresford the centre, which included Echallar, where the 7th Division was posted; and Hope the left, from the Mandale mountain to the sea. Tents were brought up, and the troops encamped on their several positions, eagerly awaiting the order to move forward; but Wellington had not yet decided finally whether to invade France or to move back into Spain and carry the war into Catalonia.

A month was thus spent, in the most inclement weather, on the summits of the bleak Pyrenees, and the allied army suffered great hardships, some of the posts being at times snowed up and cut off from provisions. Fortunately they were provided with tents—though they were a cold comfort; nevertheless, the shelter which they afforded was certainly preferable to bivouacs among the rocks.

Prior to the opening of the campaign of 1813, regiments had been unacquainted with the luxury of canvas, and it is wonderful how they managed to exist for so many years in such variations of climate. Whenever possible, the troops were billeted in the towns, villages, and farms; but when actually in the field the bivouac was resorted to, and as time went on the old soldiers became adepts at making themselves comfortable, in shelters formed of boughs of trees, or even in hastily constructed huts, when halting in the more wooded parts of the country. In 1812, tents were improvised out of blankets, two of which were fastened together by tapes sewn on to the sides, and then stretched over a pole supported by the arm piles; but these provided shelter for only four men, who, moreover, had but two blankets among them in which to sleep.

The whole matter was one of transport, and Wellington had always refused to allow the movements of his army to be hampered by excessive baggage. By this time, however, the medical officers had learnt by experience that much of the sickness of the army was attributable to exposure, and the authorities at length sanctioned the issue of four tents per company, three for the men and one for the officers, but their carriage was not to entail any increase in the number of transport animals. Hitherto the company mules carried nothing except the heavy iron camp-kettles, or cauldrons, but now these were exchanged for lighter ones of tin, which the men (six to a kettle) took it in turn to carry on their knapsacks, while the mules carried the tents.

Meanwhile, Soult had taken advantage of the inaction of his foe, and had caused to be thrown up a complete chain of entrenchments, some thirty miles long, covering St Jean de Luz on his right, and extending along the course of the Nivelle to its upper waters, whence the left of his line stretched eastward to the River Nive. The centre was guarded by outworks, erected about the Smaller Rhune and Sarre, to the east of the Greater Rhune; and so strong was this vast line that the most careful reconnaissances could discover scarcely a single weak spot in it.

At length Wellington made up his mind to move on into France, for he had now learned that Suchet would not co-operate with Soult, and he had learned also that Napoleon had met with successes in Germany. The time, therefore, was opportune to attack Soult, and to delay might result in his opponent receiving reinforcements from Napoleon. The British commander arrived at this decision early in November, and on the 9th issued his orders. His plan was to strike at the French centre, cross the Nivelle at the bridge of Amotz, and attempt to divide Soult's force. Before any general advance could be made, however, it was necessary to clear the foreground by capturing the outworks in the Pyrenees, and the Light Division, still in position about the Greater Rhune, facing the strongly fortified Smaller Rhune, not a mile distant, was ordered to push forward on the morrow. This the regiments of the famous division did in the most gallant manner, thus opening what was known as the battle of the Nivelle, and sweeping the Frenchmen from their fortified posts at the point of the bayonet.

The strength of the enemy's right determined Wellington to make no immediate advance on that side, but to bring round Hill's and Beresford's divisions in a species of gigantic wheel, so as to cross the Nivelle above and below the bridge of Amotz, and cut Soult's army in two. While, therefore, the Light Division was fighting its way through the enemy's advanced works, the 4th and 7th Divisions were sent against the forts of San Barbe and Grenada. It was a day of grand work, but we can do no more than follow the fortunes of the 51st, in Inglis's brigade of the 7th Division.

By a stroke of luck for Major Sam Rice, Colonel Mitchell had been placed on the sick list at Echallar, and the command of the regiment devolved on the major, who soon showed that he was equal to the responsibility. From the mouth of the Echallar pass, the 7th Division advanced rapidly on the Grenada fort, which covered the village of Sarre, while the 4th Division moved against the neighbouring fort of

San Barbe, the regiments carrying scaling-ladders, wherewith, if necessary, to storm the works. Such aids, however, were not needed, for the defenders, powerless to withstand the fire of the eighteen British guns which accompanied the attack, fled from the forts, and though they stood for a while at Sarre, they soon broke before the determined onslaught of the pursuers.

The victorious divisions, as they forged ahead, presently found themselves confronted by two redoubts, Louis XIV. and Harastaguia. The former was immediately stormed and carried at the point of the bayonet, and attention was then paid to the latter, in front of which the 31st French Regiment had been placed as a covering force. Upon this unfortunate regiment the 7th Division fell forthwith, breaking it and putting it to the rout, and driving the garrison from the redoubt—even to the banks of the Nivelle.

The French, pursued vigorously by the 4th and 7th Divisions, crossed the river by the various bridges, and took up positions on the heights above St Pé, whereupon Wellington, halting the other divisions, pushed the 3rd and the 7th across the river against Maransin's French division, which stood its ground and fought desperately. "After a hard struggle, in which General Inglis was wounded, and the 51st and 68th Regiments were handled very roughly,"[4] the attack succeeded, and Maransin's troops were put to flight. Thus, at nightfall, when darkness put an end to the fight, the British had established themselves in rear of the French right, and Wellington had reason to be proud of the valour of his troops. In his despatch he included the following:

> I likewise particularly observed the gallant conduct of the 51st and 68th Regiments under command of Major Rice and Lieut.-Colonel Hawkins, in Major-General Inglis's brigade, in the attack of the heights above St Pé, in the afternoon of the 10th.

On this day the 51st lost two officers and twenty-two men killed, two officers and seventy-three men wounded, and one officer (Captain Phelps) taken prisoner.

> "Major Rice," says the *Records of the 51st Regiment*, "commanding the regiment on this occasion in the absence of Colonel Mitchell, detained at Echallar by sickness, was rewarded for his bravery by a lieutenant-colonelcy and the Gold Medal."

The Peninsular Gold Medal was a much-coveted decoration, for it

---

4. Napier's *Battles and Sieges*.

was given sparingly, and only to selected officers, for certain engagements. No officer could claim the right to receive it, but as the war progressed regulations were issued from time to time, and recommendations for the decoration were restricted to certain ranks for the satisfactory performance of certain duties. It must be remembered that, at the commencement of the Peninsular War, medals were almost unknown in the British army. A few had been struck to commemorate great naval victories, but they were bestowed at first only on the chief commanders, though towards the close of the eighteenth century a wider distribution was made to the navy and marines. Soldiers, however, knew nothing of medals, and even Sir John Moore, with all his war service, died without ever having received a medal.[2]

The suggestion of granting medals to officers engaged in the war in the Peninsula probably came from Sir Arthur Wellesley, who had recently come from India, where the Honourable East India Company was accustomed to issue medals to all its native troops for the various Indian wars. Gold medals in two sizes were therefore struck and granted to senior officers, the larger medals being given to generals and the smaller to other officers, as a rule not below the rank of major. On one side of the medal was the name of the action for which it was granted, and on the principle of *bis dat qui cito dat*, the medals were distributed as soon as possible after the action, being sent out for the purpose to the seat of war.

As time went on senior officers began to accumulate many medals, since they received one for each great battle or siege; and the authorities deemed it advisable to issue no more than one medal to an officer, engraving upon it subsequently the names of all the general actions at which he was present. Presently a fresh difficulty arose: the actions became too numerous to admit of their names being engraved on the limited space of the medal; so, eventually, in 1813, regulations concerning the issue of gold medals were finally approved. It was then laid down that an officer should wear only one gold medal, upon which should be engraved the first action in which he was engaged; that for the second and third action he should receive gold clasps, inscribed with the names of the actions. The fourth action entitled the officer to the Gold Cross, upon which were engraved all four actions, and which was to be worn in substitution of the gold medal and clasps

---

2. The Gold Medal for Corunna, inscribed with his name, was subsequently handed to his relatives, and is now to be seen, with other relics of the great man, at the Museum of the R.U.S. Institution.

previously received; and gold clasps were added to the ribbon of the gold cross for each subsequent action after the original four.

As far as regimental officers were concerned, the commanding officer of a full battalion present in an action for which a commemorative medal was struck[3] was usually recommended for the smaller gold medal (or clasp if he was already in possession of the medal), even though he might have been a major temporarily in command. As a rule, no other regimental officer received the medal for services performed as such, but occasionally a major or a captain was given the decoration for some particularly brilliant service, for which nowadays he would be awarded the V.C. or the D.S.O.

But anything like a general distribution of medals to everyone engaged was not given a thought; in fact the idea of wearing medals at all was so new that the majority of officers and men of the army regarded such things as far beyond their reach; and it was not until after the issue of a silver medal to all ranks of the army present at Waterloo, that Peninsular veterans began to consider themselves slighted. Yet for upwards of thirty years they agitated in vain, and only in 1848 was justice done to them by the issue of a silver medal, with clasps. Probably, by that time, the greater number of these brave men had passed away, for, between 1808 and 1848, thousands had been killed in action, died of wounds or of disease contracted on active service, died in after-life from the effects of exposure and hardships during long years of campaigning, or died of old age.

The regimental officers, perhaps, felt the non-recognition of their services more than did the men, for they argued that they had shared in many Peninsular victories as hard-fought as Waterloo, and had nothing to show for them except the scars on their bodies. And they felt the injustice the more when they remembered the manner in which the gold medal had been awarded. Almost every officer on the staff—even the most junior in field rank—had received it as a matter of course; but no such generosity had been extended to regimental officers, few of whom had been able to fulfil the qualifications pre-

---

3. The battles and sieges for which Gold Crosses, Gold Medals, or clasps were granted were as follows: Maida, Roliça, Vimiera, Corunna, Sahagun (and other cavalry actions), Talavera, Busaco, Barrosa, Fuentes d'Onor, Albuhera, Ciudad Rodrigo, Badajoz, Salamanca, Vittoria, Pyrenees, St Sebastian, Nivelle, Nive, Orthes, Toulouse, and, in addition, Martinique (1809), Guadaloupe (1810), Java (1811), Fort Detroit, America (1812), Chateauguay, America (1813), and Chrystler's Farm, America (1813).

scribed by the authorities.

There were captains and subalterns who had fought in battles and sieges innumerable, often severely wounded and even maimed for life, yet who went undecorated; while there were majors, perhaps but once engaged, who, by a stroke of fortune, brought their regiments out of action, and thereby qualified for recommendation for the gold medal. Major Sam Rice, however, was not one of these, for he had seen as much service as any officer of the 51st. Still, but for the temporary illness of his commanding officer, his Peninsular services would have gone unrewarded.

After the battle of the Nivelle, Soult withdrew his main body to the entrenched camp at Bayonne. He destroyed the bridge at Usta-ritz, and disposed his troops along the right bank of the River Nive, so as to watch all the other crossings. The weather favoured him; for, throughout the next eight days, rain fell incessantly, the river came down in flood, and the roads, knee-deep in mud and slush, were prac-tically impassable, so that Wellington was restrained from following up his victory. Further circumstances, moreover, forced delay upon him: the Spanish troops, elated at the invasion of France, murdered and pillaged the unfortunate inhabitants far and wide, and so incensed was Wellington at their conduct that he forthwith put to death all whom he took red-handed, and sent the Spanish divisions, composed of some 25,000 men, back across the frontier, to their own country, although by so doing he foresaw the possibility of serious trouble with the Spanish Government.

Wellington now felt his way cautiously, his available troops being too few to run any great risks, and he would not have moved forward immediately except for the fact that the enemy still had a footing at one point on the left bank of the Nive. This was at the Cambo bridge, which, covered by a bridge-head on the left bank, was a source of grave concern to the British commander, since its possession could be taken advantage of by Soult to launch an attack on Wellington's right flank. On the 16th November, therefore. Hill was ordered to move out and threaten the bridge-head, an operation which was completely successful, as the enemy made no stand, but, blowing up the bridge-head and the bridge, evacuated the left bank of the river at the first sight of Hill's reconnaissance. With the Nive between his right flank and the French, Wellington knew that he could bide his time, and complete his preparations for a further advance. And it was nearly a month before he pushed on again.

Between the 8th and 13th December the fighting was heavy and almost continuous, but the 51st saw little of it, being moved about from point to point, in reserve, and being brought up at the concluding action at St Pierre only when the day had been won. But in these stoutly contested battles before Bayonne, otherwise known as the "Battles of the Nive," the Anglo-Portuguese force had met with great successes, had crossed that river, and had pushed the enemy back upon Bayonne, thus earning the well-merited praise of its commander, who himself averred that, had he gone against his conscience and brought up the 25,000 disgraced Spaniards, he would have carried Bayonne and driven Soult's army to the winds. As it was, he held the line which he had gained until he opened the campaign of 1814, and commenced the final phase of the long war.

At the time Wellington had the unpleasant feeling that the Spanish Government, smarting under the insult which had been offered to the national army, would join the French, and force the British commander to fight for the embarkation of his army. Within the next few weeks, however, the political situation cleared up, and Soult began to suffer from the calls made upon him by Napoleon to supply reinforcements for the army with which he was endeavouring to stem the tide of German invasion on the eastern frontiers of France. Soult still held the fortress of Bayonne, standing at the confluence of the Nive with the Adour, and upstream from Bayonne he held the right bank of the Adour as far as the mouth of the River Bidouse, whence his line, bending southwards almost at right angles, followed the right bank of the latter river. Wellington's immediate objective was Bayonne, the investment of which place he had determined to effect at once, and for this purpose it was necessary to throw a portion of his army across the Adour. With the sea at his command, he decided to cross the river below Bayonne, and in order to distract Soult's attention from that direction he threatened the French centre and left, about the upper Adour and Bidouse, with all the troops whom he could spare.

Towards the middle of February (1814) the operations commenced. On the 26th, Hope, with magnificent skill, threw a bridge of boats across the Adour, at the point some three hundred yards wide, and completed the investment of Bayonne forthwith. Meanwhile Soult's troops had been kept fully occupied among the rivers and streams to the eastward, and on the 27th was fought the Battle of Orthes. The 51st, which, with the 7th Division (forming part of Beresford's command), had been pushing the French north-eastward from the river

Bidouse during the previous week, found itself on the morning of the 27th near St Boes, opposite the enemy's right.

Soult had taken up a strong position along the heights extending from St Boes to the Gave de Pau about the village of Orthes, and had made up his mind to give battle. Wellington was ready to meet him. Beresford, with the 4th and 7th Divisions, was ordered to attack the right from the north-west; Hill, with the 2nd Division, moving from the south bank of the Gave de Pau, was directed to advance on the bridge of Orthes and turn the French left; while Picton, with the 3rd and 6th Divisions, and Alten, with the Light Division, held the centre.

The battle was opened by Beresford at about 9 a.m., but, although he pushed in the enemy's right and carried the village of St Boes, he was in turn forced to retire, and was roughly handled by the French guns. Picton, who had at the same time been pressing forward against the centre, met with no better success, and was also driven back. For the moment the situation was critical, and it seemed as if Soult would snatch a victory; but Wellington's master-mind realised what was happening, and, quick as thought, he hurled a counter-attack of Alten's and Picton's men in between two parts of the French army which had become separated. Beresford turned, recaptured St Boes, and cut off Soult's retreat by the Dax road; and at the same time Hill forded the Gave de Pau a little above Orthes, and menaced Soult's left.

The French, smitten in front and flank, drew off rapidly to the north-east, and the battle resolved itself into a race between Hill's Division and Soult's army for the bridge at Sault de Navailles, three miles away. The retreat was well carried out, and though Hill's cavalry pursued with a certain amount of success, Soult contrived to pass the bridge and destroy it, thus putting an end to the pursuit.

This was the last general action of the Peninsular War in which the 51st was engaged, for although the regiment crossed the Adour at St Sever, and advanced as far as Mont de Marsan, it was then detached, in order to accompany Beresford to Bordeaux, which city was wavering between allegiance to Napoleon or to the Bourbons. To settle matters, and to give confidence to the Bourbon party, Wellington sent Beresford with twelve thousand men, and the appearance of this force before Bordeaux, on the 12th March, had the desired result; whereupon Beresford, leaving Lord Dalhousie with the 7th Division and three squadrons of cavalry to occupy the place, marched back to the army. But as soon as Beresford had departed, the Napoleonists took heart and attempted an insurrection, in which they were supported by the advance of a French force from outside. For the next few weeks, therefore, the 51st was constantly engaged in skirmishes with the enemy, who was eventually dispersed by the arrival of a British fleet in the Garonne.

While these events were passing in the neighbourhood of Bordeaux, Wellington was following Soult. On the 20th March, a short but fierce fight at Tarbes resulted in the defeat of the French, who, however, retiring towards Toulouse, continued to dispute the advance of the Allies towards the upper Garonne, until, on the 10th April, Wellington caught them at Toulouse, and overthrew them. With this victory the war was brought to a close, for, the day after Wellington entered the town, the news of Napoleon's abdication was received from Paris, and the preliminaries for a permanent peace were entered into.

At Bordeaux the 51st remained in the enjoyment of a good deal of pleasure and gaiety until July, when it embarked for England, and proceeded first to Plymouth and then to Portsmouth, from which latter place it had started three years and a half before for the Peninsula. In that time the regiment had lost many officers and a great number of men, but these gallant dead had helped to gain seven fresh battle honours for the colours of the 51st. Personal rewards were restricted to the three senior officers, each of whom received the Gold Medal and brevet promotion, otherwise the officers and men found their reward only in the knowledge that they had fought for the glory of England, and had upheld the good name of their regiment. Napier, in the concluding paragraph of his *Battles and Sieges*, writes of the Peninsular army as follows:—

> Thus the war terminated, and with it all remembrance of the veterans' services. Yet those veterans had won nineteen pitched battles and innumerable combats; had made or sustained ten sieges, and taken four great fortresses; had twice expelled the French from Portugal, once from Spain; had penetrated France, and killed, wounded, or captured two hundred thousand enemies—leaving of their own number forty thousand dead, whose bones whiten the plains and mountains of the Peninsula.

But, if one turns to the lighter side of the war, one gathers from the journals and letters of officers that, in all this campaigning, with its attendant bloodshed and misery, there was usually some bright lining to the cloud. The vast majority of the officers, as has been shown, were of an age particularly susceptible to sparkling eyes and such-like things, and the Spanish and French ladies appear to have been no less susceptible to the charming manners of the brave young Englishmen—even though the latter loved and rode away. There were not a few instances, however, of attachments which ended in marriage, and some of the non-commissioned officers and men also brought home Spanish or French wives. These men of war certainly carried large hearts buttoned within their tight-fitting *coatees*, and the cordiality of the *entente* was beyond dispute, as is evident from the following words with which one of Napier's subalterns concludes his account of the war[6]—words which, when compared with the above-quoted paragraph, show with what different eyes a bachelor lieutenant and a married lieutenant-colonel looked on life:—

> But at the conclusion of the war there was such an abundance of kissing as probably the like of it was never seen before, which put one in mind of the adage, *that none but the brave deserve the fair.* There was kissing in the valleys, and kissing upon the hills, and, in short, there was embracing, kissing, and counter-kissing from Toulouse to Bordeaux.

---

6. *Narrative of Events in the South of France.* By Captain John Henry Cooke, late of the 43rd Regiment of Light Infantry. London, 1835. (Published by Leonaur, under the title *With the Light Division.*) The author was a distinguished regimental officer; was present at all the important battles and sieges; was twice wounded; received the Peninsular Medal with eight clasps and the Spanish Gold Cross; was appointed to the Corps of Gentlemen-at-Arms; became Ensign of the Yeomen of the Guard, and was knighted.

CHAPTER 13

The Waterloo Campaign

Samuel Rice's regimental soldiering so far had been full of excitement, and he had certainly borne his share of service abroad and in the field. He had suffered considerably in health, and had been invalided on more than one occasion, but his twenty-one years' service had not been without reward, although, it may be remarked, he himself appears to have thought little of his brevet or of his gold medal. His letters of this time show that, like many another senior regimental officer, he considered that he had had enough campaigning to satisfy him for some years—if not for his life-time,—and he rejoiced in the idea of a lasting peace and the quiet of garrison life at home. So convinced was he that a period of leisure and rest was in store for him that, confirmed bachelor as he had hitherto believed himself to be, he seized the opportunity to get married. Yet, within a very few months, his dream vanished; for he was suddenly called upon to leave his bride and go back to war.

Napoleon was once again the cause of all the trouble. When he abdicated in April 1814, he was deported, as a state prisoner, to the Island of Elba, in the Mediterranean; although, out of deference to the feelings of so great a man, his sentence of imprisonment was couched in the most polite terms: Elba was ceded to him, and there he was permitted to reside, with a large retinue and a pension from France. The nations of Europe hugged themselves with the hope that they had settled the troubler for all time, but early in March 1815 they received a rude awakening; for Napoleon was not the man to settle down quietly, at the age of forty-six, without making an effort to retrieve his fallen fortunes and recover his lost throne; and he astonished the world by escaping from Elba, and landing in the south of France. Here he was received enthusiastically by the people, and more especially by his old soldiers, who, again raising the cry of *Vive l'Empereur!* forthwith joined his standard and marched on Paris, whereupon the Bourbon king fled, and Napoleon once more defied all Europe.

By the Treaty of Paris (1814) Napoleon had agreed for himself and his family to renounce the throne of France, and the allied Powers had agreed to evacuate French territory. A congress then assembled at Vienna to settle various weighty questions connected with the rearrangement of frontiers, which Napoleon s high-handed conquests had upset in all directions. How long this congress would have sat it is impossible to say; no two Powers would come to terms on any point put forward, and as time went on events moved towards an open rupture between certain of the Powers. Napoleon's escape, however, put an end to all differences, and the nations one and all determined to combine against the common "enemy and disturber of the world." The armies of some of the Powers had not retired far beyond the frontiers of France, and these turned about and prepared for an immediate invasion, while those at a distance began to move up.

Towards the close of 1813 Great Britain had sent an army, under the command of Sir Thomas Graham, to the Netherlands (Holland and Belgium), to assist the Prince of Orange in holding his own against the French, and the bulk of that army, still remaining in these countries after the peace of 1814, formed the nucleus of Wellington's army of 1815, reinforcements being despatched rapidly from England.

On the 30th March, the 51st landed at Ostend. Lieut.-Colonel Rice was in luck again, for he found himself in command of the regiment, Colonel Mitchell having been appointed to the command of a brigade. Travelling in barges on the canal, the regiment moved through Bruges to Ghent, where it halted for a few days, and then marched to Brussels, a week later moving into cantonments at Grammont.

The command of the Anglo-Dutch or Anglo-Belgian army was given to Wellington, who soon assembled, in the Netherlands, some 100,000 troops. Acting in conjunction with him was the Army of the Lower Rhine, consisting of Prussians and Saxons, under Blücher, numbering another 100,000 or perhaps a little more. Next came the Austrians and Bavarians (under Schweidnitz), who, to the number of 250,000, were known as the Army of the Upper Rhine; while, away in rear, 170,000 Russians were moving up in reserve. Moreover, the Spaniards, Portuguese, Swiss, Sardinians, Danes and Swedes, were all ready to close in on France, in the event of their co-operation being required. As a matter of fact, Wellington and Blücher hewed their road to victory without the assistance of the others.

Had Wellington had his way, he would have moved into France and assumed the offensive before Napoleon should have time to re-organise his army, but for political and other reasons this was found to be impossible, and April and May were spent in making arrangements for the defence of Belgium; for it was judged that Napoleon would strike at Brussels as soon as possible. He himself would have preferred to have bided his time, but he was forced into immediate action by the knowledge that, if he were to delay, he would be overwhelmed by the Austrians and Russians. He despised the army of Wellington, and he thought little of the British commander, against whom, however, he had never as yet been pitted. For these reasons he was not long in making up his mind to invade Belgium.

Meanwhile Wellington and Blücher had disposed their armies so as to watch the approaches to the Belgian capital, and by the beginning of June the general situation was as follows: At Brussels Wellington had his headquarters, and kept Cole's and Picton's divisions in reserve. In front, *i.e.*, towards the south, Hill's corps was on the right, stretching from the Scheldt up to about Ath; and the Prince of Orange's corps at Mons, Enghien, and Nivelles, prolonged the line to the left; while the Dutch and Belgian cavalry, covering these two corps, were posted well out in front, and Lord Uxbridge's British cavalry was kept in rear, about Grammont. To the left again came the Prussians, with the head-quarters of their corps at Charleroi, Namur, Ciney, and Liège. So that the whole line covered a front of about one hundred miles, and was, roughly speaking, forty to fifty miles to the south of Brussels.

The 51st was in the 4th British Brigade (Mitchell), belonging to the 4th Division (Colville), in Hill's corps, and the regiment remained in its cantonments at Grammont until the morning of the 16th June. How little was known up to this time of the coming campaign is vouched for by a letter which Colonel Rice wrote at Grammont on the 9th June, but which was not posted till the 13th. He wrote as if the army generally had no idea of any immediate fighting taking place.

We are at present quiet," he said; "all a matter of conjecture as to what is to be done. The Great Duke knows, but we poor devils know nothing.

But at this time even the Great Duke himself did not know what was going on at any great distance beyond his outposts. Up to the 12th June he had not heard that the French were actually moving towards the Belgian frontier, though he may have suspected it; and so badly served was he by his intelligence officers (who, it is only fair to say, were themselves kept in ignorance of events by the Prussian staff), that it was not until the afternoon of the 15th that he was able to decide whether Napoleon intended to advance on Brussels in one column, by the direct road *via* Charleroi, or whether he would divide his force so as to send a portion of it by the western route through Mons and Hal.

Meanwhile Napoleon, with his customary energy, had matured his plans rapidly, and had pushed forward his several corps towards the frontier; so that, when he himself left Paris on the 12th June, he had made up his mind that he would cross into Belgium on the 15th, and be in possession of Brussels shortly afterwards, having defeated Blücher's Prussians and Wellington's British and allied troops. He concentrated rapidly, and on the night of the 14th nearly the whole of his army was in bivouac close up to the Prussian outposts. At dawn on the 15th he saw the first item on his programme carried out, the French forcing back the Prussians, occupying Charleroi, and advancing northwards towards Quatre Bras.

At 3 p.m. that day Wellington was apprised of these movements, but so certain was he of the soundness of his dispositions that he feared nothing. Learning that no French troops were moving in the direction of Mons, he knew that his right flank was safe, so at 5 p.m. he issued orders for a general concentration of his force towards Quatre Bras—the point where the Nivelles-Ligny road crossed the road from Charleroi to Brussels—and at 10 p.m. he supplemented these orders by detailed instructions as to routes and objectives. Then he attended the famous ball given by the Duchess of Richmond in Brussels, whereat a great many British officers were present, though all had been warned that they were to leave early and join their regiments marching to the front. Straight from the festive scene, therefore, many rode all night to overtake the troops only as they were becoming engaged with the enemy.

At daybreak on the 16th the 51st (with Mitchell's brigade) left Grammont for Braine le Comte, where, after a weary march, it halted for the night in pouring rain. During the march the sounds of guns were distinctly heard in the distance, yet no one in the regiment knew what was taking place, or the whereabouts of the enemy. But not far away stirring events had been in progress. At 11 a.m. Wellington, riding from Brussels, had reached the position which his advanced troops were taking up at Quatre Bras, though by that time only some 7000 Dutch and Belgians, under the Prince of Orange, had arrived. Fortunately, however. Napoleon appeared to be directing all his energies against Blücher's 80,000 Prussians, in the neighbourhood of Ligny, and Wellington rode across to confer with the Prussian Field-Marshal, eventually agreeing to go to his assistance at 4 p.m., if not himself attacked.

Wellington then returned to Quatre Bras, and within a couple of hours realised that the Prussians would have to look after themselves; for Napoleon, aiming at a double victory, sent Ney against Wellington early in the afternoon, and the battle which raged around Quatre Bras for the remainder of the day only ended in a victory for Wellington by the timely arrival of the reserves from Brussels. Blücher, in the meanwhile, had been severely handled by Napoleon, who, after a bloody conflict of nearly six hours, succeeded in breaking the centre of the Prussian line and driving the defeated army from the field. But of the forced retreat of his Prussian allies from Ligny Wellington heard nothing definite until next morning, when he learned that Blücher had retired upon Wavre.

No sooner did Wellington become aware of the Prussian retreat than he decided to fall back from Quatre Bras to the position at Waterloo which he had had in his mind all along, and at about 10 a. m. on the 17th June he sent word to Blücher that he would fight at Waterloo if a Prussian corps would join him there. He then issued orders for the retirement from Quatre Bras, and sent instructions to Prince Frederic's Dutch-Belgians and such troops of the 4th Division as were at Braine le Comte or on the road to Nivelles to assemble at the former of these two places and await orders, while all other troops were to retire at once to Waterloo.

Now it happened that Mitchell's brigade alone of the 4th Division, marching early from Braine le Comte, had reached Nivelles before the order arrived, and thus avoided sharing in the ill-luck which befell the remainder of the division—*viz.*, being posted on the flank at Tubize, near Hal, while the great victory of the 18th June was being won.[1] Mitchell, therefore, paraded his brigade with the 2nd Division, already

---

1. The 35th, 54th, 59th, and 91st Regiments, forming the 6th British Brigade (4th Division) received no acknowledgment of their services in the Waterloo campaign, their absence from the battle debarring them from obtaining the battle honour for their colours. But the officers and men were granted the medal, and took their share of the prize-money voted by Parliament.

at Nivelles; and at noon the 51st was marching north by the Brussels road.

The march of the afternoon was hot and dusty, and was made all the more disagreeable by the road frequently becoming blocked by troops, guns, wagons, and ambulances withdrawing from Quatre Bras. The prospects of a fight, however, kept the men going, and the sight of some French columns in motion during the afternoon put new life into them. It was evident that an engagement could not be long delayed, and many imagined that it would take place before nightfall. Towards evening Mitchell marched his brigade on to that part of the position allotted to it—on the extreme right near Braine la Lend, and there the 51st and the other regiments of the brigade bivouacked. In all directions troops could be seen moving into position; and though darkness was approaching it still seemed as if the fight could not be postponed till the morrow. Masses of French troops were visible at no great distance, and a few British guns were already opening fire on some of the enemy's infantry, while parties of cavalry were briskly engaged in more than one part of the field.

But the night closed in without matters going further, and it was a night not easily forgotten by those who slept out in it. Rain fell in torrents, so that the bivouacs became a sea of mud, and the soldiers, lying out in the open, were drenched to the skin. When at length day broke and the heavy rain ceased, the situation became fully apparent, and no doubt remained as to the severity of the coming struggle. Less than a mile separated the two great armies, drawn up and facing one another. Between them lay a shallow valley, some two or three miles in length, and averaging half a mile in width, the sides sloping gently, but being everywhere uneven and undulating.

The trend of the valley was east and west, and Wellington's army occupied the northern crest and ground in rear, slightly in advance of the village of Mont St Jean; while the French were in position on the southern crest. From south to north, and dividing each position into two almost equal parts, ran the great paved cause-way from Charleroi to Brussels. Such was the field whereon was fought the memorable battle of Waterloo, so named from the village a little in rear of Mont St Jean; and within that cramped area there were at one time engaged no fewer than one hundred and eighty thousand combatants.

It is not proposed to treat here of the battle of Waterloo in detail—a task to which numerous bulky volumes have been devoted,—but in describing the small part played in the fight by Lieut.-Colonel

Sam Rice and his regiment, it will be necessary at any rate to sum up the situation at various times, in order to make the narrative complete. Still it may be said at once that the bulk of Mitchell's brigade kept to the one part of the field throughout the day, at times gaining ground, at times forced back, yet ever awaiting attack in the vicinity of Hougoumont. The brigade was weak in numbers, mustering no more than 1800 bayonets, of which the 51st supplied 540. The duty allotted to Mitchell was an important one, since Wellington considered it probable that Napoleon would attempt to turn his right flank and push through to Brussels by way of the road through Hal, and it was for that reason that he had detached the Dutch-Belgians and part of the 4th Division (numbering in all some 18,000 men) to the neighbourhood of Hal. These troops were some five miles from the field of battle, and at the outset Mitchell's brigade was called upon to hold in check any determined movement of the enemy in this direction until fresh dispositions could be made.

Wellington had taken up a strong defensive position, with most of his troops drawn back below the actual crest, and with his reserves well concealed by the folds of the ground. Napoleon, on the other hand, deigned to little concealment, and sought to break down his opponents' defences by sheer weight of numbers. At a little before noon the fight commenced. Napoleon sending forward his brother, Prince Jerome, against the advanced post of Hougoumont, which, as the key of the position, was strongly held by the Allies. At the same time an artillery duel opened all along the line, and a tempest of shot and shell raged across the valley; but the defenders of Hougoumont, reinforced by the whole of Byng's British Guards, resisted every onslaught of the French columns, even though parties of the enemy established themselves close up to the buildings and set them on fire. Almost continuously during the afternoon the attacks on this vital point went on, and so numerous at times were the assailants that they were able to overlap it and threaten the right of the Allies' main line. Here Mitchell's men came into action, and assisted in forcing back the assailants.

Early in the day Mitchell had advanced several companies, for the purpose of closing the gap between Hougoumont and Braine la Leud, and one company of the 51st was posted close to an abatis which had been placed across the main road a little in rear of the entrance to the avenue of Hougoumont. Four other companies of the regiment were extended farther to the right, along the hollow way leading to Braine la Leud, with instructions to engage the enemy's skirmishers as they advanced, and then to endeavour to harass with heavy musket fire the solid columns following their skirmishers. As had been expected, the French columns came on, covered by skirmishers, but so advantageous was the ground over which they advanced, and so high the standing corn through which they moved, that the companies of the 51st could not observe their approach until they were almost upon them. Then, rising, the British soldiers poured in their fire at forty paces, and, cheering wildly, dashed forward at the charge. And the impetuous onslaught had the desired effect, for the enemy, although supported by cavalry, were beaten back. The four companies of the 51st were then ordered to retire some two hundred yards, and rejoin the regiment.

While this was in progress, Napoleon was busy making preparations for his grand assault, designed to break the left centre of the British position. For this great effort, seventy-four guns were moved up, so as to bring their fire to bear, at a range of less than half a mile, on the Allies; and Marshal Ney was placed in command of 18,000 men in four columns, supported by Kellerman's cavalry division. Napoleon hoped that this combined attack would be final and decisive; that, having captured the advanced post of La Haie Sainte, the columns would be able to sweep onwards to Mont St Jean, cut off Wellington from Brussels as well as from the Prussians coming from the direction of Wavre, and thus make victory complete.

At 1 p.m. Ney's masses of columns moved down into the valley, and passed the seventy-four guns, which immediately opened fire over their heads, and caused havoc in the ranks of the Allies. Three of the columns pressed forward towards the Allies' centre, while the third moved away north-east, with the intention of driving in the left flank. Whether by design or by accident, Ney's principal attack was directed against the portion of the front line held by Bylandt's brigade of Dutch and Belgians, and no sooner did the French skirmishers, covering the advance of the columns, begin to make use of their muskets than panic seized their adversaries, who turned and fled in disorder. Then was Wellington's forethought, as well as the wisdom of his dispositions, apparent, for doubting the loyalty of the Dutch-Belgians, he had been careful to support them everywhere by British brigades, and here, close in rear, stood Picton's division, ready to take the place of the disloyal or cowardly Dutch-Belgians.

Although barely recovered from the effects of their recent fighting at Quatre Bras, Picton's 3000 gallant men responded to the call, and advanced in two thin lines to meet the 12,000 Frenchmen, already flushed with victory. Nearer the columns approached, and the British lines halted to receive them. Then, when within a few yards, Ney ordered his columns to deploy into line, Picton, taking advantage of the momentary check, delivered a withering volley and then charged in with the bayonet. The head of the leading French column was hurled back in confusion, and the 3000 British soldiers flung themselves upon the disorganised 12,000 Frenchmen, before they could recover from their first surprise. Picton was shot dead as he led the charge, but his gallant action had saved the situation, and it remained for the cavalry to complete Ney's discomfiture in this part of the field, charging the broken infantry, overthrowing the cavalry, and putting the seventy-four guns out of action for the remainder of the day.

Thus ended the second phase of the great battle, and so far Napoleon had made no headway. Yet he was by no means disheartened, and, ordering all his remaining guns into action, he pounded the British line from a distance, while he prepared for his next assault. At 4 p.m. began another phase of the fight, when Wellington's right wing was assailed by squadron after squadron of *Cuirassiers*, fresh bodies of infantry moving at the same time against La Haie Sainte and Hougoumont. The charges of the French cavalry were magnificent, but the squares in which Wellington had rapidly formed his troops resisted all the enemy's efforts to break them.

The British guns also stood firm, firing grape at the charging horsemen, until they arrived within forty yards, when, discharging a salvo, the gunners quitted their guns for the time being and fell back to the shelter of the infantry squares. Four times did the French cavalry charge home, using some 12,000 men for the purpose; yet were they able to do no more than to ride round and between the squares, which, being arranged chequerwise, met them with bristling bayonets and a rattling musketry fire in all directions, throwing them into disorder and obliging the greater number to draw off, with heavy losses in killed, wounded, and prisoners.

It was just before this that the company of the 51st, still posted near the abatis on the Nivelles road, was able to do some execution. A party of Cuirassiers, captured by the British cavalry after riding into the position, broke away from their escort and endeavoured to make their way back to their own lines. Galloping down the Nivelles road, hotly pursued by the escort, they first came under fire of a detachment of the 51st, out in front of the regiment; but from this fire they suffered little, as it became masked by the pursuing British dragoons.

The sound of the firing in his rear, however, attracted the attention of Captain Ross, commanding the 51st company near the abatis, and he soon became aware of the approach of the fugitives, who, ignorant of the fact that the road was blocked, came on at full speed. Then Ross turned his men about, and, opening fire, emptied many saddles. "Eight of the *Cuirassiers*," says Siborne, the historian, "and twelve of their horses, were killed, and the remainder, about sixty, taken or dispersed."

The greater part of Napoleon's famous heavy cavalry was now *hors de combat*, and had effected little, except that perhaps their several charges had helped Donzelot's infantry to gain a footing in the vicinity of La Haie Sainte, and thus enabled them, a little later, to capture that post. This success to be of any value Napoleon realised would have to be followed up forthwith, for he was already aware that the Prussians from Wavre were approaching his right flank. It was past seven o'clock in the evening, and there was no time to lose; consequently, Napoleon bestirred himself, and prepared for his final grand assault on Wellington's position. The capture of La Haie Sainte proved of great value to the Frenchmen, for Donzelot's men were able to prevent, with their musketry fire, the British gunners in their front from fighting their guns.

French guns were then brought up to the post, and at a range of less than a hundred yards, poured grape into the ranks of the Allies. Napoleon felt confident that victory was within his grasp; his grand reserve—his veterans of the Old Guard—still remained at hand, fresh and ready for a supreme effort, and he determined that they should make that effort. Placing Ney in command of the two massive columns of infantry, he ordered them to take a line between La Haie Sainte and Hougoumont, and assail the position. As his beloved veterans passed him on the way to the front, he sat on his white horse with outstretched arm, pointing in the direction which the attack was to take, and the cheers which came from the old soldiers convinced him that if it were possible at this juncture for any troops to break down Wellington's defences, then his Imperial Guard would do it.

Down the slope in front of La Belle Alliance, into the shallow valley marched these 10,000 warriors, headed by the drummers beating the *pas de charge*.[2] Then, as they began to ascend towards the British

2. In the Peninsular War a considerable amount of theatrical effect was given to the French attack by the bold advance of the drummers, whose drumming was called by the British soldiers *Old Trousers*.

position, they pushed forward a cloud of skirmishers, who, joining hands with those of Donzelot, opened a heavy fire. The two columns, advancing to the attack in close order, were now seen to be heading straight for that part of the line held by Maitland's brigade of Guards. On the right of Maitland, Adam's brigade had been moved up, so as to prolong the line as far as the northern enclosure of Hougoumont, to the right rear of which, again, stood Mitchell's brigade, in support of the gallant garrison of the *château*.

Barely four hundred yards separated the head of the leading French column from the British position, when Sir John Colborne, commanding the 52nd, of Adam's brigade, swiftly realised the situation. Acting on his own initiative, he gave the order to his regiment to advance in quick time towards the flank of the attacking columns, and the long red line moved forward in perfect order. Then suddenly he wheeled his whole line up, so as to face the flank of the columns, and threw out a company of skirmishers with orders to open fire on the Imperial Guard. The Frenchmen, thus challenged, halted and replied, and by so doing brought destruction upon themselves, for Colborne's line was ready for them.

The ranks closed up; the bugles rang out; and with one mighty roar from the regiment, eight hundred British bayonets bore down on the veterans of France. But the latter did not stand to receive the charge; the sudden onslaught appalled them; the leading battalions broke and fled to the rear, and in their flight carried with them the whole of the Imperial Guard—the flower of the French army, and Napoleon's last hope. No time was given to them to re-form, for the remainder of Adam's brigade and Maitland's Guards opened fire upon them from the higher ground as they fled; and Wellington, with the light of victory in his eyes, ordered a general advance towards La Belle Alliance, where Napoleon and Ney could be seen rallying their men for a last stand.

But when, as the sun fast approached the horizon, Blücher's Prussians were observed to be moving in rapidly from the east and northeast, the French knew that the squares into which they had been hastily formed would be powerless to stem the tide of the advancing hosts. One man alone amongst them all remained resolute. Napoleon even then refused to acknowledge himself beaten, and enjoined on his soldiers to stand firm, and, if necessary, die by his side on the field. His generals, however, saw that all hope had gone, and begged their emperor to make good his escape while there was yet time. Then, as the squares gave way and melted into the great mass of fugitives pressing south, Soult and the others rode off with their mighty leader—away from his last field of battle. In Wellington, the "*Sepoy*-General" at whom he had scoffed, Napoleon had met his match.

The pursuit did not slacken for an instant, and Wellington led on his victorious troops as far as Rossomme, when, assured that victory was complete and that the Prussians were following on the heels of the flying Frenchmen, he drew rein, and in the moonlight rode back towards Waterloo. At Genappe he met Marshal Blücher; and, amidst the cheers of those around them, the two great warriors gripped hands, as they congratulated each other on the brilliant result of the battle. Then it was arranged that the Prussians should continue the pursuit; while the British army, worn out by nine hours' hard fighting, bivouacked on the actual battlefield.

The 51st and the 14th lay on their arms for the night in the wood of Hougoumont; the 23rd, having taken part in the general advance, bivouacked near La Belle Alliance; and next morning Mitchell's three regiments, having united again, marched to Nivelles, where they halted for a day to get rations, and were congratulated, in special orders issued by Lord Hill and by Sir Charles Colville, on the part that they had played in "the glorious and forever memorable battle of the 18th June." For their share in this victory both Colonel Mitchell and Lieutenant-Colonel Rice were appointed Companions of the Bath. Thus once again fortune smiled on Samuel Rice, who, until the autumn of 1813, had considered himself the most unlucky of officers. A stroke of luck, as has been shown, gave him the temporary command of the 51st at the battle of the Nivelle, the Peninsular Gold Medal, and a brevet lieutenant-colonelcy; by luck he obtained the temporary command of the regiment at Waterloo, the Waterloo Medal, and the C.B., as well as the sum of £433, being a field-officer's share of the prize-money granted by Parliament to the victorious army.

And by pure and simple luck alone did the 51st take part in the great battle, instead of being at Tubize with the rest of the 4th Division. Moreover, all this led subsequently to Colonel Rice receiving the further honour of being appointed a Knight of Hanover. Yet there are some who maintain that there is no such thing as luck. Without it, Colonel Rice would have missed four decorations—in an age when decorations were not freely given; and without it, he would have gone to his grave unrewarded for his many campaigns, for the Silver Medal for the Peninsular War was not granted until eight years after his death.

The services rendered by himself and his regiment at Waterloo may not have been very remarkable, though it is certain that they did all that was required of them.

Some years afterwards, when Captain William Siborne was constructing his famous model of Waterloo, now in the Museum of the R.U.S. Institution, (*The Royal Armouries, 2010.*) Colonel Rice, among other survivors of the battle, was requested to describe the movements of the regiment which he commanded on that eventful day. His reply[3] was characteristic of the man: he claimed no honour or glory for himself, but he set forth the bald facts:—

> The 51st Regiment was in the Corps of the Army immediately under Lord Hill—brigaded with the 14th and 23rd, under the command of Colonel Mitchell, being a Light Corps, and standing at the head of the column upon its first formation at the crest of the position. Companies were in succession ordered in front, and occupied ground to the right of the Nivelles road, pretty nearly in line with the Hougoumont farm. Lastly, the remaining companies under my command descended and took possession of a favourable rising ground, covered with thick brushwood, and very defensible against any sudden attack of cavalry. Here we remained posted, waiting orders.
>
> Late in the day, I forget the hour, an *aide-de-camp* from Lord Hill came down with an order to keep *this ground* to the *last*, as he was withdrawing his whole force to the left, and that I must not expect *any support*. Consequently I prepared myself to render as defensible as possible the post committed to my charge.
>
> Being so separated from the army, you will perceive we bore no decided part in the action, and were but holding ground during the great movements. The French had a line of cavalry—*vedettes*—in our front; and to their rear, at a considerable distance, I could perceive a body of lancers, who no doubt were waiting some favourable moment to advance.
>
> Situated as I was, I could see but little of what was going on to my left, except the charge of the French *cuirassiers*, on the left of Hougoumont farm, on the position. After being foiled in this attempt against the squares, a considerable body passed down

3 In *Waterloo Letters*, edited by Major-General H. T. Siborne, late Colonel R.E., son of Captain W. Siborne, the historian. These letters were selected for publication out of several hundreds, the originals of all of which are now in the Library of the British Museum.

the Nivelles road, on which there was an *abatis*. I was so placed as to perceive this, and gave my parties in advance orders to fire, for being so much in their rear, I could not well distinguish friend from foe. The fire was successful, though some few miraculously cleared the *abatis*. I mention this merely to show our ground more than anything else.

What I have offered I fear you will not consider very satisfactory, but you must remember we were not connected during any part of the memorable day with any of the principal movements. In fact, I have considered my regiment as a picket detached from the main body, throwing out skirmishers and supports, according to my own view, and in covering a certain space of ground.

I have been frequently questioned respecting the battle of Waterloo and movements, and my reply has invariably been that I was so situated as to have but a partial view of the field, and not engaged in the great conflict that was raging to my left. In fact, I may say that I was stationary throughout the day, and the only order I received was the one I have already mentioned.—I beg, &c.,

S. Rice,
Colonel late 51st Regiment.

CHAPTER 14

Paris and Peace

To capture the French capital as rapidly as possible, and before Napoleon should have an opportunity of rallying his defeated army, now became the object of the allied forces. On the 20th June the Prussians had passed the frontier in hot pursuit of the fugitive Frenchmen, and by the 23rd Blücher was at Catillon and Wellington at Le Cateau Cambresis. Meanwhile, the French had begun to recover from their panic, and twenty thousand had assembled at Laon, where Soult was working strenuously to get them into order, hoping that when Grouchy arrived with his corps it would be possible to do something to check the advance of the Allies. After Ligny, Grouchy had pursued the beaten Prussians towards Wavre, where he defeated their rearguard on the 18th and 19th June. Then, retreating, he beat off an attack by Pirch at Namur on the 20th, and withdrew into France. Wellington and Blücher were aware of all this, and debated whether to turn aside and attack Soult forthwith, or whether to pass him by and push on to Paris. They decided on the latter course.

From the Belgian frontier four principal roads converged on Paris. On the easternmost road the French were collecting at Laon, while scattered fugitives, making for the capital, were pressing along the other three roads, of which the two on the west were allotted to Wellington's columns and the third to Blücher's troops. On the 24th June Mitchell's brigade, which had marched from Nivelles to Le Cateau, received orders to proceed to Cambray, which was still held by a French garrison. The reduction of the place was entrusted to Colville's division, and the garrison was summoned that night, but refused to surrender.

Next morning: Colville ordered the assault of the works, detailing the light companies of Johnstone's brigade to storm the Valencienne gate, while the 23rd and 51st simultaneously assaulted the Paris gate. The two regiments succeeded in breaking open the outer gate of the Couvre Port with little difficulty, but the Paris gate itself resisted every effort. Close by, however, there was found a breach in the walls under repair, and by storming this an entry was effected, without much loss—the 51st having no more than two men killed and ten wounded. The Valencienne gate was carried by Johnstone's brigade, and the garrison withdrew to the citadel, which held out until the evening of the 25th.

The advance on Paris was then resumed; Peronne was captured by the Guards division and Ham by the Prussians; and a few days later Soult and Grouchy, retreating towards Paris, made a feeble attempt to cut in on Blücher's flank, but failing to make any impression continued the march to the capital, which they reached on the 29th June. Napoleon himself had arrived there on the 21st, but had been forced by the Chamber of Deputies to abdicate, and had then retired to Malmaison, a few miles out of Paris.

On the 29th Blücher was at Gonesse, with his advanced troops close to Aubervilliers, near St Denis; and Wellington was at Senlis. Although the Chamber had asked for a suspension of hostilities, no agreement had been arrived at, and knowing that the French now had some 80,000 soldiers in Paris, Wellington and Blücher decided that the Prussians should move round to the south of the city, while the remainder of the allied troops pushed in from the north. On the 30th, therefore, the Prussians crossed the Seine near St Germains, and two days later Blücher was at Versailles.

On that day (July 2) Wellington threw a bridge across the Seine at Argenteuil, to better his communications with Blücher, and on the following day the last shots of the campaign were fired, the Prussians having a smart skirmish at Issy, and the opposing piquets on the north of the city exchanging a few shots. In the evening part of the 51st moved to the village of Aubervilliers, which had not been wholly abandoned by the French troops, so that, as had frequently occurred in Peninsula times, one half of the village was held by the British and the other by the French, without molesting one another. And here occurred one of those curious incidents illustrative of the friendship of enemies which were not uncommon in Peninsular warfare. Ensign Mainwaring tells the story:—

> We soon grew friends, and on the full security of honourable warfare some of us crossed the streets and entered into conver-

sation with the officers. They good-naturedly asked us how we were off for eatables, and offered to send us some white bread and tobacco; and the nearest picket was immediately furnished with a good supply, for which their sutler-woman was well paid, though the French refused at first to take payment. They asked us into the house and gave us an excellent luncheon, and whilst we were all laughing and talking away, one of the officers, by his epaulettes apparently a major, took hold of the button of my jacket, and looking at it exclaimed, 'Ah, 51st! Was monsieur with his regiment in Spain? for I saved the life of one of your captains, whom we captured at the battle of Nivelle; he was *un brave homme, bel homme*. Is he alive? I should so much like to see him.'

It was rather singular that the person of whom he spoke was the captain of my company (Phelps),[1] and I accordingly told the Frenchman that his wish could be instantly and easily gratified, that the *Brave* was in a house not a hundred yards distant, and I immediately sent for him. He soon came; the Gaul was delighted, flew into his arms, kissed him on one cheek and then on the other, talked with the utmost rapidity, asked a hundred questions and never waited for one answer from my gallant old chief, who, when he got breathing-time, recognised him instantly, shook him heartily by the hand, acknowledged that he had saved his life, prevented his being plundered or ill-used, and that he behaved in the kindest and most generous manner possible to him.[2]

No one who saw us all clustered together in this friendly manner, amongst these *mustachioed* veterans of Napoleon, would ever have imagined that we were foes, and that perhaps in a short half hour we might be seeking each other's lives, with bayonets clashing and bullets whizzing from those hands so cordially grasped in kind and grateful feeling without one spark of national hate or animosity between us.

1. James Henry Phelps, K.H.; ensign, 51st, 1798; major, 4th Foot, 1834; retired (lieut.-colonel), 1838; police magistrate, Liverpool; died at Sydney, 1842.
2. In the affair near Sarre (during the battle of the Nivelle, 10th November 1813), Captain Phelps held on too long, and was cut off. He then ran for it, but the Frenchmen discharged their muskets at him, surrounded him, and took him prisoner. Even then he would have been bayoneted but for the timely arrival on the spot of the French officer. By a miracle, none of the shots fired at him had taken effect, though several bullets had passed through his clothes and cap.

In all probability, although young Mainwaring was not in the secret, the senior officers on both sides had an inkling that the campaign was over, for, earlier in the day, an agreement to suspend hostilities had been negotiated at St Cloud. This was known as the "Convention of Paris," by the provisions of which the French army was to be withdrawn to the south of the River Loire within eight days, and Paris to be handed over to the Allies. During the two following days the French troops marched out of the capital, and the Allies encamped in the Bois de Boulogne, the occupation of the actual city being completed on the 7th July, on which day Adam's brigade made a triumphant entry and pitched camp in the Champs Elysees. Thus within three weeks of the firing of the first shot of the campaign Napoleon had been crushed, his capital captured, and Louis XVIII. restored to the throne.

The fate of the greatest Frenchman who ever lived was certainly pitiable, yet for the peace of Europe it was impossible to allow him liberty. From Paris he fled to Rochefort on the 2nd July, hoping to escape to America, but discovering that the Bourbons were about to arrest him, he surrendered to Captain Maitland of H.M.S. *Bellerophon*, and was at once conveyed to Plymouth. Here he made the bold request to be permitted to reside in England, as a country gentleman, on his parole; but the allied Powers refused his request, and politely intimated to him their decision that the remainder of his life should be spent at St Helena. There, accordingly, he lived, in open arrest, until the end came on the 5th May 1821.

Paris was the second European capital into which Samuel Rice and the 51st, as part of a triumphant army, had marched within the past three years, and as all chance of further fighting was at an end, they thoroughly enjoyed the life which they led for the next few weeks. Great numbers of English people visited Paris, to see their relations and friends in the army of occupation, and as the Parisians themselves were both friendly and hospitable, there was no lack of amusement. There were, of course, plenty of guards to be found and other duties to be performed, the most interesting of which, perhaps, were in connection with the removal of art treasures from the Louvre.

For many years Napoleon and his victorious generals had made it a custom to bring back as spoils of war the choicest paintings and statues to be found in the museums of conquered countries, and to place them in the Louvre, to become heirlooms for the French nation. Now, however, that the Allies were masters of the situation, they decided to restore all these things to their rightful owners, and the various regiments furnished working parties, to assist in packing up the treasures, as well as guards, to prevent possible French interference, for many days in succession. Curiously enough, the Parisians paid very little attention to what was going on, and the removal of everything that was claimed by foreign nations was effected without trouble.

Gay times the British subaltern had in Paris, with dances, dinners, and theatres galore, and many a one lost everything he possessed at the gaming tables. Yet the young officer cared little for his losses, and the Frenchmen wanted every scrap of British gold that they could collect, since they were called upon to pay a war indemnity of thirty million pounds for espousing the cause of Napoleon and defying all Europe.

Until the 30th October, the 51st remained encamped in the Bois de Boulogne, and then moved to the village of Verrieres, some ten miles from Paris, five weeks later receiving orders to march to Calais and embark for England, since the regiment was not required to form part of the army of occupation of France. So Samuel Rice returned from his last campaign, covered with honour and glory, to rest on his laurels, and to settle down to the dull monotony of peace-time soldiering—the comparison between which and campaigning is well described in the following words:—

Those were spirit-stirring days indeed, and although it may perhaps be wrong to say so, yet what has life to offer now that can compare with them? How tame, how stupid, how insipid, does all the monotony of the daily routine of drills, peace-guards, and dress-parades, which now fill up and fritter away our time, appear to them whose lives for years were passed in camps, living in the open air, seeing the glorious sun rise every day, or watching by the piquet-fires at night the beautiful stars; their minds elevated by the thought that they were doing their duty to their country, that the eyes of all Europe were upon their slightest movements, their hearts beating with enthusiasm, as victory followed victory; and if death some-times came in the midst of all this, its sting was scarcely felt, since the soldier's soul winged its flight to heaven 'mid the roar of cannon, the blaze of musketry, and the victorious cheers of his gallant comrades.

Thus soliloquised Frederick Mainwaring, when, some years afterwards, he was setting down stray reminiscences of his fighting days. He was then, with eighteen years' service, still only a lieutenant in the 51st, and a decade of garrison life must have weighed heavily on him. But his lot was shared by plenty of other Peninsular and Waterloo heroes, and amongst them, his commanding officer, Colonel Rice. Yet Mainwaring was more fortunate than many of his brother officers, who, when the reductions consequent on peace took place, were placed on half pay, and so debarred from even following the profession to which they had devoted the best part of their lives.[3] Hundreds of officers were thus thrown on their own resources, and for years the country was flooded with half-pay lieutenants. It was, of course, impossible to retain the services of all of them, and the Government cannot be accused of meanness, for the half pay of the infantry lieutenant was increased very considerably, and he was allowed to count two years for Waterloo towards service qualifying for the higher rate.

The 51st arrived in England in January 1816, to commence a five years' tour of garrison duty, being quartered first at Blatchington and then at Chichester, with a detachment for duty at the Pavilion, at Brighton. In 1817 it moved to Chatham, and later in the year to Portsmouth, Samuel Rice being promoted to the command of the regiment, on the death of Colonel Mitchell, on the 20th April. In 1818 the 51st marched from Portsmouth to Plymouth, and in the following year moved by sea to Chatham and Sheerness, whence company detachments were furnished for Harwich and for the island of Heligoland.[4] In 1820 the regiment was on the move again, changing quarters an extraordinary number of times, and being frequently split up into detachments.

Romford, Brighton, Chichester, Croydon, Woolwich, Greenwich, Deptford, Bow, Stratford, Teddington, Twickenham, Isleworth, and Winchester all provided temporary homes for headquarters or detachments during the year. Three months in barracks at Winchester was the longest resting-time allowed the regiment, for though the officers had begun to hope that these were to be their quarters for a year or two, in February 1821 they were ordered to Portsmouth, and, after all these incessant movements, it came almost as a relief to them to receive, in April, further orders to prepare for immediate embarkation for the Mediterranean.

---

3. On the reduction of the establishment of the regiment, a captain and twelve subalterns of the 51st were transferred to the half-pay list. None of them rejoined the 51st, and only three ever served again. 4. Heligoland was a British possession from 1807 to 1890, when, by the Anglo-German Agreement, it was ceded to Germany.

In spite of its distracting changes of quarters, the regiment had found time to gather recruits and to recover from the effects of active service, so that by 1820 it was up to full strength, and most favourably reported on by the inspecting general for "its movements and appearance." With regard to the latter point, it may be of interest to remark on the dress of the officers and soldiers of this time. It will be remembered that in 1809, when the 51st was made a light infantry regiment, it received a new uniform, and in this it fought through the Peninsular War and the Waterloo campaign, though during the former strict regulations in the matter of dress were, by force of circumstances, seldom adhered to. It was frequently impossible for officers to replenish their worn-out garments, and at times they presented a most ragged appearance—very different from that in which they are handed down to posterity by painters of the various battle-scenes. Still, so much was thought of the smart turn-out of a regiment even on active service, that it was a point of honour with both officers and men to clean up on every possible occasion, and it is on record that the men who stormed Badajoz spent the hours previous to the assault in polishing themselves up, "as if for a review."

The light infantry uniform which should have been worn by the 51st from 1809 onwards, consisted principally of a short-tailed, easy-fitting red jacket, white breeches, black cloth leggings, and shoes, with a light felt *shako* (having an oilskin covering for wet weather) as head-dress. At first the officers wore cocked hats, but in 1811 these were replaced by *shakos* with a green feather in front. Probably it was found that the breeches and leggings were difficult to keep in repair, for it is certain that they soon disappeared in favour of blue-grey cloth trousers, with short spat-gaiters underneath; and the officers, who were supposed to wear long boots (to the knee), took to the trousers also, wearing leather gaiters over them, if they were able to obtain them. In the interval between the Peninsular War and the Waterloo campaign regiments had time to return to a strict uniformity of dress, and the grey trousers became the regulation covering for the legs on active service; otherwise there was no change until after Waterloo.

As soon as peace was established and regiments began to return home, the military tailors, who had had idle times for some years, cast about for openings for innovations; but since the army had now established the fact that it was intended for fighting more than for show, and since the uniform worn in 1815 was considered both serviceable and showy, the tailors found some difficulty in introducing alterations. The opportunity came, however, in 1816, when someone took a fancy to the head-dresses worn by some of the foreign troops forming part of the army of occupation of France, and forthwith a new *shako* was designed for the British army. This was heavy and cumbersome, being seven and a half inches high and eleven inches in diameter at the top, but its shape and size gave the tailors wide scope for lace and other adornments. So appearance, not for the first or the last time, was made to override utility.

Other innovations in dress soon followed, and by 1821 the uniform in which the 51st had fought in the Peninsula and at Waterloo was almost entirely altered. The grey trousers had gone, and the white breeches and black leggings had come back; the curved light infantry sabre, worn by the officers suspended from slings, was replaced by a straight sword, hung in a frog from the white shoulder-belt; and for the short-tailed light infantry jacket there had been substituted the long-tailed *coatee*. The 51st still wore grass-green facings, but in April 1821 His Majesty conferred upon the regiment the additional title of "The Kings Own Light Infantry," when its facings were changed to blue and the lace to gold (oak-leaf pattern). A year later the historic breeches and leggings finally disappeared, and trousers, grey or white according to the season, were ordered to be worn.

In May 1821 the 51st, six hundred and fifty strong, embarked at Portsmouth for the Ionian Isles, and reaching Corfu in the following month, occupied the Citadel and Fort Neuf. It was just twenty-four years since Samuel Rice and the regiment had arrived at Gibraltar from Elba, when the general scuttle from the Mediterranean had taken place, but in those twenty-four years Great Britain had established a firm footing in that sea, having taken and retained possession of Malta (1800) and the Ionian Isles (1809), and having at different times occupied, but subsequently evacuated, Minorca, Sicily, and Alexandria. The Ionian Isles, in which the 51st remained for thirteen long years, were seven in number—viz., Corfu, Cephalonia, Zante, Ithaca, Santa Maura, Cerigo, and Paxo—and, though essentially Greek, had been under Neapolitan and Venetian rule previous to being ceded to France in 1797.

In 1801 they were formed into a republic (The Septinsular Republic) under the protection of Turkey and Russia, but only to pass again to France in 1807. Collingwood captured Cephalonia, Zante, Santa Maura, and Ithaca in 1809, and by the Treaty of Paris (1815) all seven islands became a British Protectorate, remaining such until

1863, when they were transferred to Greece. As a foreign station for British troops the islands were always most popular, at any rate with the officers, the climate being good and the shooting excellent.

Probably no officer was better acquainted with the Ionian Islands than was Colonel Samuel Rice, for during the last ten years of his command of the 51st the regiment furnished detachments at different times to all the islands, and the colonel transferred his headquarters from one to another, though residing principally at Cephalonia, Zante, and Corfu. Life there was devoid of all excitement, except, perhaps, that afforded by the wrangling between the High Commissioner of the Islands, Sir Frederick Adam (of Adam's brigade of Waterloo fame), and the British Resident of Cephalonia, Charles Napier, the eventual conqueror of Sind; but Rice's twenty odd years of campaigning had left him none too strong, and he was apparently content to finish out his regimental service by devoting himself to the welfare of the corps of which he was so justly proud.

That under his command the 51st retained its high reputation there is ample proof in the reports made by various inspecting generals; and when he gave up the command, in July 1831, he had the satisfaction of feeling that, as the last officer of the 51st who had served in it under Sir John Moore, he had carried out the teachings of his illustrious chief for thirty-eight years, and handed the regiment over to his successor not only in as good a state as he had found it on joining as an ensign in 1793, but also with added laurels which, moreover, he himself had helped to win.

During the period of Samuel Rice's regimental service the 51st was abroad for no less than thirty years; but those were strenuous times, and no regiment could count on a lengthy sojourn at home, for, in addition to the long war in Europe, Great Britain was kept busily engaged in the East Indies, in the West Indies, and in America. Still it was exceptional even then for a regiment to be so continuously on foreign service, but in this respect, it may be remarked, the 51st was always exceptional. Apart from the campaigning, and apart from the bad climate of foreign stations, the life of the regimental officer was ever without rest, for the slight repose which might have come with service at home was broken into by the authorities, who seem to have been at pains to deny a resting-place to a regiment for more than a few months at a time.

Yet we people of today find fault with the unfortunate officer of a century ago, because he did not read military history and study the theory of his profession! There can be little doubt, however, that the effect of all this harassing service was to wear out the officer before his time. Some veterans there were, of course, who, being particularly robust, lived to a ripe old age, but the majority of those officers who fought for England in the great struggle from 1793 to 1815 passed away long before attaining the allotted span of three-score years and ten. And Samuel Rice was one of these.

Under the usual purchase system arrangements, a purse was made up to induce Colonel Rice to vacate the command of the regiment, but, hoping for further employment, he exchanged to the half-pay unattached list. Having no son of his own to carry on his name in the 51st, he did his best to make amends by getting two of his three Rice nephews[5] appointed to the regiment, thus pro-longing the family connection with it for a further period of twenty-three years. He remained on half pay until 1834, when he was appointed Inspecting Field Officer of the Leeds Recruiting District, an appointment, however, which he held for only a little more than a year, as his health gave way and obliged him to lay down his sword. He died in London on the 7th March 1840, in his sixty-fifth year, leaving a widow and a daughter.[6]

Such was the career of a typical regimental officer of the old school, who served his country throughout, perhaps, the most critical period of its existence, who witnessed the rise and fall of England's inveterate enemy, who shared in the victories which won for England fame, and who never claimed that he had done more than play a very minor part in the epoch-making drama. Still, Samuel Rice was one of those who helped to raise the power and name of England to the loftiest position in Europe—and, indeed, in the world.

5. Percy John Rice, ensign, 51st, 1828; lieutenant, 1834; captain, 1837; major, 1849; died (unmarried) at Bangalore, India, 1850.

Augustus Thomas Rice, ensign, 51st, 1831; lieutenant, 1837; captain, 1841; major, 1852; brevet lieut.-colonel, 1853; retired as colonel on full pay, 1854; died (unmarried), 1888. He served with distinction in the Burmese War, 1852; severely wounded at the capture of Bassein; mentioned in despatches; promoted for gallantry; and received the medal for Pegu.

Samuel Rice's third nephew, Horatio Morgan Rice, took holy orders, and died in 1863, leaving a son, the Reverend John Morgan Rice (who died without issue in 1895), and a daughter. Miss Lucy Augusta Rice, who is the sole surviving member of the family bearing the name of Rice.

6. The daughter, Margaret Rice, married Captain B. T. Foord Bowes, 95th Regiment, and died (without issue) in 1842. Samuel Rice survived all his twelve brothers and sisters except one—*viz.*, Sir Ralph Rice, who lived for another ten years.

LEONAUR

ALSO FROM LEONAUR
AVAILABLE IN SOFTCOVER OR HARDCOVER WITH DUST JACKET

IRON TIMES WITH THE GUARDS *by An O. E. (G. P. A. Fildes)*—The Experiences of an Officer of the Coldstream Guards on the Western Front During the First World War.

THE GREAT WAR IN THE MIDDLE EAST: 1 *by W. T. Massey*—The Desert Campaigns & How Jerusalem Was Won---two classic accounts in one volume.

THE GREAT WAR IN THE MIDDLE EAST: 2 *by W. T. Massey*—Allenby's Final Triumph.

SMITH-DORRIEN *by Horace Smith-Dorrien*—Isandlwhana to the Great War.

1914 *by Sir John French*—The Early Campaigns of the Great War by the British Commander.

GRENADIER *by E. R. M. Fryer*—The Recollections of an Officer of the Grenadier Guards throughout the Great War on the Western Front.

BATTLE, CAPTURE & ESCAPE *by George Pearson*—The Experiences of a Canadian Light Infantryman During the Great War.

DIGGERS AT WAR *by R. Hugh Knyvett & G. P. Cuttriss*—"Over There" With the Australians by R. Hugh Knyvett and Over the Top With the Third Australian Division by G. P. Cuttriss. Accounts of Australians During the Great War in the Middle East, at Gallipoli and on the Western Front.

HEAVY FIGHTING BEFORE US *by George Brenton Laurie*—The Letters of an Officer of the Royal Irish Rifles on the Western Front During the Great War.

THE CAMELIERS *by Oliver Hogue*—A Classic Account of the Australians of the Imperial Camel Corps During the First World War in the Middle East.

RED DUST *by Donald Black*—A Classic Account of Australian Light Horsemen in Palestine During the First World War.

THE LEAN, BROWN MEN *by Angus Buchanan*—Experiences in East Africa During the Great War with the 25th Royal Fusiliers—the Legion of Frontiersmen.

THE NIGERIAN REGIMENT IN EAST AFRICA *by W. D. Downes*—On Campaign During the Great War 1916-1918.

THE 'DIE-HARDS' IN SIBERIA *by John Ward*—With the Middlesex Regiment Against the Bolsheviks 1918-19.

LEONAUR

ALSO FROM LEONAUR

AVAILABLE IN SOFTCOVER OR HARDCOVER WITH DUST JACKET

FARAWAY CAMPAIGN *by F. James*—Experiences of an Indian Army Cavalry Officer in Persia & Russia During the Great War.

REVOLT IN THE DESERT *by T. E. Lawrence*—An account of the experiences of one remarkable British officer's war from his own perspective.

MACHINE-GUN SQUADRON *by A. M. G.*—The 20th Machine Gunners from British Yeomanry Regiments in the Middle East Campaign of the First World War.

A GUNNER'S CRUSADE *by Antony Bluett*—The Campaign in the Desert, Palestine & Syria as Experienced by the Honourable Artillery Company During the Great War .

DESPATCH RIDER *by W. H. L. Watson*—The Experiences of a British Army Motorcycle Despatch Rider During the Opening Battles of the Great War in Europe.

TIGERS ALONG THE TIGRIS *by E. J. Thompson*—The Leicestershire Regiment in Mesopotamia During the First World War.

HEARTS & DRAGONS *by Charles R. M. F. Crutwell*—The 4th Royal Berkshire Regiment in France and Italy During the Great War, 1914-1918.

INFANTRY BRIGADE: 1914 *by John Ward*—The Diary of a Commander of the 15th Infantry Brigade, 5th Division, British Army, During the Retreat from Mons.

DOING OUR 'BIT' *by Ian Hay*—Two Classic Accounts of the Men of Kitchener's 'New Army' During the Great War including *The First 100,000* & *All In It.*

AN EYE IN THE STORM *by Arthur Ruhl*—An American War Correspondent's Experiences of the First World War from the Western Front to Gallipoli-and Beyond.

STAND & FALL *by Joe Cassells*—With the Middlesex Regiment Against the Bolsheviks 1918-19.

RIFLEMAN MACGILL'S WAR *by Patrick MacGill*—A Soldier of the London Irish During the Great War in Europe including *The Amateur Army*, *The Red Horizon* & *The Great Push.*

WITH THE GUNS *by C. A. Rose & Hugh Dalton*—Two First Hand Accounts of British Gunners at War in Europe During World War 1- Three Years in France with the Guns and With the British Guns in Italy.

THE BUSH WAR DOCTOR *by Robert V. Dolbey*—The Experiences of a British Army Doctor During the East African Campaign of the First World War.